COUNTRY**GUITAR**
METHOD**COMPILATION**

Three Books in One! Master Country Guitar Licks, Techniques and Soloing

LEVI**CLAY**

FUNDAMENTAL**CHANGES**

The Complete Country Guitar Method Compilation

Three Books in One! Master Country Guitar Licks, Techniques & Soloing

ISBN: 978-1-911267-72-0

Published by **www.fundamental-changes.com**

www.fundamental-changes.com

Twitter: @guitar_joseph

Twitter: @LeviClay88

Over 10,000 fans on Facebook: FundamentalChangesInGuitar

Instagram: FundamentalChanges

For over 350 Free Guitar Lessons with Videos Check Out

www.fundamental-changes.com

Cover Image Copyright: Carson Hess

Instagram @carsonhess81

Foreword

Welcome to the Complete Country Guitar Method Compilation, and thanks for taking the time to check it out, you're on the way to country guitar mastery!

This book is all about creating a one-stop shop to take you from beginner to advanced country guitarist quickly, and efficiently. There's a distinct lack of country guitar instructional books available, so I've compiled three of my best-selling books into one great value package.

This compilation contains Country Guitar for Beginners, Country Guitar Soloing Techniques, and Country Guitar Heroes: 100 Licks for Country Guitar.

This compilation will give you everything need, no matter what level you are playing at.

You will:

• Get a fundamental understanding of chords and rhythm guitar in various sub-genres of country music.

• Learn the theory that connects chords, arpeggios, and scales, and how these are used in country music

• Understand the phrasing tricks used by country guitar players that don't rely on playing fast to sound good

• Get a solid understanding of the CAGED system and how it's used for chords, scales, arpeggios and for playing over chord changes.

• Develop the techniques needed to improve speed and accuracy, including alternate picking, hybrid picking, slurs, banjo rolls, double stops, and more.

• Learn hundreds of real-life licks inspired by the genres most distinguished players

• Master multiple tracks composed for each book, each with their own backing tracks for fun and exciting practice.

While the book has been organized to suit a beginner player who will begin at page one, you can also quickly dig into the chapters that cover the material that interests you.

The material is structured to provide you with the theoretical tools you'll need to play the style and introduce you to basic soloing concepts (Country Guitar for Beginners), develop the technique needed to play the genre at a high level (Country Guitar Soloing Techniques), and finally present you with authentic vocabulary used by the greats (Country Guitar Heroes: 100 Licks for Country Guitar).

About each book:

Country Guitar for Beginners

Country guitar is a genre rich in history, which more people are turning to in 2017. As with studying any music, the best way to sound authentic is to understand and pay tribute to its roots.

Country Guitar for Beginners covers The Carter Family and Jimmie Rodgers, right through to cowboys like Hank Williams, Western swingers like Eldon Shamblin and outlaws like Merle Haggard

You'll learn the chords needed to play each style and the correct approaches to rhythm guitar. You'll understand how to develop this knowledge into scales, solos, and licks.

Finally, you'll look at three tracks composed in a pop, rockabilly, and outlaw setting. You will learn the rhythm parts and solos, and practice them with the supplied backing tracks.

Country Guitar Soloing Techniques

Country Guitar Soloing Techniques arms you with expert technique to help you play in the style of Brent Mason, Albert Lee, and Johnny Hiland.

There's an emphasis on the CAGED system and understanding of harmony, however, the bulk of the book develops your alternate picking technique, cross picking, hybrid picking, banjo rolls, slurs, double stops, and more.

Included is a full track titled Hot Dang Twang that uses each concept covered, and features two full solos that test your guitar technique.

Country Guitar Heroes: 100 Licks for Country Guitar

Now you've built the skills to play country guitar, the final step is to get to grips with some real-world vocabulary and licks

Music is a language, and being able to communicate with other musicians or listeners means being able to speak to them using words they will recognize.

Country Guitar Heroes teaches you 100 licks in the style of 20 of the best players in the genre. Each one of these licks is broken down and explained theoretically so you'll be able to develop them further and combine them at will.

Finally, I've included a selection of solos that use these licks exclusively, but transposed and adapted them to work in a new context. This is where you'll learn to turn other people's licks into your own unique language.

There's a lot of content, and will provide you with years of study... but practice makes perfect, so grab your guitar and get ready to twang!

Levi

The audio files for this book are available to download for free from **www.fundamental-changes.com**

Contents

Book 2: Country Guitar Soloing Techniques

Book 3: Country Guitar Heroes – 100 Country Licks for Guitar

COUNTRYGUITAR FORBEGINNERS

A Complete Method to Learn Traditional and Modern Country Guitar Playing

LEVI**CLAY**

FUNDAMENTAL**CHANGES**

Introduction

Considered by many to be the sound of America, surveys will tell you that there's no more popular genre of music than country music. Country and Western has a rich history, but to many only conjures up images of cowboys. However, the reality is that there's so much more to the story than this.

Born in the 1920s, country music shares many similarities with the blues, in that country is a fusion of music from other continents that found a footing in a new location. While we might think of the birthplace of the genre as the Appalachian Mountains, many would argue that the music was actually conceived in in the traditional folk sound and instrumentation of countries like Ireland and Scotland.

After many generations in the Appalachian melting pot (where music was played socially for entertainment), residents began to move south to work in cities like Atlanta, Georgia. This brought country music to ears of a different type of person; the business man. It was here that the recording industry would start to experiment with the commercial potential of country music. By the end of the '20s, the American people would come to know these early country sounds through success stories such as Jimmie Rodgers and The Carter Family.

During the '30s, the Great Depression saw a dramatic drop in record sales. The solution for music lovers was the radio renaissance, with the Grand Ole Opry filling the ears of anyone willing to listen. Thanks to Hollywood, the idea of the cowboy ballad caught on, with artists like Roy Acuff having hits with classics such as Wabash Cannonball.

Things really changed in the 1940s as western swing took off, with Bob Wills and his Texas Playboys bringing amplified electric guitar and even drums into his band. This may sound trivial now, but at the time these changes were revolutionary and despised by purists. Simultaneously there was an explosion in the bluegrass scene, as Bill Monroe and the Blue Grass Boys took the traditional unamplified folk and gospel music to new commercial heights.

Country music would continue to grow and branch into numerous sub-genres over the next sixty years, not to mention become one of the driving sounds behind rockabilly, and eventually, rock and roll. From the ballads of Hank Williams to the stardom of Johnny Cash… the simple sounds of Merle Travis to the sophistications of Chet Atkins… the class of Merle Haggard to the rebellion of Willie Nelson… the pop of Dolly Parton to the rock of the Allman Brothers… or the traditions of Alan Jackson verses the progression of Carrie Underwood: Country music is a genre you could spend a long time getting to know, as it runs deep in the DNA of the music of the 20th century.

Country guitar is a fascinating genre and will require serious dedication and passion to achieve the mastery of Albert Lee or Brent Mason's hot licks. On the other hand, it's very easy to achieve a good command of the genre by playing songs and solos typical of the style.

I really do believe that Scotty Anderson may be one of the most terrifyingly technical players to ever pick up the guitar, and this should come as no surprise when you hear the playing of Jimmy Bryant, way back in the '50s; long before 'shred' guitar appeared!

If you want to get technical, then stick at it, but remember that the foundations of timing, tone and stylistic awareness are the bedrock on which these skills should be built.

Country Guitar for Beginners is split into two sections that are designed to develop the specific skills needed to become proficient in the many elements of the genre.

Part One focuses on chord playing and rhythm guitar skills. By developing a good feel now, you will sit tightly on the groove later when you're running up and down the neck with open string cascades and punchy double stops. Remember, the guitar didn't really function as a lead instrument until much later in the genre's development. It's all well and good being able to play Hot Wired (in fact it's pretty impressive!), but you also need to be able to know how to play something like Hey Good Lookin' or San Antonio Rose when required.

Once you've completed Part One, you will be ready to play anything you'd hear from Jimmie Rodgers, Hank Williams, Johnny Cash or similar icons of the genre. Building a sense of this style is imperative if you want to study players like Chet Atkins or the great Jerry Reed.

Part Two takes you through everything you need to play lead guitar solos typical of the earlier styles of country music. You'll look at basic picking concepts and how to *flat pick* and *thumb pick*… how to embellish rhythm parts with typical double stop riffs… scales in multiple keys… the use of triads as soloing guides… bending ideas, diatonic intervals and arpeggios. The goal is to teach you to fill the shoes of legendary guitarists like Roy Nichols, James Burton, Luther Perkins, and Eldon Shamblin.

While your ultimate goal may be to become the next Danny Gatton or Johnny Hiland, never lose sight of the roots. There's a reason these guys sound wonderful, and it's their understanding of everything that country music is. They don't sound like rock players who learned a few old country clichés.

At times, this journey may seem tough, but speaking as someone who got into country music relatively late in my life, I can say with absolute confidence that your skills will develop in time. Take it slow and make sure every movement is calm and calculated.

Remember the old adage: don't practice until you get it right, practice until you can't get it wrong. Stick at it, and with slow repetition, you're sure to get where you want to be.

Music isn't just about where you're going; it's about enjoying the journey.

Have fun,

Levi

Part One: Chords and Rhythm Guitar

In this section, you'll revisit the essential chord voicings found in everything from cowboy ballads to western swing. You may know some of these chords already but don't skip them as everything will matter by the time you reach the end of the chapter. There are plenty of country guitar secrets thrown in too… so pay attention! Once you've refreshed these voicings, you will look at the many ways they're used in real country rhythm guitar.

This section covers:

- Many usable chord diagrams

- Tips for changing chords

- Rhythm counting exercises

- Common chord progressions

- 'Alternating Bass' strumming

- Theory of chord construction

- Western Swing-style chord voicings

- Adding jazz influences

- Inversions and applications

- Western Swing chord progressions

- Modern strumming patterns

By mastering the skills in this section, you'll prepare yourself to dig deeper into other areas. Along with building dexterity in the fretting hand, you'll build the skills needed to tackle lead guitar too.

While it may be tempting to skip over some of these sections if you are a more advanced player remember that your sense of groove and timekeeping can *always* be improved, and the most efficient way to develop your abilities is by locking in with a good rhythm part and stay in the zone for hours.

The rhythm guitar skills we're looking at in part one are the ones most often required for singers and band work. So once you've got these rhythms and chords solid, try playing with a singer, or sing a melody yourself. Your focus should always be the music, and as you become more comfortable with these rhythms, you'll find yourself free to listen when playing.

I promise you'll thank me later!

Chapter One: Country Chord Refresher

At this stage, I assume that you're already familiar with basic open chords and some simple chord progressions, but really *understanding* these chords is the key to success in country guitar. Ignoring this aspect of music would be akin to building a house without foundations; everything may appear fine, but it could collapse at any time.

It would not be an understatement to say that chord knowledge is the most important aspect of playing country guitar - not just as a rhythm player, but as a lead guitarist too.

Before we begin, I want you to play a note on the guitar, absolutely any note, and ask yourself, "is this a good note?".

The answer is always "Eh?!"

It's a question that doesn't make any sense because a single note is nothing without context. If I play the note A against an A chord, it sounds fine. If I play that same A against an F chord it sounds great too. If I play that same A against a G# chord, it normally sounds pretty awful! The distances between these notes are called intervals.

The lesson is that in music, everything is intervals. Even in the key of E, the E won't sound great over every chord. Some intervals are pleasing to the ear, and others are less effective.

It's important to learn about chords because this knowledge will give you great insight into which notes will sound good, and which notes won't.

First, let's look at five of the most common Major chords found in country music. These crop up often in songs in the keys of C, G, D and even F.

In these early diagrams, I've included finger numbers to show you how these are often played. 1 represents the index finger, 2 is the middle finger and so on.

I've included these fingerings as most guitarists *don't* finger the G Major chord this way. It may feel a little uncomfortable at first, but it works great when combined with the C Major chord.

The fingering for F Major is also an eye-opener to many students who are used to a six-string barre. However, this 'mini-barre' is how Jimmie Rodgers would have played the chord. Understanding that this is a completely acceptable way to play the chord will come in handy later on when you're playing chord voicings common in Merle Travis or Chet Atkins style.

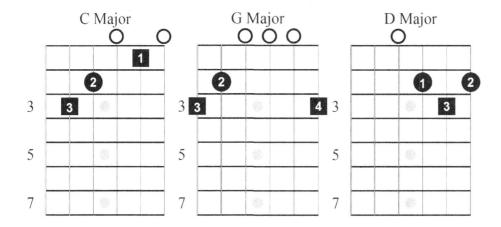

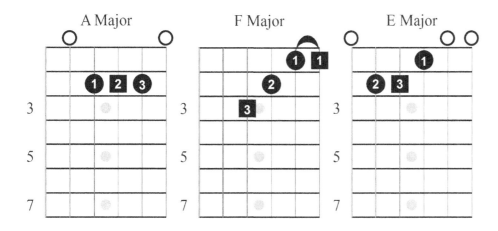

If you combine some of these chords into a simple progression, you're able to practice both timing and fretting-hand dexterity.

Your first goal is to move each of your fingers from one chord to the next simultaneously, rather than one at a time, as this can result in a perceptible delay in the chord changes.

The only way to master any chord is by building *muscle memory*, so take time to look at the previous diagrams and see each chord as a whole unit in your mind before placing your fingers on the guitar. Slowly practice forming each chord from nothing. Take your hand off the fingerboard, move to the chord, take your hand off the neck and repeat.

Time in music is divided into bars. Each bar of music contains four beats, and in the following examples, each chord lasts for two of those beats. As we count 1, 2, 3, 4, we're going to play a chord on both beat 1 and beat 3. The most important tip I can give here is that your strumming arm should be used as a time keeping device, so your arm moves up and down on every beat. This process begins as I count in with the metronome, so my first strum will be placed accurately on beat 1.

Always strum the beats (1, 2, 3 and 4) with a down strum. Notes that fall between the beats will be played with an up-strum.

Example 1a:

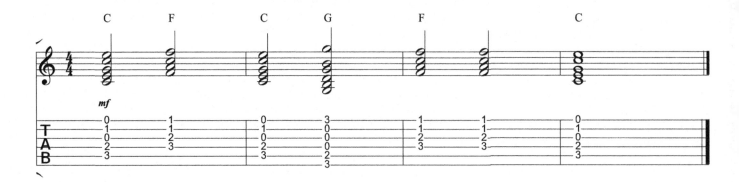

Let's look at simple variations to these chords that will turn them from *Major* chords into *Dominant* chords.

We learn the theory of this when we discuss Western swing later, but at this stage, it's important to train the fingers and the ears without complicating the music with theory. It's more important to be able to *hear* the difference between Major and Dominant chords, so when you play the Dominant chords try to describe in words how it *sounds* to you.

There are no wrong answers! It's all about associating an idea or feeling with the sound of a Dominant chord so that it jumps out at you when you hear it. Play through the following Dominant chords. In most cases, there is only one note different between the Major and Dominant versions of each chord.

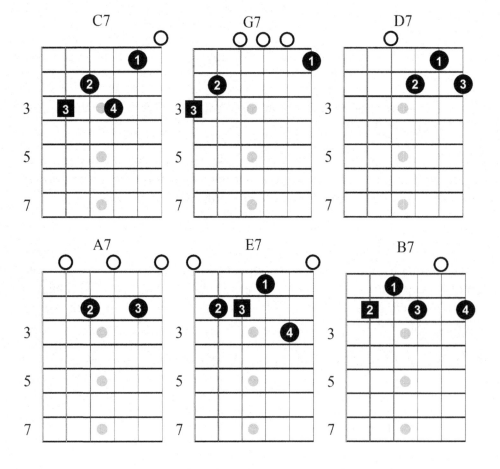

As with the Major chords, we can use these new chords in a progression to learn how they function, and to give our fingers a chance to start moving between them.

Example 1b:

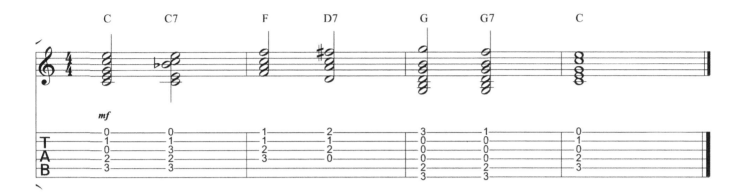

Next, we will learn some Minor chords.

To me, these chords sound "sad" or perhaps "longing"… but that's just me! The ultimate goal is to be able to *hear* these chords and say, "oh, that's a Minor chord!".

Practice changing between the following chords.

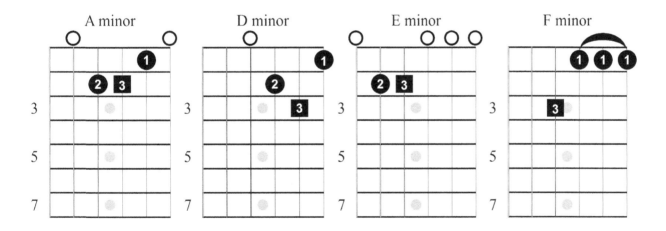

Now we can start to combine all the different chord types to create a chord *progression*.

This example contains some strumming. In this example, there are four chord strums per bar, and each is played with a down-stroke. Many more strumming ideas will be covered in the next chapter.

The following country ballad can be played very slowly and the key is to lock into the metronome by strumming a chord each time the metronome clicks. Count this out loud as, "1, 2, 3, 4, 1, 2, 3, 4". This is referred to as 4/4, or *common* time, with each beat being a 1/4 note (as it takes up 1/4 of a 4/4 bar).

Example 1c:

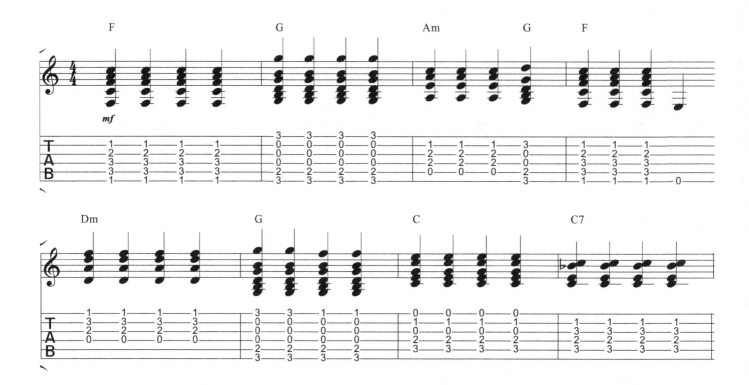

Early country music was closely related to gospel music. Amazing Grace is a wonderful hymn dating back as far as 1779. We play it here in the key of G and use a mixture of Major, Minor and Dominant chords.

Unlike the previous example, this piece has a 'three' feel, meaning there are three beats in each bar. Count "1, 2, 3, 1, 2, 3", and accent the first beat a little louder to help keep the feel.

I encourage you to sing the melody if you're familiar with it. It's surprising how complete a chord progression like this can feel just by adding the melody.

Example 1d:

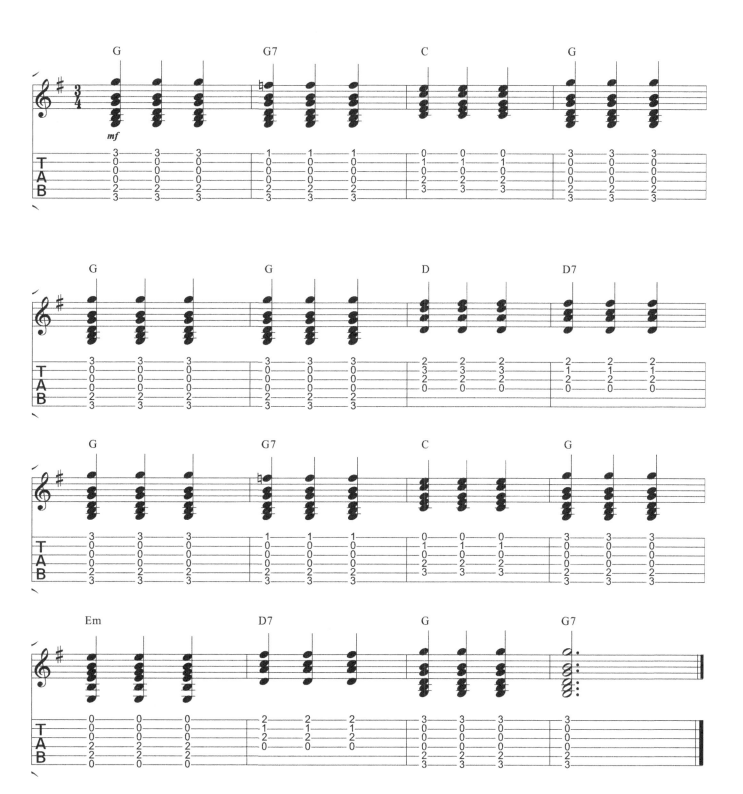

Don't forget to use the proper fingering for the G Major chord!

The intention here is to demonstrate how these simple chords can form the basis of many songs. Using them shouldn't be looked down on in any way.

Take the time to practice these simple chord progressions and attempt to distinguish the difference in sound between each chord family (Major, Minor, Dominant). I find the best way to do this is to play the chord progressions so slowly that I am able to think ahead. When playing the G Major chord from the previous example, I attempt to 'hear' what the G7 chord is going to sound like in my mind before I play it. Focusing on these harmonic shifts is one of the best ways to train your ears.

Chapter Two: Basic Strumming and Playing Songs

Now you know some chords, let's use them to make music in the style of the early country players.

The first thing to consider is the *function* of the guitar in country music; how it developed, and what is required to create an authentic sound when backing a singer or creating a rhythm track.

As mentioned in the introduction, drums in country music didn't occur until many years after the genre had taken off, and even then it was something the purists were adamantly against. There are stories of the Grand Ole Opry refusing to let artists use drums, despite there being a drummer in their band. This essentially cut out a huge avenue of exposure for any artist trying to move with the times by bringing in pop or rock influences, rather than sticking true to a 'pure' genre that was dwindling in popularity.

The period without drums resulted in the other instruments having to create a driving, percussive sound in other ways. As such, the guitar acted as both an instrument that provided harmony, and a percussive instrument to keep time so that people could dance. One might argue that the guitar is best used as a source of percussion because many country bands (especially in Honky-Tonk bars) had pianos which always outclassed guitars as harmony providers.

The 'classic' country feel that developed was a combination of the bass playing on beats 1 and 3 of the bar with a heavy accent on the guitar on beats 2 and 4. This 2 and 4 accent is commonly known as a *backbeat*, and is the defining sound in contemporary 4/4 music, from early jazz, right up to the pop music of today.

Let's recreate this feel on a C Major chord to really get the effect locked in our ears and muscles. To keep the playing interesting, we'll imitate what a bass player would play on our lowest strings.

Listen closely to the recording of the following example because the *dynamics* are important. We'll begin by playing the root note on beat 1, then a chord on beat 2. Next, we play the 5th degree of C Major (G)[1] and then accent the chord again on beat 4.

Repeat this sequence repeats as long as is required to commit it to muscle memory. Take your time with this example and get comfortable with the alternating bass note.

Example 2a:

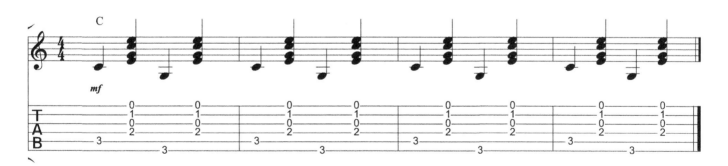

This movement of the root, followed by the 5th is extremely important in country music. To find the 5th of a chord simply count up five notes from the root. The 5th of A is E (A, B, C, D, E), the 5th of G is D (G, A, B, C, D) etc.

---

1. The note G is the fifth note in the scale of C Major: C, D, E, F, G.

When we change from the C Major chord to the A Major chord, everything in the strumming pattern remains the same, with the root on the fifth string and the 5th on the sixth string. This needs a little more care though, as you don't want the bass notes to ring out into each other. Try to cut off the bass notes with the palm of the strumming hand before hitting the chord stabs.

In bar three and four, the A chord changes to an A7. As this is still an "A-type" chord, the alternating bass pattern doesn't need to change.

Example 2b:

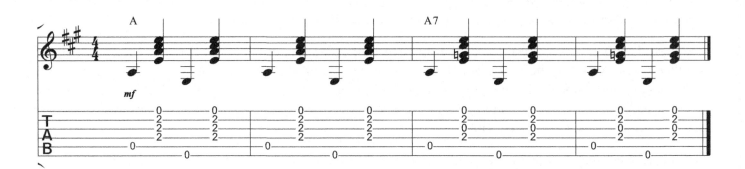

One last example of the root and 5th movement is the following B7 chord. Assuming you've got to grips with the fingering of this chord from the previous chapter, all you need to do is alternate the 2nd finger between the fifth and sixth string. As with the previous chords, move between the root (B) and the 5th (F#). You may notice that if the root of the chord is on the A string, then the 5th will always be on the same fret of the E string.

Example 2c:

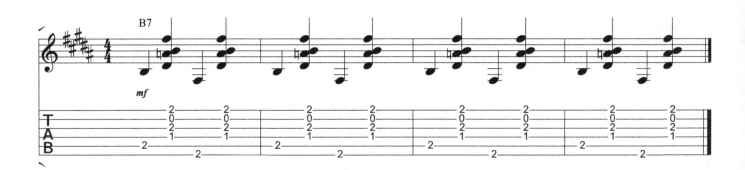

One challenging part of this style is that not all chords have the root on the A string!

This is demonstrated with a G Major chord. With this chord, the root note is on the low E string, and the 5th (D) is on the open D string. This means jumping over the A string to the D string to play the alternating bass. Skipping over the A string can feel awkward at first, but this is an important movement to master.

As with the A Major chord, switch to the Dominant chord in bars three and four.

Example 2d:

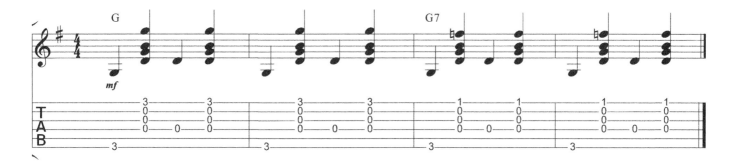

On an E Major chord, the root is on the low E string, and the 5th is on the A string. Moving between these notes will probably feel easy after working on the G chord. As with the previous examples, changing to the Dominant chord in bar three shows you the alternating bass pattern remains consistent here.

Example 2e:

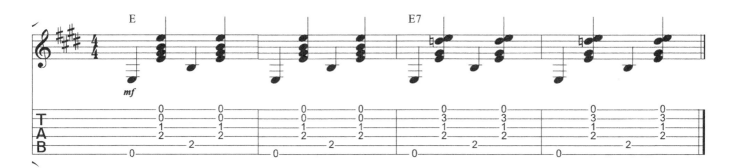

D Major chords have root notes on the open D (fourth) string, and the 5th is played on the open A (fifth) string.

Example 2f:

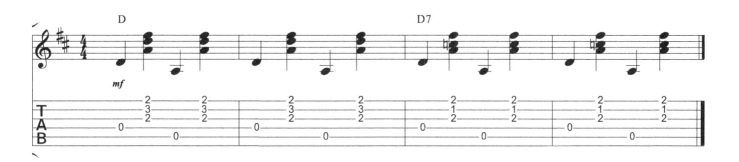

When I really got into playing country rhythm seriously, I noticed that many of the greats would play a 'mini barre' version of the F Major chord, with a root on the D string instead of the low E string. Aside from being easier on the hand than the full barre chord, this voicing also has the benefit of allowing an easy movement to play the 5th on the A string.

Example 2h:

To add more life to these parts, let's develop the backbeat by adding by adding another strum on the upstroke of beats 2 and 4. This creates a count of "1, 2&, 3, 4&, 1, 2&, 3, 4&". The important thing to understand is that the movement in the strumming hand shouldn't change. Continue to strum down on each beat but now simply catch the strings with the pick on the way up too.

Play the previous strumming pattern applied to a C Major and C7 chord.

Example 2i:

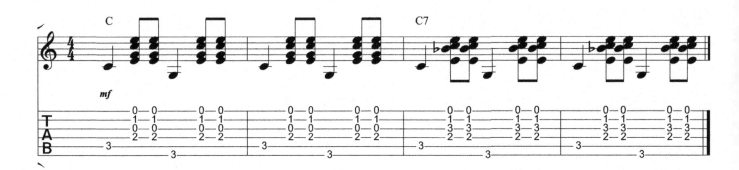

Let's use the previous exercises to make some music! This example is typical of Johnny Cash's approach to rhythm guitar on songs like Walk the Line or Folsom Prison Blues. Johnny was one of the most iconic, best-selling country artists of all time, and his music still touches millions of people the world over, even after his death in 2003.

The chord progression is very close to a standard twelve-bar blues but with a pause on the V chord (B7) for two bars. The bass movement sticks to the root and 5th movement you've just spent time mastering.

Example 2j:

Next, let's add the 'down up' stroke on beat 2 to make a rhythm that is typical of Hank Williams.

As with the previous examples, continue to alternate between the root and the 5th in the bass part to create a solid, driving sound. This is an essential part of the genre, and an important feel to master before moving on to look at the style of legends such as Merle Travis or Chet Atkins.

Example 2k:

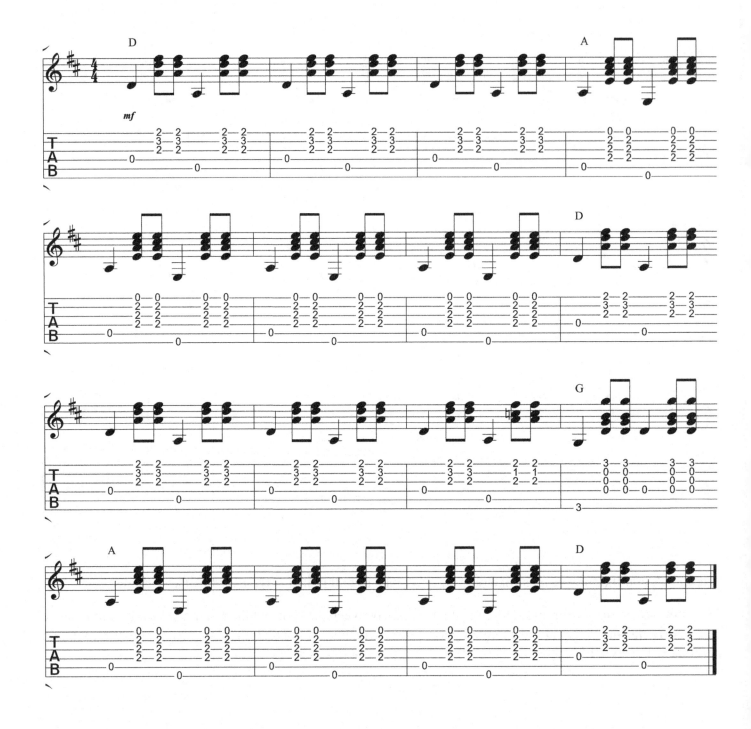

The next example is in the style of Jimmie Rodgers, and similar to his playing on classics such as Blue Yodel No.1, or Waiting on a Train.

This example has the same feel as before, but now with added bass notes other than the root and 5th.

Beat 3 of bar two sees you playing the 3rd (E) of the C7 chord. There are no hard and fast rules for choosing these bass notes; it's all about creating an interesting melodic movement to keep the song moving forward. All these extra bass notes simply happen to be within easy reach of the chord fingering.

Example 2l:

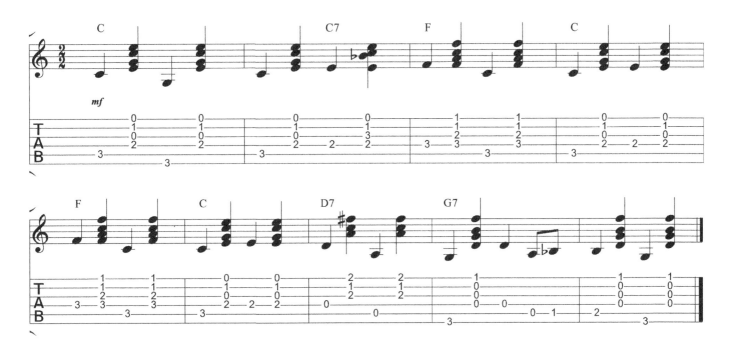

Let's stick with Jimmie's approach to rhythm, but this time play in 3/4. This feel is similar to Amazing Grace from Chapter One, but now you will play a bass note on beat 1 and chord strums on beats 2 and 3.

In this example you'll notice some interesting notes added in the bass, in particular the B played against the C Major chord (bar seven) and the F# played against the G Major chord (bar fifteen). As a rule, you can always approach any chord from a fret below and it's going to sound great.

Example 2m:

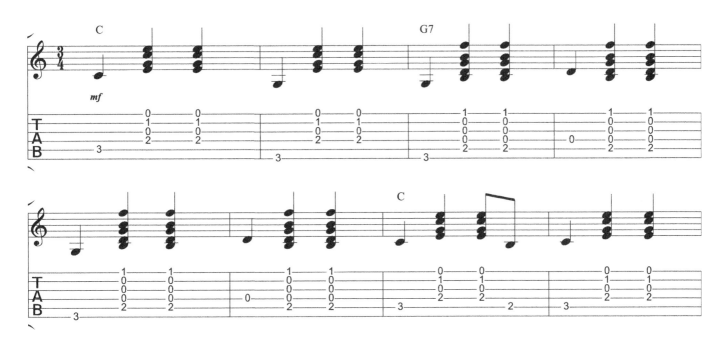

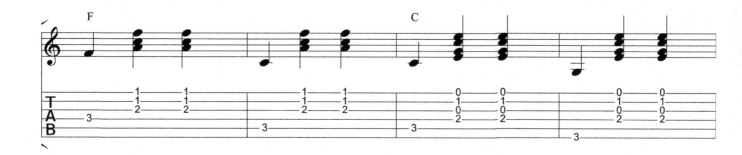

You should now be getting a sense of how to create a country backbeat by accenting beat 2 of the bar with a slightly harder strum. If not, listen carefully to the audio examples and try to mimic my playing. This feel is the life-blood of country rhythm guitar, so listen to as much music as you can and try to emulate this feel in your playing.

Syncopation is the act of offsetting a beat so an accent falls somewhere it would not normally be expected.

In reality, this is simply displacing a chord or note that you would expect to fall on a strong beat. On paper, this idea may sound complicated, but it's actually something you'll have heard hundreds of times.

The first syncopated example accents a chord played on the "and" of beat 4. This is held though beat 1 of the following bar.

Remember, the strumming technique here is identical to before. Your hand moves down on the beats and up between the beats. The trick is to keep your hand moving all the time, even though you're not actually striking the strings on beat 1 of bar two.

Keep a strong backbeat by accenting the 2 and 4 where possible. The exception is when you're syncopating, as it sounds best to accent the notes that are off the beat as it helps to make the music sound more human, and less mechanical. My best advice here is to listen to the audio examples: These ideas look complicated on paper but make much more sense once you hear them. Learning music is all about listening and copying what you hear.

Example 2n:

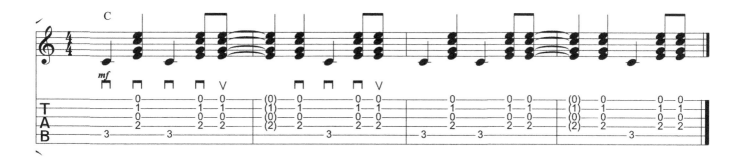

The next example takes the previous idea but moves the syncopated chord to the "and" of beat 2.

You can vocalise bar one by saying; "1, 2 & … & 4". This counting looks quite complex when written down, so listen closely to the audio example and you'll soon realize this is a rhythm you hear all the time,

Practice this rhythm on the first two bars of the following example. When you start to get the idea, add the second two bars which contain an F Major chord to keep you on your toes.

Example 2o:

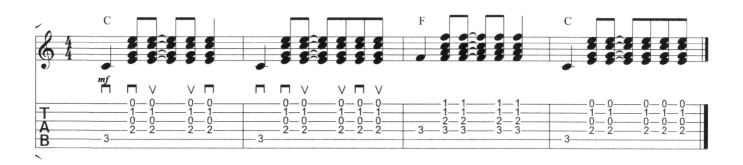

The 3rd example places the syncopated strum on the "and" of beat 2 moving into beat 3.

This rhythm could just as easily be played in the second half of the bar to fall on the "and" of beat 3 moving into beat 4.

It is important to notice that this example affects the backbeat because the syncopated note effectively moves the beat 2 accent earlier than expected.

As always, listen carefully to the audio recording to get a feel for this example. It's always easier to hear these ideas than to learn them by reading.

Example 2p:

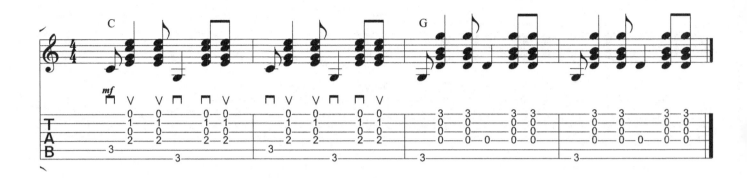

The final example in this chapter applies syncopated ideas to a common country chord progression.

Played in G, the example begins on the I chord (G Major) before moving to the IV (C Major) then V (D Major), this idea then repeats but moves from the V (D Major) to the IV (C Major).

The second section moves to the vi (Em) followed by the V (D Major), this repeats but is varied by a syncopated V7 chord (D7) that pulls you back home to G Major.

Example 2q:

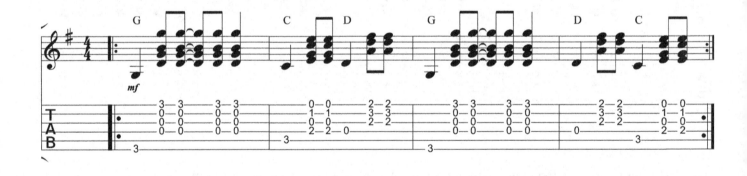

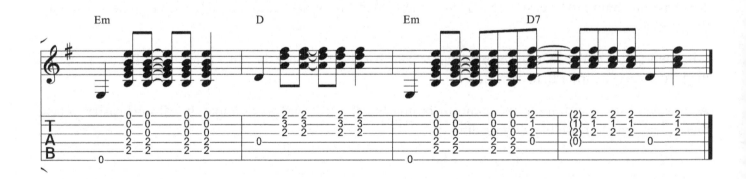

After working through this chapter, you will be armed with the tools to play most common country acoustic strumming parts. You should now be able to explore more rhythm playing and develop your inner pulse while working on simple tunes.

Listen to the country greats and imitate their strumming patterns. The more you listen to legends like Merle Haggard, Waylon Jennings, David Allan Coe, Ernest Tubb and Glen Campbell, the more you'll develop a feel for how these guys played.

What you'll quickly learn is that once you've really mastered strumming, you don't improve by *thinking* more. The best way to improve is by *listening* and *replicating* what you hear. Remember, the strumming hand moves down and up to the music, simply hit the strings as and when you want to hear them.

Chapter Three: Western Swing Rhythm

During the late '20s and early '30s, a new sub-genre of country music began to evolve when the jazz music of the era met the instrumentation of country music found in the South.

Suddenly, bands popped up all over the country playing this new *Western Swing* music for people to dance to. Notable pioneers like Bob Wills, Milton Brown, and Spade Cooley began using drums to add excitement to their driving jazz-based rhythm sections. They were still playing songs, but the more involved chord changes gave guitarists like Eldon Shamblin, Jimmy Wyble, and Junior Barnard something new to experiment with in both their rhythm style and their solos (which were plentiful!).

Unfortunately, the genre saw a sharp decline in the '40s when the US introduced a nightclub tax for "dancing nightclubs" to help raise funds for the war effort. This steep 30% tax saw countless clubs ban dancing, which was enough to all but kill the movement. While the genre never saw a true renaissance, it lived on in the works of bands like The Hot Club of Cowtown, The Lucky Stars, and The Swing Commanders.

One of the defining aspects of Western swing rhythm playing is the driving 'four on the floor' rhythm (four 1/4 notes per measure) and almost dizzying use of chord *inversions*; think Freddie Green in Count Basie Orchestra's Orchestra or Django Reinhardt's rhythm work, but with a redneck twist.

A chord inversion is a voicing where a note *other than the root* note appears in the bass. So while a G Major triad contains the notes G, B, and D, this could be played with any of the three different notes (G, B or D) in the bass; each being a different inversion.

A G Major chord with the root in the bass (G, B, D) is called a *root position chord*.

Playing the 3rd in the bass (B, G, D, or B, D, G) is a *1st inversion* triad and is written as G/B (pronounced 'G over B' and meaning a G chord over a B bass note).

Playing the 5th in the bass gives you a *2nd inversion* triad of G/D.

Example 3a demonstrates three inversions of a G chord beginning with an E-shape barre form.

Each voicing contains just three notes, the root, 5th, and 3rd. This is an open-voiced triad, sometimes called a 'shell voicing'. Stripped down voicings like this have two advantages: not only do they sit well in this musical setting, but using fewer notes makes changing between voicings at faster tempos much easier.

In the following diagrams, the notes that are played are shown as black dots, while the bigger barre chord 'CAGED' shape is shown with hollow notes to give you some context. Don't play the hollow notes.

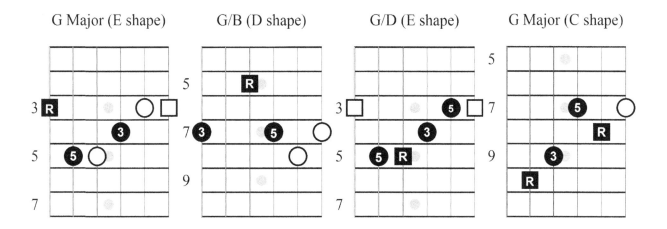

G Major (E shape)   G/B (D shape)   G/D (E shape)   G Major (C shape)

Example 3a:

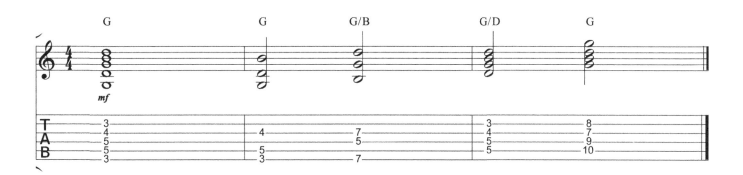

In swing, inversions are used in two ways. While they are used to create smooth changes from chord to chord, they're also used to create interest for the listener when one chord is held for a prolonged period of time. The Bob Wills classic 'Stay a Little Longer' is a good example, as it begins with four bars of a G Major chord. The following example demonstrates how four bars of G Major might be played in *early* country music

Example 3b:

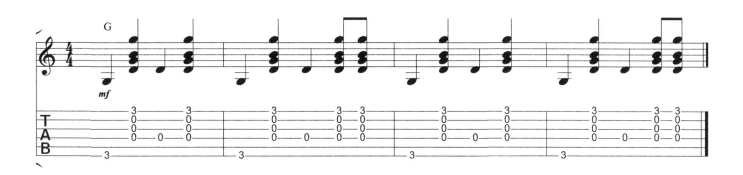

The next example takes that G Major chord but this time moves between some of the inversions above to create interest. Not only are parts like these both fun and challenging to play, they also sound great too.

Example 3c:

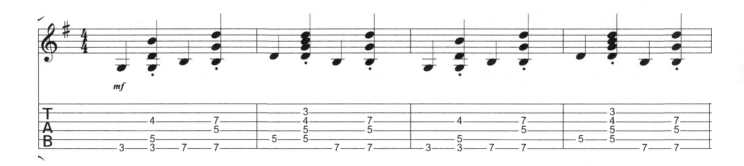

Example 3d demonstrates how a swing player might approach a long stint on one chord. When you look closely, you'll notice this riff contains a melody in the bass. This helps tie the part together and make it feel more like a riff than a stream of chord changes.

Also, the rhythm has been notated a bit literally here, so it's important to get a feel for the dynamics of this style by listening to the audio. There's also definitely a lot of cross-pollination with the famous Gypsy jazz 'la pompe' rhythm. Use a heavy accent on beats 2 and 4, so much so that beats 1 and 3 often only include a single note.

Don't take this too literally! The idea is to have a small, soft strum followed by a bigger, more aggressive strum to push the beat along. Listen to the audio carefully to hear for this yourself.

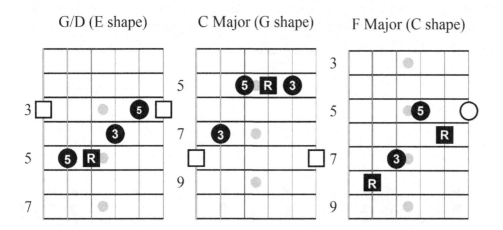

Note the melody in the lowest part of the chords above. While the C/E and F aren't inversions of G, the movement in the bass ties them together nicely.

Example 3d:

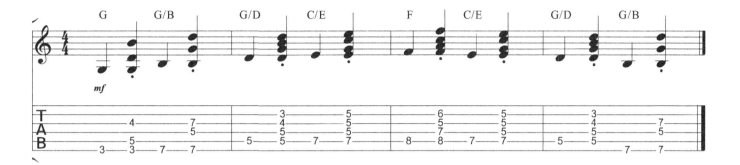

Aside from these fast-paced inversions, Western swing chord vocabulary also contains more extensions, such as 7th- and 6th-chords. As time goes by you'll learn more chord extensions, but the following basic sounds will always serve you well.

Example 3e:

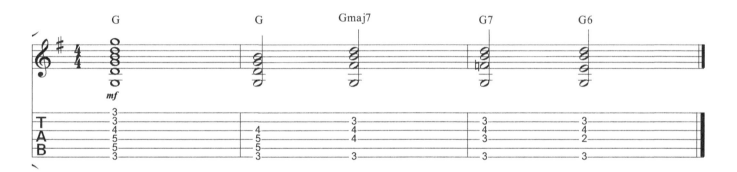

The next example showcases how a swing player might use these sounds when comping on a blues. The first four measures sit on a G Major, but the inner voice of the chords changes the chord from a G Major to a Gmaj7 to a G6 to a G7 which finally resolves to a C7 in bar five. On the return to G Major, there's a repeat of the three inversions studied earlier.

Example 3f:

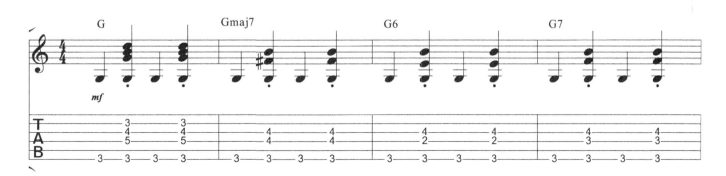

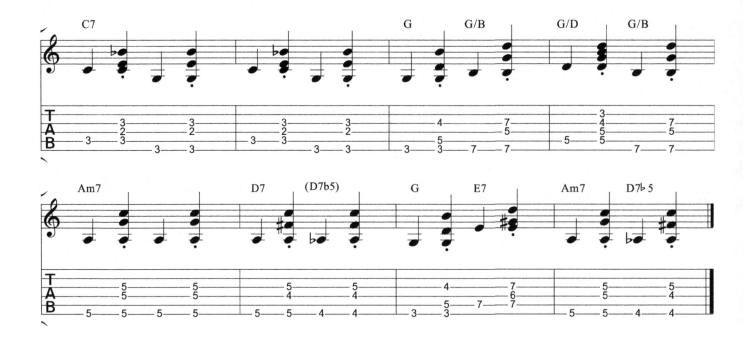

There are also useful inversions and extensions that fit under the hands with an 'A shape' chord While this collection of chords isn't comprehensive, it's certainly enough to draw a decent amount of ideas for a C Major barre chord.

Example 3g:

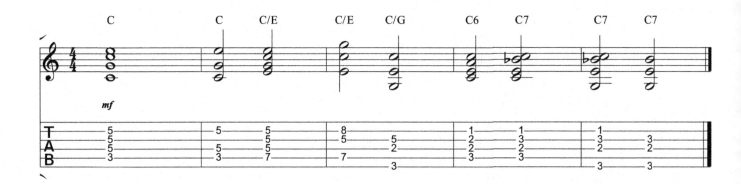

One of the most intriguing parts of swing players is how they're able to create both motion on a static chord, but also connect chord changes fluently. In the following example, begin on a G Major chord and move up the neck using inversions. The transition to the C Major happens via a G7 chord, before moving down the neck in inversions and resolving to the original G Major chord.

Example 3h:

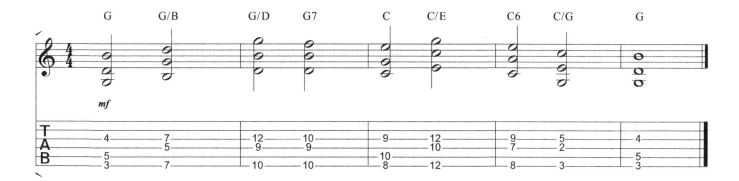

Another common approach that creates harmonic interest is playing chord-scales. The next example features voicings for chords in the key of G Major. Note the use of the C6 in measure two as a sweeter sound than the expected Cmaj7.

Example 3i:

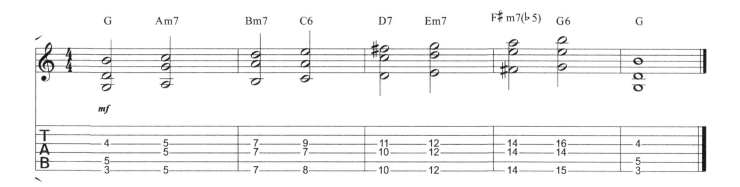

The next example shares many chords with the previous *chord-scale* idea, but instead of playing chords like Bm7 and D7, these have been replaced inversions of the G Major triad and results in the same bass movement, but stays strongly related to the original G Major chord.

Example 3j:

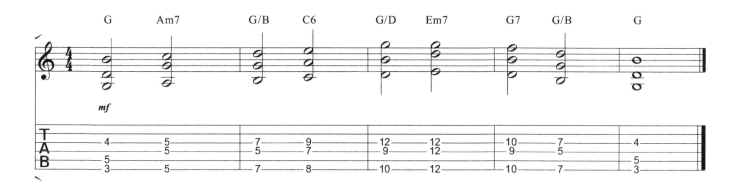

Another common trick is to play *diminished chords a semitone below the chord* they're moving to. For example, playing a G#dim7 between the chords of G Major and Am7. This creates a very smooth transition between the voicings.

As a general rule, you can always play a diminished 7 chord a semitone below the root of the chord you are moving to.

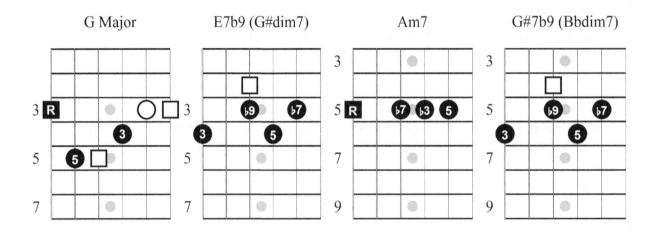

Example 3k:

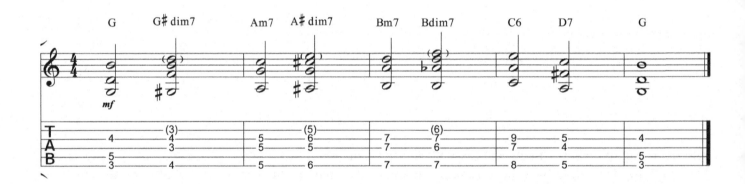

Here's an example of that idea used to create a chord riff on a C Major vamp. First, the C Major moves up the chord-scale to Dm7 (via a diminished chord), then up to a C/E via another diminished chord. This then moves down via a ii-V (Dm7 - G7) back to C Major to turn the riff around. You'll find ideas like this all over Light Crust Doughboys recordings.

This all sounds very complicated, but the important part is to listen to the bass movement and treat it as a melody rather than a complex collection of substitutions and theory.

Example 3l:

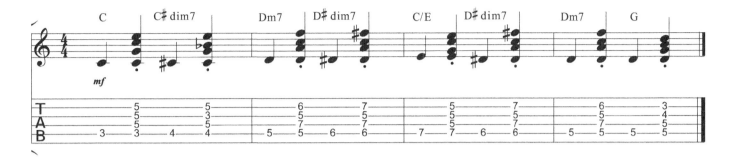

Next is a similar idea, but this time on the lowest strings and in the key of G Major.

Example 3m:

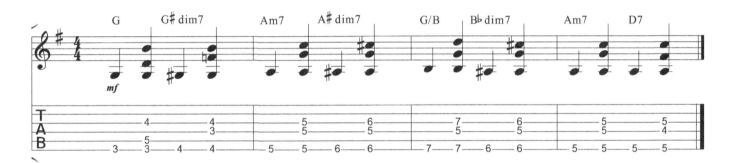

Here's an example similar to something the great Eldon Shamblin might have played. Eldon's work with Bob Wills and His Texas Playboys is a shining example of the style. This idea contains some new chords, including a tricky voicing for G7, and an Eb6. Both of these voicings are based on a C Major barre.

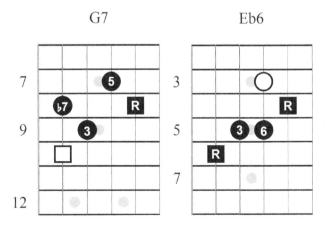

Beginning with a G Major triad, G7 is formed by moving the root note down two frets to the b7, and creating a G7/F. By itself, this voicing it pretty hard on the ears, but sandwiched between the G Major and C/E, the F in the bass works well as it walks down the scale.

Example 3n:

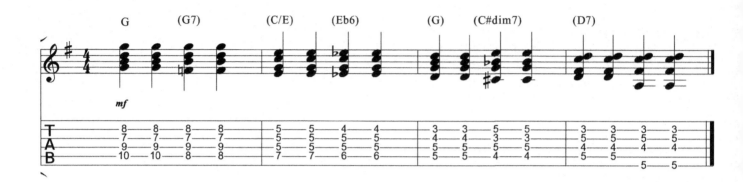

The final example is a little more in-depth, and outlines a sixteen-bar Western swing-type progression. The chord progression in the first four measures could be thought of as G - A7 - D7 - G7 - E7 - A7 D7, but with the guitar playing two chords per bar, and running up and down the neck, things get interesting quite quickly.

Over the G Major chord, a chord-scale approach has been used which contrasts with the inversions played over the A7 chord.

Over the D Major chord we play a walk-down in the bass, starting with the root (D), and moving through the b7, 6th, and 5th.

For the turnaround, we begin with G Major, then move up to a 2nd inversion E7 voicing. This voicing moves down chromatically to return to G Major.

The second eight bars starts with the same movement of G Major to A7. A new trick is shown on the A7 chord, simply move the chord down one fret and back up again! This doesn't need a theoretical explanation; it just sounds great!

The final four bars feature another walk down in the bass, this time beginning on an Em7 chord. To end there is a 'ii-V-I' in G, ending on a clichéd 6/9 voicing that is common in country and early rockabilly music.

Example 3o:

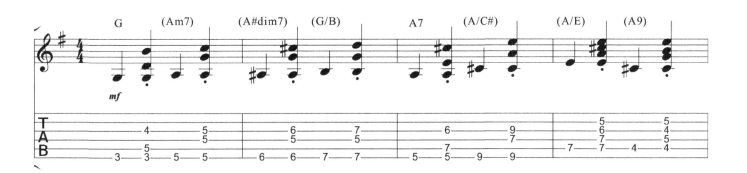

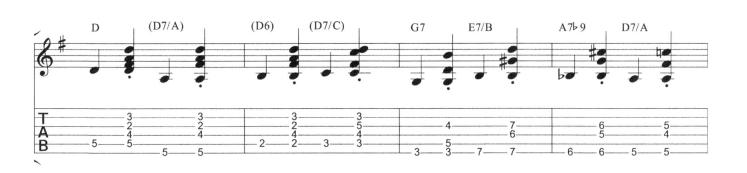

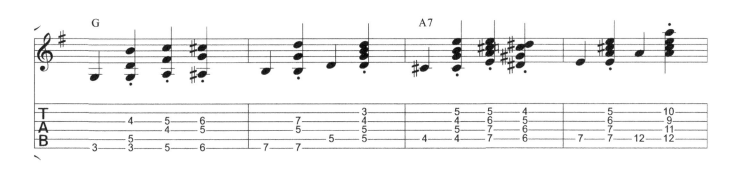

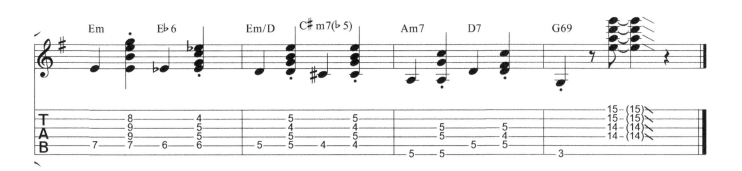

These examples should open your ears up to the sound of this exciting and unique genre of music.

Spend some time listening to the music of Bob Wills and His Texas Playboys, and Milton Brown and His Musical Brownies to become familiar with the standards of the genre. You'll also hear a lot of cross-pollination with the Gypsy Jazz music of Django Reinhardt and the Quintette du Hot Club de France as songs like "After You've Gone" were played by both.

This genre of music influences music that came years later, such as the much beloved Bakersfield sound, that used swing as a main component. Buck Owens would become well known for this music, and players like Vince Gill keep it alive today with his band, The Time Jumpers.

Chapter Four: Hybrid Picking Riffs

After Rock and Roll took over the world and Rockabilly (itself coming from a portamento of rock and hillbilly) gained a cult following, Nashville began producing music with commercial success at the top its the list of priorities. The pop element of country music certainly wasn't a bad thing as it introduced acts like Glen Campbell and Dolly Parton to wider audiences of young people who didn't want to listen to the same music as their parents.

As time went by, more and more flavours were brought to country music and were adapted to country's traditional tastes. No influence was stronger than the mildly overdriven guitar sounds of rock music. This influence went both ways, as rock acts like the Rolling Stones, The Allman Brothers, Lynyrd Skynyrd and The Eagles started using more country-influence ideas. This sound is still strong today, even in the more pop-focused songs of Brad Paisley, Miranda Lambert, and Carrie Underwood

Eventually incorporation of rock into country led to *Truck-Driving* country music, that combined elements of Outlaw, Rock, Honky-Tonk and Bakersfield to create a sound that formed an exciting direction for established artists like Merle Haggard and Jerry Reed, while also creating a vehicle for artists like Alan Jackson and Junior Brown to reach a new audience of their own.

A big part of playing this style authentically is the use of the pick and fingers together, commonly known as *hybrid* picking. Not only does hybrid picking make some things technically easier to play, it also sounds quite different. With hybrid picking, you can play more than one note simultaneously, rather than slightly apart (which is impossible to avoid when strumming with a pick). Hybrid picking also adds a little more 'spank' to the notes as you pull the strings away from the fretboard… After they're plucked, they slap back aggressively against the fretboard.

First up, let's get used to how hybrid picking sounds and feels. Play this example with the middle and index finger simultaneously. Place them on the string before plucking and pull outwards to sound the notes. Some players like Brent Mason use acrylic nails to give these notes a pick-like attack, but, personally speaking, I just use the flesh of the fingers. Both options are fine.

Example 4a:

Now add the pick. Here's a short example based around an E Major chord. The first note is plucked with the pick then the *double stop* is played with the fingers. Simply alternate between the two.

As an experiment, try playing this idea with just the pick. While it is possible, it's a lot more work and doesn't sound the same at all.

Example 4b:

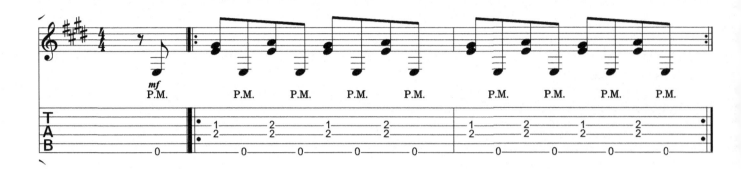

Next it's important to practice the 'pinch', which is when you use the pick and fingers together.

Example 4c:

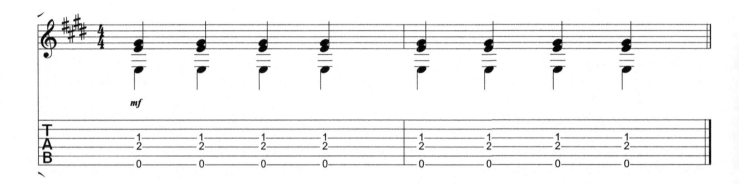

Before adding syncopation, it's important to get used to the pick alternating between the sixth and fourth strings. This example teaches that idea by playing the bass notes with down-strokes.

Example 4d:

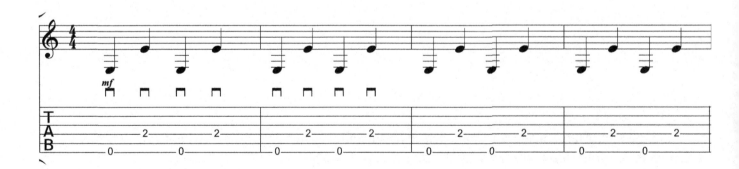

As with the previous example, the pick continues to play on all 4 beats. The pinch only occurs on beats 2 and 4. The pick still plays the low notes. The notation uses downward facing stems for notes played with the pick and upward facing stems for notes played with the fingers.

Example 4e:

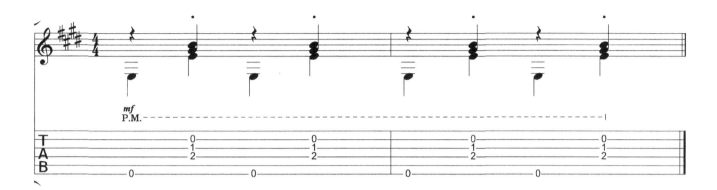

The next example expands on the previous idea by adding syncopation. The second double stop is pulled forward by an 1/8th note to create an accented offbeat. This is a big part of the rockabilly style, though the Travis picking country fingerstyle subject will be covered much more deeply in book two.

Example 4f:

Here's an example that requires you to double-pick the double stops to create an interesting rhythmic pattern consisting of two groups of three, followed by one group of two. Although the bar contains eight notes, the traditional backbeat has now been removed. Instead of accenting the 2 and 4, count "1 2 3 1 2 3 1 2" and accent the 1s to give you a better idea of the feel.

Example 4g:

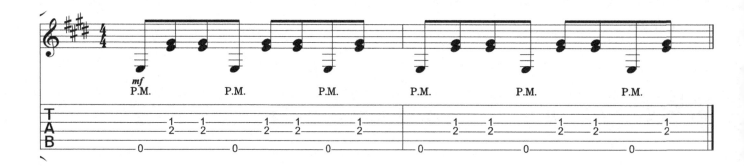

The next example is similar to the rhythm playing you'll to hear in Merle Haggard's band. Based around an E7 chord, use the pick for the notes on the low E string, and the fingers for the double stops. This example requires tight time keeping skills in the fretting hand as you're required to pluck open strings and hammer onto a fretted note. Use the 1st finger for the hammered note, then fret both notes on the 2nd fret with a 2nd finger barre.

Example 4h:

Example 4h embellishes the previous riff to cover four bars. In the second measure you'll need to play the high E string and let all the strings ring. As with the double stops, use a picking hand finger to sound this note. In the final measure the same idea is played, but this time ends with an alternate-picked idea on the D and A strings.

Example 4i:

The next example draws influence from Boogie-Woogie bands by using a solid stream of 1/8th notes. In order to execute the double-stroke with the pick it is easiest to play an up-stroke followed by a down (as indicated above the tablature). Ideas like this are as at home in the blues as they are in country music.

Example 4j:

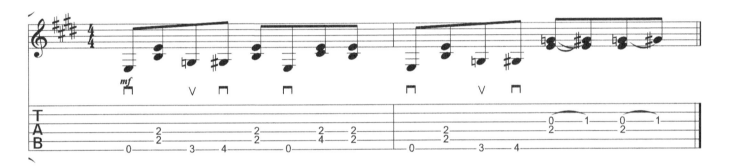

Here is an idea similar to example 4g, but this time in the key of A. In the second bar there's a little melodic trick in the double stop that takes an A5 chord and moves the lowest note down from the 5th to the b5th to the 4th. Not only does this give a pleasing bluesy edge, but it opens up some sonic options when riffing.

Example 4k:

The next example expands on the previous idea by adding more single notes while leaving the double stops as accents in the rhythm. While there are notes here that could be seen as part of a scale, they're more about linking chord tones together than a scale in their own right. We will look at scales later!

Example 4l:

Here's an example that uses the low open E and finger-picked double stops as a starting point, but adds a walk-up for melodic interest in the bass. Use the pick for the single notes and fingers for the double-stops.

Example 4m:

The next example applies the hybrid picking concept to a chord progression to give you a better idea of how someone like Brad Paisley would use it in a song. Played in the key of E, this I, V, vi, IV progression is outlined with simple chord-patterns, so don't lose sight of the original barre chord when adding the single notes.

Example 4n:

The final example in this chapter uses hybrid picked *riffing* to a chord progression in the key of G. The G Major chord is played in open position while the C Major and D7 use barre chords in higher positions.

Example 4o:

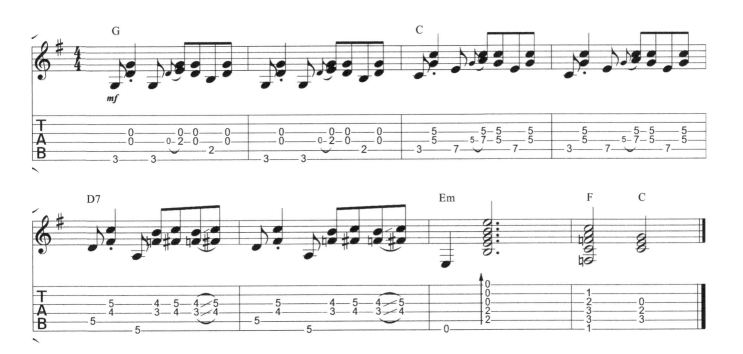

Hopefully, you can see that in Country music, chords are thought of as *individual events* and are embellished as such. Rather than playing the scale of G Major over a whole progression in G, the thought process is much closer to jazz, where each individual chord is treated and embellished as an entity in its own right.

Part Two: Scales, Arpeggios and Lead Guitar

In Part Two, you'll develop a full range of scales, arpeggios and soloing approaches that can be applied to of country music.

In this section, you'll learn:

- Scale theory

- Open position scales

- Movable scales

- The CAGED system

- Soloing with intervals

- Relationships between chords, arpeggios and scales

- How to use patterns to make real music

- Arpeggio concepts

- Soloing ideas

Mastering the skills in this section will free your mind from thinking too much about the neck when playing, as well as preparing your fingers for the more technically demanding aspects of country guitar like banjo rolls and open string ideas.

Don't rush through these ideas, take your time and don't be afraid to jump back to earlier chapters to review concepts, techniques, and theory. Listen to country music as much as possible and try to recognise the techniques in everything you hear.

Chapter Five: Country Scale Primer

In order to develop your knowledge of chords, harmony, and soloing, it's important to get to grips with the sounds and common fingerings of a selection of country music scales.

This chapter will build your knowledge of intervals and create proficiency in:

- The Minor Pentatonic scale

- The Blues scale

- The Major Pentatonic scale

- The "Country" scale

- Open position fingerings

- Movable forms

- Parallel vs derivative modal theory

Coming from the Greek penta, - meaning "five", and tonic, - meaning "based on the key note", a Pentatonic scale is any scale that consists of five notes.

The Minor Pentatonic scale is the workhorse of countless respectable country, blues, rock, metal, and even jazz players; many of the greatest of all time use it exclusively, never feeling the need to look elsewhere to create genre-defining signature sounds, so it would be foolish to overlook it!

Example 5a shows the E Minor Pentatonic scale played in the open position. At this stage, don't worry too much about picking technique or theory, just concentrate on hearing the sound of the scale.

Example 5a:

As previously stated, much can be achieved with this scale, including moving the entire form up or down the neck to suit any key. For example, here's the same scale shifted up the neck three frets to give you the G Minor Pentatonic scale. Note that the root note is found on the low E string, and is played with the 1st finger.

Example 5b:

Looking at this scale on a diagram gives you the chance to see the intervals at play. Intervals are what gives the scale it's character. Consisting of the Root, b3, 4, 5 and b7, the scale contains the same notes as a Minor 7 chord (R, b3, 5, b7) but with an added 4th.

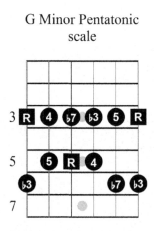

G Minor Pentatonic
scale

One might surmise that this means the G Minor Pentatonic scale will work exclusively over Minor chords, but the truth is a little surprising. In fact, while the Minor 3rd of a G Minor Pentatonic scale should clash horribly with the Major 3rd of a G Major or G7 chord, the result is pleasing tension best described as "bluesy" or "gritty".

Example 5c demonstrates the G Minor Pentatonic played against a G Minor chord vamp. It sounds like a good fit, capturing the quality of the chord in a pleasing way.

Example 5c:

The next example uses a different G Minor Pentatonic lick against a G *Major* chord to see how it sounds.

You'll notice that I'm bending those b3rds (Bbs) a little sharp to create a bluesy quality, this is known as a "blues curl" and doesn't *quite* raise the note from Bb to B, but hints at something in between.

Example 5d:

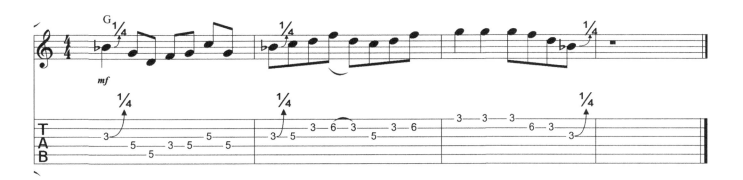

When getting to grips with scales on the guitar, it is important to understand that your ear must match your technical proficiency, if not surpass it. You must practice all your ideas and exercises in some sort of harmonic context so you're not just learning how to play the lick, but you're also building a *relationship* with it in context, and internalising how it makes you feel.

To create an instant backing track, I use a looper pedal by TC electronic when practicing. This repeats a chord indefinitely so that I never lose the harmonic context; there are numerous options when it comes to recording backing tracks, but this feels the quickest and best-sounding to me.

While it is important to learn scales that cover the entire neck, at this stage there's more benefit to be had from building control of a scale in one area before introducing multiple fingerings and position shifts. That said, it's also useful to have little "bolt-on" notes that can be added to the top or bottom of a pattern to extend your vocabulary.

For example, below is the G Minor Pentatonic scale from the previous example, this time with a little additional range at the top and at the bottom. This will come in handy quite soon.

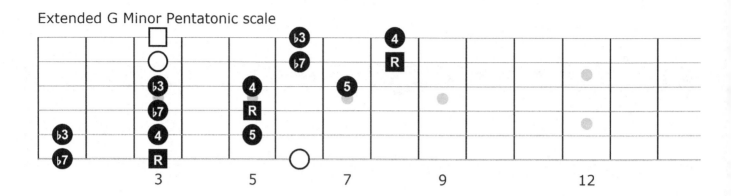

Extended G Minor Pentatonic scale

You'll notice that some of the notes are hollow, this is to help outline a "roadmap" used to move up the neck. The white notes are possible fingerings of the scale notes, but re-fingered in the following example to create an easier line.

In order to play the three consecutive notes on the A string, use the 1st finger on the 1st fret, the 3rd finger on the 3rd fret, and then shift with the 3rd finger to play the 5th fret.

Example 5e:

The following lick is an example of how common this bolt-on approach is: I opt to slide to the 5th fret on the G string rather than picking the same note on the B string. Not only is this easier, but the articulation is different. The slide adds something to the lick and is a big part of why it sounds the way it does.

Example 5f:

This final Minor Pentatonic example uses the previous position shift idea, but this time played back in the open position. Here, the scale is used to create a fill between the backbeat on the E Major chord in a way that is typical of the style.

Example 5g:

The next scale *could* be called a *hexatonic*, meaning that it contains six notes. However, looking at the following diagram, you'll notice that it's the same shape as the earlier Minor Pentatonic scale but with one added note. Throughout my years of teaching, I'm yet to meet anyone that thinks of this as a new scale as it's so obviously a Minor Pentatonic scale with an added extra note. The extra note is a b5 interval (often called the *blues note*).

G Blues scale

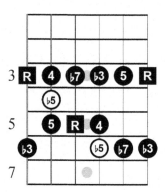

This b5 has a very distinctive sound, and is normally used as an interesting passing note but can be played as a dark note to pause on. Learn how this note sounds until it's something you're able to add to your playing as and when you hear it.

Example 5h:

The "problem" with the above scales is that while they're usable in country music, they tend to add a blues influence to the country vocabulary, creating a sad, minor vibe. When you listen to timeless country music, a large portion of it is in Major keys, so being able to play a Major sound is essential to the genre.

The first port of call for any serious country player is the Major Pentatonic scale, the Minor Pentatonic's Major, yet soulful, cousin. The intervals in the G Major, and G Minor Pentatonic scales are compared below:

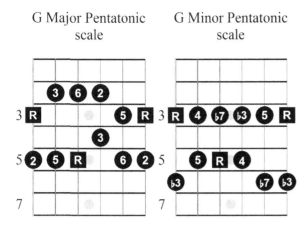

G Major Pentatonic scale   G Minor Pentatonic scale

When compared to the Minor Pentatonic, there's clearly a different set of intervals at play in the Major Pentatonic scale. While the Minor Pentatonic scale contains R, b3rd, 4th, 5th, and b7th, the Major Pentatonic drops the darker b3rd, 4th, and b7th in favour of the sweeter sounding 2nd, 3rd and 6th giving a formula of 1, 2, 3, 5, 6.

I find it helpful associate a chord sound to every scale, so that when someone asks, "what does the Major Pentatonic scale sound like?", I'm simply able to play a chord that instantly creates the correct vibe of the scale. Remember, chords come from scales, and a chord is nothing more than certain notes of a scale played at the same time.

With the G Minor Pentatonic scale, the R, 3rd, 5th, and 7th gives you R, b3, 5, b7 - or a Minor 7 chord.

Example 5i:

Using the intervals of the Major Pentatonic scale, the R, 3rd, 5th and 6th create a G6 chord.

Example 5j:

One trick often used by guitar players is to use the Minor Pentatonic scale shape to play the Major Pentatonic scale.

It is easy to use the Minor Pentatonic scale shape you already know to form a Major Pentatonic scale with the same root note. Simply move the Minor Pentatonic scale down three frets. Your little finger should now be on the root where your first finger was originally.

For example, Play the C Minor Pentatonic scale by placing your first finger on the 8th fret of the low E string. Then, move the whole shape down three frets so your 4th finger is now on the 8th fret. Play the notes of the Minor Pentatonic scale shape beginning and ending with your little finger on the 8th fret. You are now playing a C Major Pentatonic scale. Play this over a C Major chord vamp to hear the effect.

Example 5k:

Here's a classic country lick using this pattern. Note the use of the Eb to approach the E; this movement is very common in this style.

Example 5l:

We can use the Blues scale too, and apply it to the Major and Minor relationship. Playing the Blues scale shape as a Major Pentatonic idea is very common and is referred to as the *Country* scale.

C Country scale

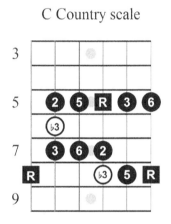

This isn't an all-encompassing scale that will turn anyone into a country-picking master, but the combination of that sweet Major Pentatonic tonality, along with the added bluesy b3, creates a unique sound heard in most country guitar solos.

As with the b5 in the Blues scale, the b3 in the Country scale is a tension note which should be handled carefully, its most common use is as a chromatic approach note to the natural 3rd, as shown in the following lick.

Example 5m:

Another common approach to country music soloing is to use a Major scale over a full chord progression in one key. For example, the Major scale will work over any chord in the key of the G Major, so for chord progressions like G / Em / C / D7, you can treat all four chords as coming from the G Major scale. Let's take a look at some of those major scales and learn some licks.

Here are the most important Major scales in the played in the open position. These are a big part of the country music style.

Play the notated chord first to get the sound of the key in your ear, then play the scale slowly enough to really *hear* what you're playing. Try to hear each note before you play it, as not only does this help develop your ear, but also puts you in a position of *reactive* improvisation.

First up is an open C Major scale

Example 5n:

Here's a lick typical among bluegrass players. It sticks closely to the scale, aside from the added b3 (Eb) towards the end of the lick.

Example 5o:

Next is a G Major scale (G, A, B, C, D, E, F#). When you play this scale, pay attention to the location of the new note (F#). Not only will this help you to see the difference between scales, but it will also help you start learning where notes are on the neck.

Example 5p:

Here's a great little country melody using that scale.

Example 5q:

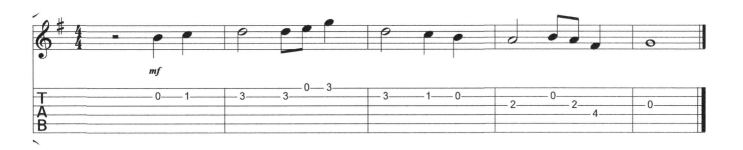

And one more lick that's a little more challenging.

Example 5r:

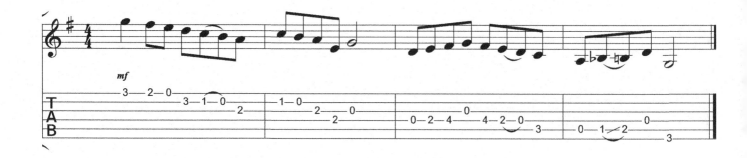

Next is a D Major scale, which introduces the note C# (D, E, F#, G, A, B, C#).

Example 5s:

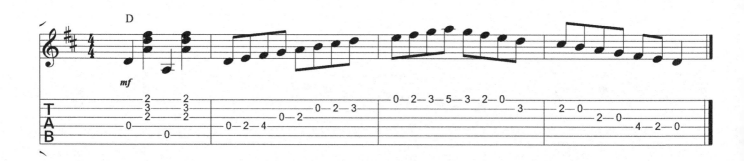

Here's a lick using that scale. As with previous examples, the b3 (F) has been used to make it sound a little more country.

Example 5t:

The A Major scale adds a G# to the mix (A, B, C#, D, E, F#, G#).

Example 5u:

This lick in A Major shows that as you add more accidentals, these licks can become a little trickier to play.

Example 5v:

One last open scale to learn is E Major, which introduces a D# (E, F#, G#, A, B, C#, D#).

Example 5w:

Here's a lick you'll see in one of the later solos. Notice how notes that are a tone apart are connected with chromatic passing tones. This isn't something that needs to be analysed in great detail; it fits nicely under the fingers and sounds great.

Example 5x:

The next example it a typical bluegrass-style solo line using the G Major scale to give an idea of how incredible pickers like Tony Rice or Doc Watson use open positions.

The trickiest part of this style is the discipline of playing open-string notes with equal rhythmic values to the fretted notes. Many players use the fretting hand to keep the picking hand in check; a finger goes down - you pick a note. However, when we introduce open string notes, this automation can get lost. Take your time and make sure you're comfortable combining open strings and fretted notes evenly in these scales, as this technique will become very important later on.

Example 5y:

Here's another bluegrass type melody, this time in the key of D Major.

Example 5z:

The obvious challenge with the five 'open' scales studied so far is that they're all fingered differently. However, it is possible to use a movable form (just like a barre chord) to play any scale, no matter which key you're in.

Using the Major Pentatonic scale as a starting point, let's fill in the other notes needed to create a movable Major scale.

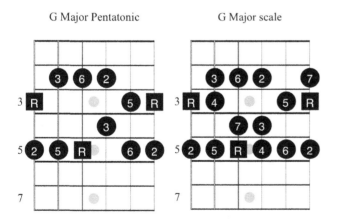

While this isn't the only movable form, it's a good starting point when soloing in a Major key.

The following example demonstrates one country lick played in four different keys ,by simply moving the shape up and down the neck. In comparison to developing vocabulary using open position scales, this should feel easy, all while opening up the fretboard.

Example 5z1:

Each example so far has been played over major chords. While major chords absolutely occur in country music, it's often more common to find progressions built from Dominant chords.

A Dominant 7 chord consists of a Major chord with an added b7th degree. The "correct" scale to play over a Dominant 7 chord is often called the "Mixolydian mode", but in country music, the Mixolydian mode is normally just called the Dominant 7 scale, or viewed as a major scale with a b7.

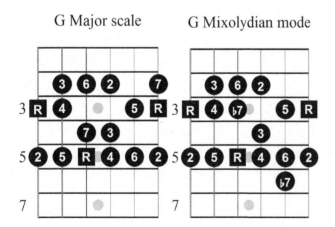

I'll often think of the 'G Mixolydian' scale as the 'G7' scale, because it's the scale that fits over a G7 chord. It contains the intervals of that chord and is my first choice for creating melodic ideas.

The following example showcases the sound of the Dominant 7 scale to closely outline the G7 harmony. Note the use of Bb as an approach to the 3rd of G7 (B).

Example 5z2:

Here's another lick using that scale.

Example 5z3:

The ultimate goal is to start seeing all available notes as simply sounds at your disposal. There are twelve notes, and each one has its own unique sound over different chords. While it's common to pool sets of notes that sound great together as 'scales', the other notes aren't unplayable, they're just acquired sounds that take time to master. It's also O.K. to mix and match scales to get the sound you want.

There are many more scales, modes, and arpeggios to learn, but musicians don't build knowledge by simply knowing music theory. The most important knowledge is acquired through musical experience, so the next step is to get a feel for traditional country licks and vocabulary, and learn how many country players see this language on the guitar neck.

Chapter Six: CAGED Positions

One of the most rewarding aspects of country guitar is how harmonically aware the genre will make you, and also learning to navigate the entirety of the neck is a big part of the sound of everyone from Albert Lee to Johnny Hiland.

The most common guitar neck visualization method is to see licks and phrases as embellishments to small chord forms. This technique goes right back to the '20s and is nothing more than common sense: Each small chord form is a three-note fragment (triad) that is used as a harmonic anchor. It is then easy to decorate this anchor with melodies without ever losing the sound of the chord.

Over time, this anchor approach has expanded into a full system of visualization, which is taught at institutions the world over due to the importance it places on harmony. It is a perfect way to think when playing blues, jazz, and country music. This 'CAGED' system is really nothing more than the result of the natural geometry of the neck. Despite being named The CAGED system, the approach actually completely 'uncages' you, allowing you to play freely anywhere on the guitar neck.

So far you've looked at a selection of scales that began with the root note on the low E string. This amounts to 1/5th of the system. This is a pretty sizable chunk, but let's move back a step and look at how that scale fits into the CAGED system.

The CAGED system begins by looking at the five C, A, G, E, and D open-position chords.

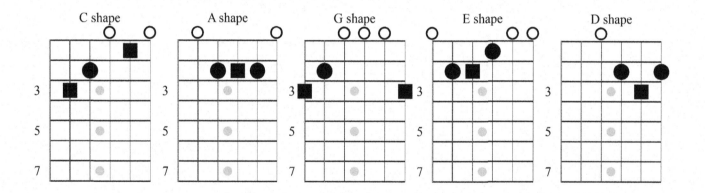

I break each chord down into one of two categories; chords where the notes are 'behind' the root note, and chords where the notes are 'in front of' the root note.

For example, on the C Major chord, the root is played with the 3rd finger. The other notes in the chord are *behind* this note as they're on lower frets (closer to the nut of the guitar). The same is true of the G Major chord.

In the A Major chord, the root is on the open A string, and the other notes of the chord are *in front* (on higher frets) of that note. The E Major and D Major chords both fit into this category.

Each of these CAGED chord shapes can be played as a barre, and therefore moved anywhere on the neck. For example, moving the 'C Shape' up in semitones allows us to play the chords of C# Major, then D Major, The D# Major, etc.

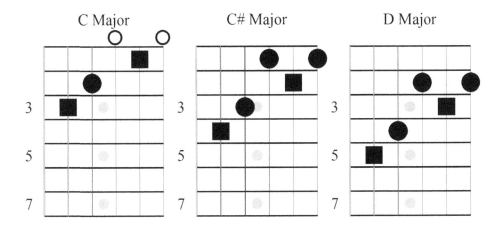

Using each of the CAGED shapes (and with a little awareness of where the root notes are located on the fretboard), we can now play *any* chord in five different places on the guitar neck.

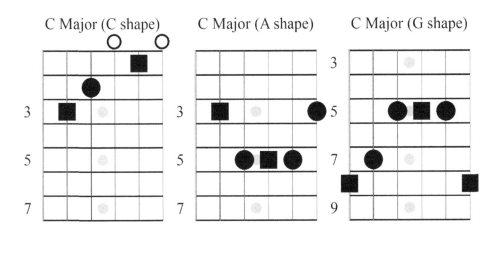

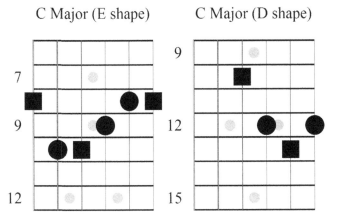

Some of these shapes share the same root location (for example, the 'A' and 'C' shapes of C Major both have a root on the 3rd fret). This is where the idea of 'forward' and 'backward' shapes is important. Try not to have too much bias towards one shape otherwise you might find develop some grey areas in your fretboard knowledge. It's ok to feel stronger in some positions than others, but you don't want any blank spots on the neck.

The next example demonstrates how these small harmonic fragments (triads) fall on the neck, and how they relate to the CAGED chords. Each three-note grouping contains the adjacent notes C, E, and G.

Measure 1 falls around the A shape of the CAGED system.

Measure 2 falls around the E shape, and measure 3 falls around the C shape.

You'll soon notice that a huge amount of country guitar is built around these basic chord forms.

Example 6a:

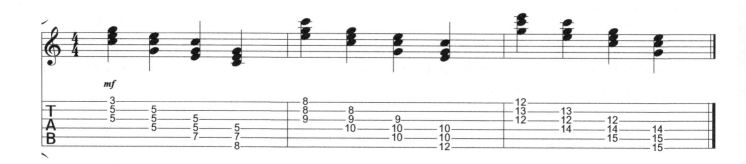

These triads can be used to play interesting chord ideas around any chord progression:

Example 6b:

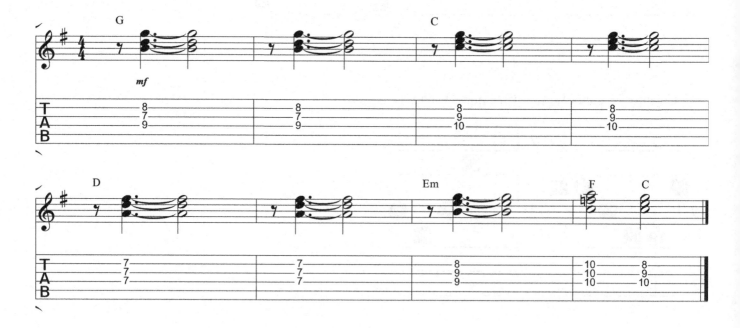

Here's the same triad roadmap, but outlined melodically. The great thing is that this approach doesn't sound at all like playing scales; for the most part you're playing the notes of the triad but embellishing them with notes a semitone below. This is how early country players approached soloing as it results in solos with a strong sense of harmony

Example 6c:

This is also my approach when I solo. Even when I play a lot of notes, all I'm normally doing is decorating small three- or four-string chord voicings that I visualise on the neck.

To see how this approach is applied in country music, I've written an example over an A7 vamp. Check out the following three diagrams which show an A triad and a G triad (three notes found in the A Mixolydian scale).

The triads are shown as black notes, while the other notes of the A7 chord (which I use for melody) are hollow.

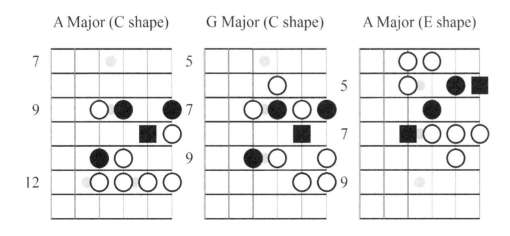

Let's use this roadmap to navigate from the 9th fret area down to the 5th fret in an interesting and harmonically strong way. This lick doesn't sound like running up and down scales but instead creates something exciting and unpredictable.

Example 6d:

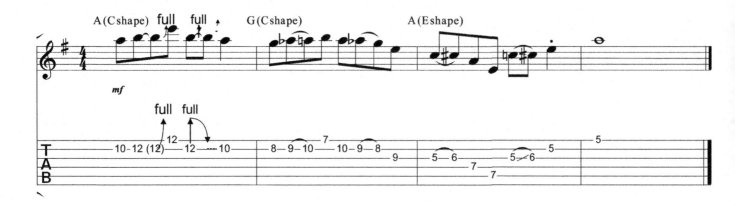

Here's another lick using the same roadmap. This one is a little more challenging to play and demonstrates that it's possible to interpret CAGED positions in a variety of ways.

The lick begins by approaching the 3rd from a semitone below and ascends the scale before playing two notes from A7 the chord as a double stop. In measure two, the double stop moves down to target two notes from the G Major chord and create a nice G/A sound, before shifting down to the E shape at the 5th fret with a typical country lick to finish.

Example 6e:

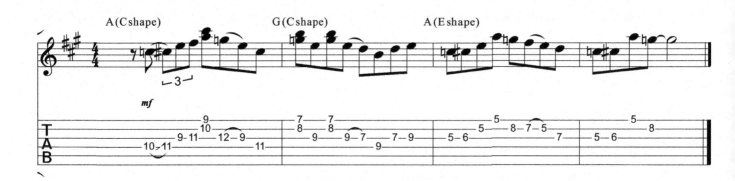

Building the connection between chords and scale patterns is essential when navigating the neck fluently, so take time to work through each of the following diagrams carefully. First find the root note of the chord (shown as a black square), then the chord should light up in your mind (black notes in the diagrams), before finally adding the notes of the scale around it (indicated by hollow notes).

First up is the C shape. In black, you'll see the notes of the chord. Around this, you have the notes needed to pad the chord out to become a scale.

E7 (C shape)

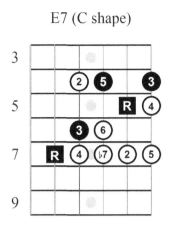

The following is an E7 lick played in the C shape. As usual the b3rd is used as an approach note to the 3rd of the chord.

Example 6f:

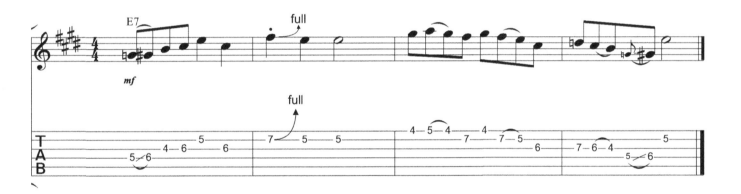

Here's another lick in that position.

Example 6g:

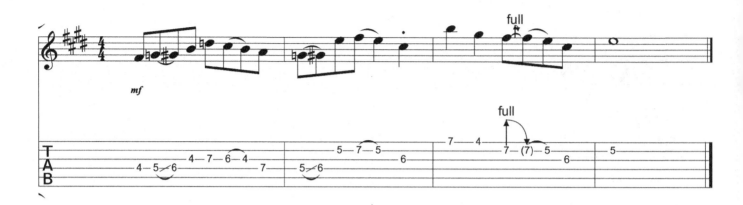

Next up is E Major played with the A shape. The root can be found on the A string and is played with either the 1st finger (for the chord) or the 2nd finger (for the scale).

E7 (A shape)

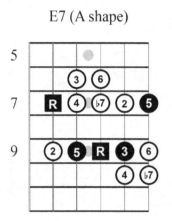

And here's a lick in that position to give you an idea of how this area can be used.

Example 6h:

Here's another lick based around the A shape, this time using some double stops that fit nicely under the fingers.

Example 6i:

The G shape is often overlooked but contains many great opportunities for melodies.

E7 (G shape)

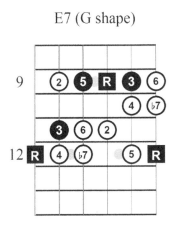

This lick uses a classic pedal steel style bend and some Country scale ideas.

Example 6j:

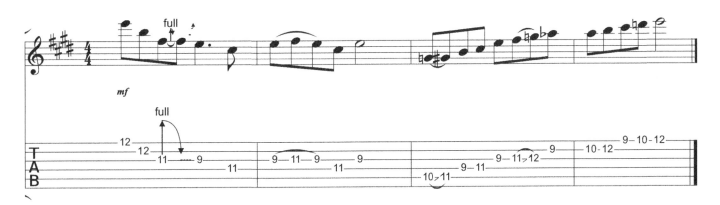

Here's a second lick in that position to demonstrate the endless possibilities found in each area of the neck.

Example 6k:

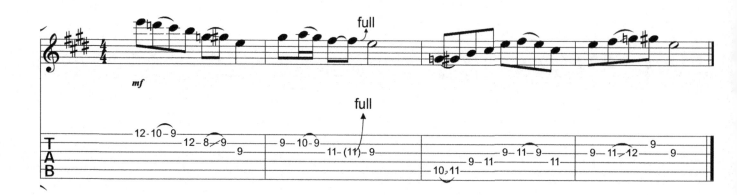

The E shape is the most common position. In fact, it was covered in the previous chapter. It's included here for completion.

E7 (E shape)

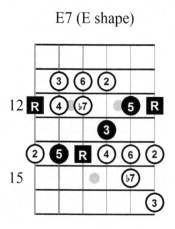

Here's another lick in this position to expand your vocabulary further.

Example 6l:

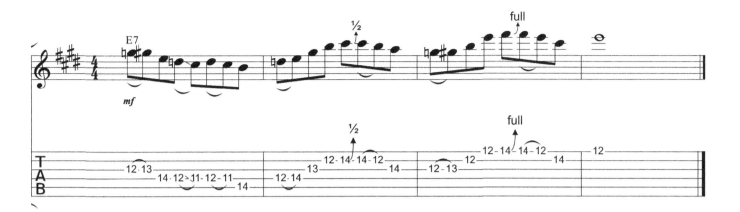

And one more idea here, this time using a few more chromatic passing notes to connect notes of the scale.

Example 6m:

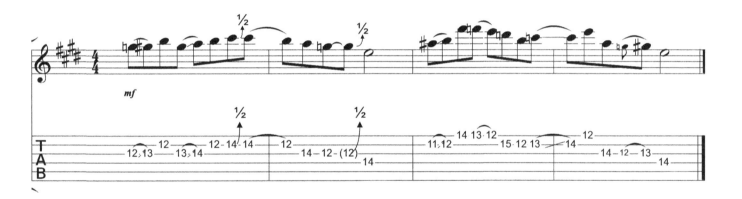

Finally, here's the D shape.

E7 (D shape)

I find this shape a little harder to use when soloing. I do use it, but usually while moving up to the C shape, or down to the E. Here's an idea that stays in position.

Example 6n:

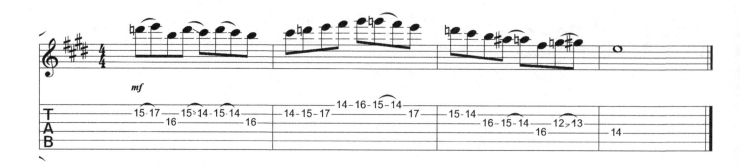

Here's an example that links multiple positions of the E Major scale together. Pay attention to the markings above the tab to see where the CAGED point of reference changes.

Example 6o:

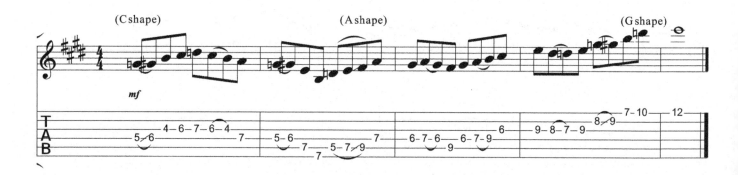

Here's one final E Major idea that stars up high on the neck and moves downward in a manner that conjures up images of Nashville ace, Brent Mason.

Example 6p:

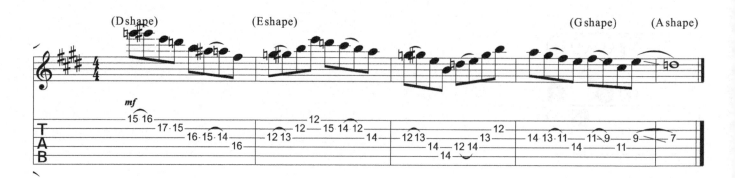

Now to draw this all together, here's an example of some of this vocabulary being used over the chord changes of G7 - A7 - D7 - G7.

Over the G7 chord, we play the lick found in example 6p, but here it is moved down the neck to fit a G7 chord rather than the E7 looked at previously.

To hit the A7 chord, move up the neck by two frets and play within the E shape again, moving to the A shape to switch to the D7 chord with a lick reminiscent to example 6h. This then resolves down to the E shape, targeting the 3rd of G7 (B).

Example 6q:

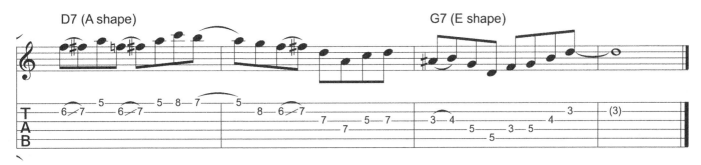

Here's another example over those same chord changes.

This time you begin in the A shape with a lick similar to example 6h, but moved up to a G7 chord. As you're in the 10th fret area, changing to the A7 chord is as easy as moving to the C shape, which is targeted by landing on the 5th of the chord (E).

It's possible to stay in this area of the neck for the D7 chord by switching to the E shape (played at the 10th fret), and to hit the G7 I've moved down the neck by playing the C shape over the G7, targeting the 3rd (B).

Example 6r:

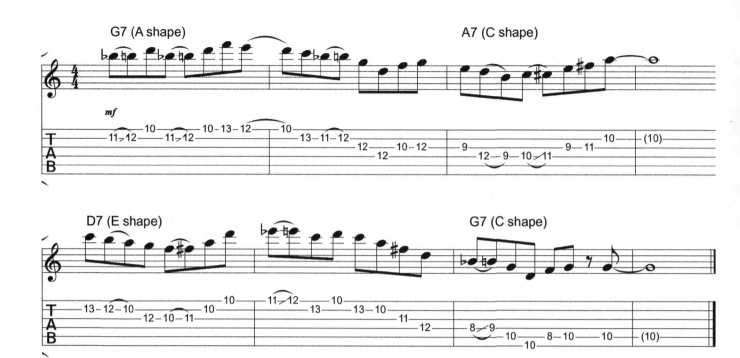

Being aware of the little chord forms as you move around the neck will help your licks feel musical, rather than just running up and down scales because they automatically place emphasis on chord tones. This approach takes a while to master, but once these frameworks are opened up, you'll be connecting the whole neck in no time at all.

Chapter Seven - 3rds & 6ths Interval Licks

Country guitar playing is heavily influenced by other instruments, and none are more notable than the double stop ideas found on the fiddle or lap/pedal steel guitar.

Not only will these intervallic ideas give you an authentic country sound, they will open up your ears to new ideas and also encourage you to move away from just playing scales up and down.

Playing diatonic 3rds consists of taking a note, and then playing a note a 3rd higher in the scale. For example, In C Major, (C D E F G A B) a 3rd above C is E, a 3rd above D is F, and so on.

Playing intervals alone won't instantly give you country sound though. The following example consists of diatonic 3rds within the G Major scale, but this has a more mechanical, 'neoclassical' sound that you'd expect from a player like Paul Gilbert.

Example 7a:

You'll notice that some intervals are on the same strings and some are on adjacent strings. Playing intervals on different strings has two benefits. Firstly, the notes are able to ring into each other if that's the desired sound, and secondly, you are able to play up and down the neck on string pairs instead of across the neck in a scale shape.

Here's an example using diatonic 3rds in the G Mixolydian scale to outline a G7 chord. The pattern consists of playing the lower note of the pair, the higher note, repeating the lower note and sliding up to the next interval.

Example 7b:

When doing this, it's very useful to be able to see the bigger chord forms as a point of reference. This gives you a route into the interval and a way to resolve it.

Below are 3rds of G Mixolydian on the G and B strings, visualized around the E, C and A barre forms. Note that the chord grips are shown as hollow notes, with the notes of the 3rd-pairs given in black and connected with lines.

3rds around E7 shape   3rds around C7 shape   3rds around A7 shape

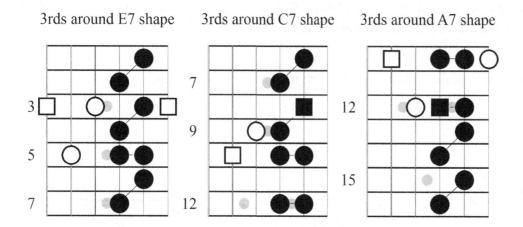

Here is a lick that uses these 3rds as a way to get from the E shape at the 3rd fret to the A shape at the 10th fret.

The lick in measure one is lick similar to an idea played many times in this book; a hybrid of the pentatonic scale and the G7 chord, using both the Minor and Major 3rd. Measure two slides up the neck using 3rds and resolves to the A shape.

Example 7c:

A clearer framework for this type of idea might be to see it on the neck rather than as a lick. It's not important how you get from point A to point B, just focus on the concept.

3rds Around G7 CAGED Shapes

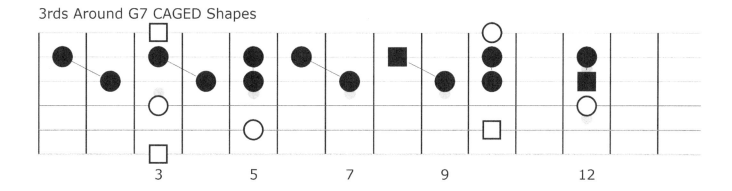

Another way to use these 3rds is as extensions to melodic fragments you're already familiar with. The following lick sits around an E shape and uses notes which are already familiar. To develop the idea a little more I've added the 3rd interval below the chord shape.

Example 7d:

A similar approach can be applied to any position. Playing 3rds with the C chord as a framework might result in the following idea. As with many licks, combining the Minor and Major 3rds is an essential part of the sound.

Example 7e:

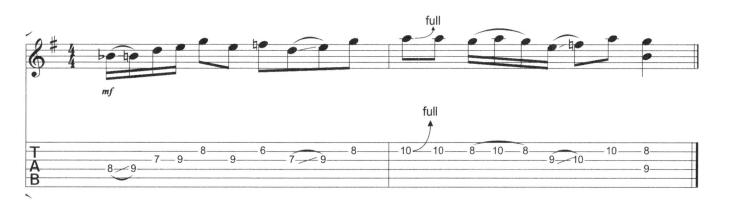

One of the exciting options presented by 3rds is the possibility of connecting two shapes together with chromatic passing notes. These work great when playing rhythm guitar as shown in the following pedal steel-inspired example.

Example 7f:

Here's another chordal example, this time moving down from the E shape of a G7 chord to give an ending that would fit well on a swing tune.

Example 7g:

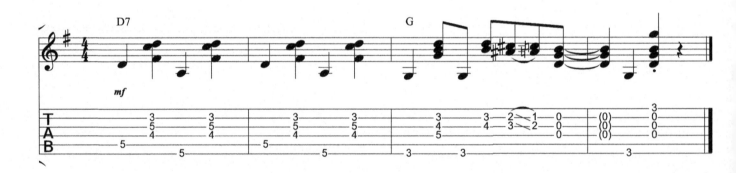

It's worth considering that like these aren't just limited to the G and B string, as this example on the B and E string shows.

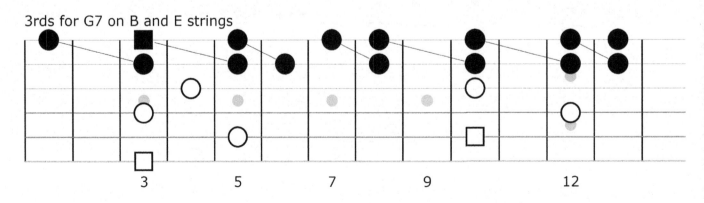

3rds for G7 on B and E strings

Example 7h:

Here's an example on the D and G strings. This would be a great way to play some modern country rhythm guitar on a slow ballad.

3rds for G7 on D and G strings

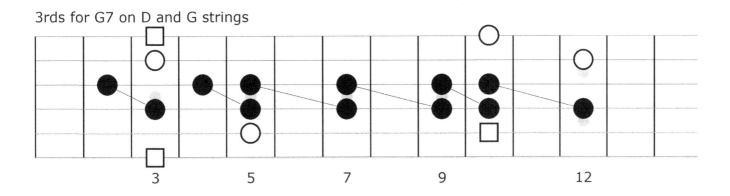

Example 7i:

3rds are often thought of as being 'sweet' sounding when used melodically, but their close cousin, the 6th, has just as much sweetness to it's sound.

The interval of C to E is a 3rd; but if you *invert* that interval and go from E to C, you create a 6th (E F G A B C). 3rds and 6ths are very closely related, despite each having their own unique sound.

The following example demonstrates how a classical guitarist might play diatonic 6ths in the key of G. They sound nice, but they're very tricky to play like this.

Example 7j:

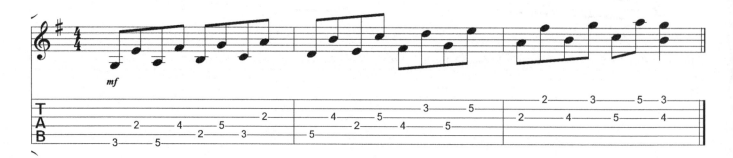

An easier (and more practical) way to play 6ths is on string pairs, like the G and high E shown below in the key of G.

Example 7k:

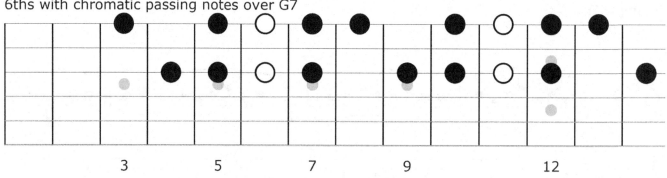

Here's the same basic idea, but this time I've linked the parallel shapes with chromatic passing notes. The non-diatonic (chromatic) 6ths have been marked in brackets. They sound great as passing notes, but you wouldn't want to sit on them on a strong beat of the bar!

Example 7l:

Here's an example of how these 6ths can be used when soloing and creating melodies. Beginning with the G Major Pentatonic scale, the lick quickly moves up to the 7th fret and descends down in 6ths, ending on the 3rd (B).

Example 7m:

Next up is an example that uses chromatic passing notes between 6th intervals. The lick begins with a bluegrass cliché before moving up the neck and playing 6ths around the E and C shapes.

Example 7n:

As with the 3rds, you may find these concepts easier to see on the fretboard rather than as a lick.

6ths around E7 shape   6ths around C7 shape

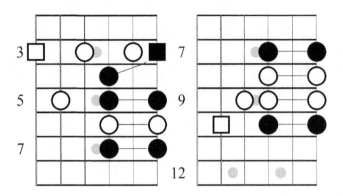

Again, these ideas aren't limited to just one string set, and should be explored on the D and B, A and G, and E and D sets.

6ths with chromatic passing notes over G7

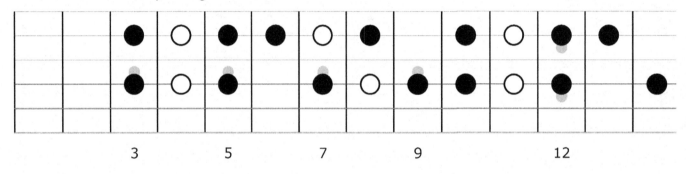

Here's an example on A7 that features 6ths on the A and G strings. The lick begins in the open A shape and moves up to the E shape. The second half of the lick jumps to the G and E strings for an ending similar previous ideas.

Example 7o:

Another common way to embellish these 6th ideas is with this *chicken pickin'* idea. The lowest note of each 6th is approached chromatically from a tone below before the higher note is plucked aggressively with a picking-hand finger. Early country players would often play all three notes by sliding the third finger. It's certainly not as accurate as using one finger per fret, but it's full of attitude.

Example 7p:

Here's a similar example but this time descending the neck and resolving with a typical pedal steel imitation bend.

Licks like this are very common in the playing of greats like Roy Nichols.

Example 7q:

Here's a final, more advanced lick in A that features 3rds and some sliding 6ths.

Example 7r:

While 3rds and 6ths aren't the only intervals you'll find in the playing of country guitar icons, they're certainly the most common and idiomatic.

Chapter Eight - String Bending Skills

One of the most common tools in the arsenal of the country guitarist is the bend, and it is one of the more unique effects available on stringed instruments like the guitar.

The electric guitar draws influence and inspiration from fiddle, as well as steel guitar players. One of the best ways to get to grips with country vocabulary is to listen to other instruments and adapt their ideas to your own instrument.

Developed from the lap steel guitar, the pedal steel was developed in the '40s to give players more musical options. The lap steel guitar is an instrument with ten strings tuned to an open chord (normally E9), and played with a large metal bar (known as a tone bar). This felt quite limiting to many players, so engineers started creating complex mechanical systems that could change the pitch of a string via the use of a pedal. Over time this would result in a common set up of three foot pedals, and four knee levers that all raised or lowered the pitch of different strings.

These pedals allowed players to play a chord and then change the pitch of one or more of those notes while others stayed static. This is an iconic sound, integral to the sound of country music, so give it the attention it deserves by listening and mimicking its unique character when you can.

Notable steel players include, Speedy West, Buddy Emmons, Paul Franklin, and Randle Currie to name just a few.

One of the biggest differences you'll find among country guitar players vs blues or rock players, is that in country there is great importance placed on the note you're bending *to*, rather than just bending to create a musical effect.

The other big difference between bent notes in country and bent notes in other genres, is that in country you'll often bend one note *while* sustaining others. In order to execute these bends, the force must come from the finger rather than the wrist. Remember that you're imitating a pedal steel guitar, so you want the bend to sound as mechanical as possible. Don't take your time! - Bend straight up to the note as though it were done with a mechanical pedal.

The first pedal steel example is in the key of A Major and takes the notes B, and E, and bends the B (the 9th) up a tone to C# (3rd) to create an A Major triad. In order to execute this bend, fix the 3rd finger on the 5th fret, while the 1st and 2nd finger rest on the 4th fret and work together to support the bend.

Example 8a:

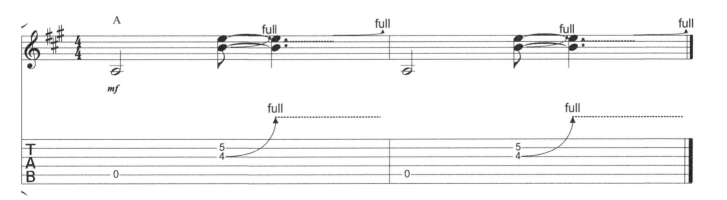

The previous example can be expanded by adding the root (A) on the high E string.

When looking at these diagrams, the notes played are black, while the notes of the chord are hollow. This allows you to see the notes you're playing, and where each bend targets.

Steel Bend 2-3

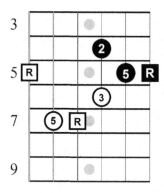

Example 8b:

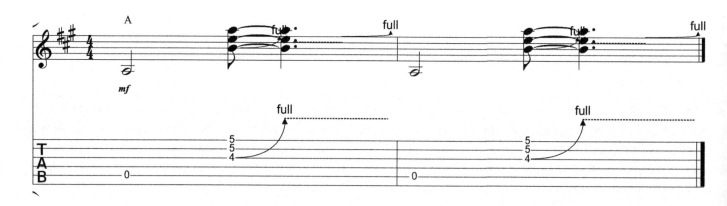

The next example jumps up the neck to bend the 9th (B) up to the 3rd (C#), while holding the 5th (E) on the high E string. This fits into the A shape of the CAGED system.

Steel Bend 2-3

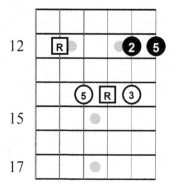

Example 8c:

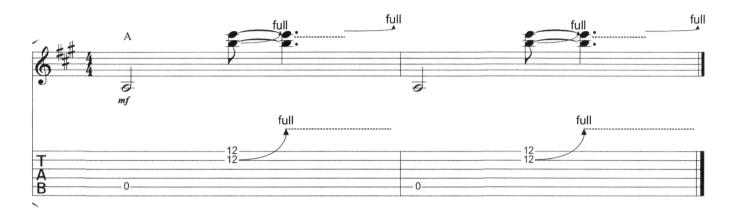

Here, this bending idea is used in a lick that descends the neck while outlining an A Major chord. Note the use of 3rd intervals from the previous chapter.

Example 8d:

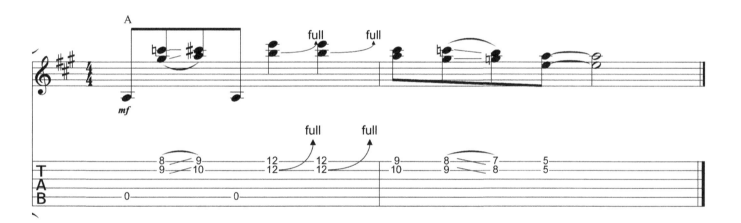

Another common idea taken from pedal steel players is to bend one note and hold it while playing other notes.

Example 8e:

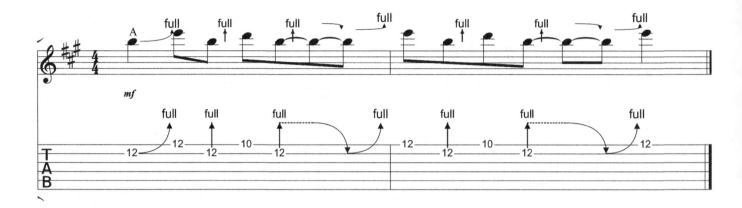

The following example bends the b7 on the B string (G) up to the root (A). This is played against the 3rd (C#) and the 9th (B).

Example 8f:

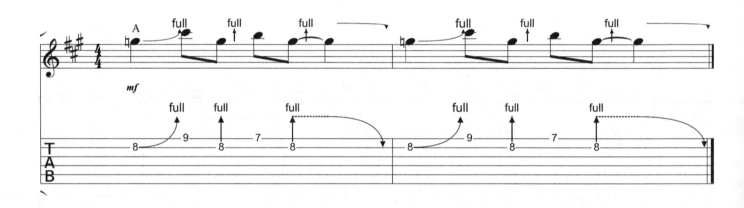

The next lick combines some of the previous ideas to create a line that would work in any solo.

Example 8g:

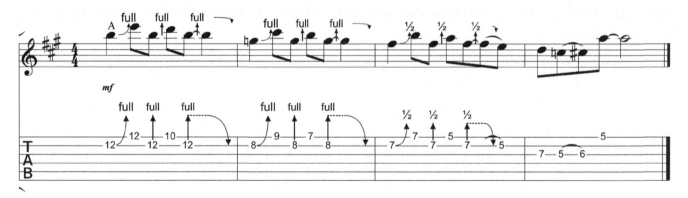

Here's an idea that combines the 6ths from the previous chapter with the pedal steel-inspired bend from the first example.

Example 8h:

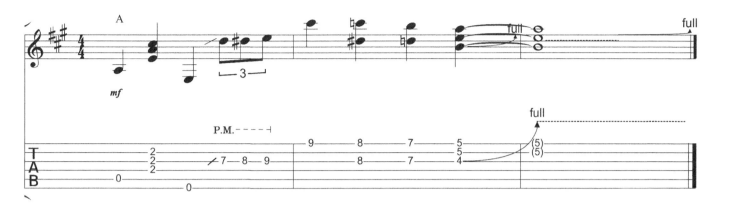

We can also use these bends at the *top* of the melody and place the static notes at the bottom.

Here's another way to play an A chord. Hold the notes on the A and D strings static and bend the note on the G string with the 1st finger.

Steel Bend 2-3

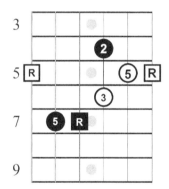

Example 9i:

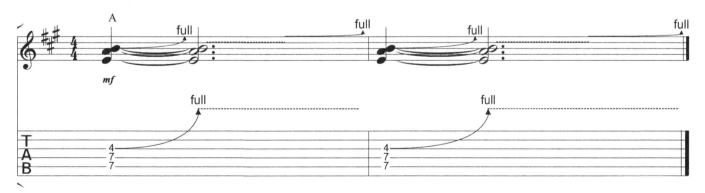

Here's another great way to use this concept, with the b7 and 3rd on the bottom and bending the 5th up to the 6th.

Steel Bend 5-6

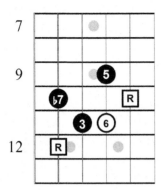

When used in context, this is a great way to lead from A to D.

Example 8j:

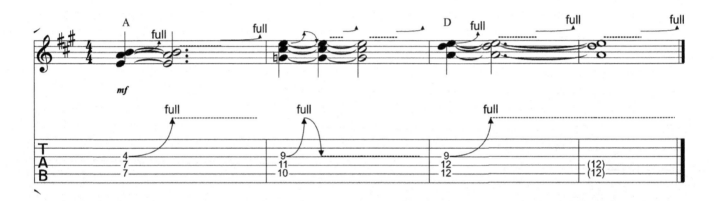

It's also possible to bend notes in the middle of chords, though this requires the use of a B-bender (a mechanical bending system activated by attaching the strap to a lever inside the strap pin). Numerous companies such as Hipshot and Bigsby make retrofit devices to achieve this sound.

Example 8k:

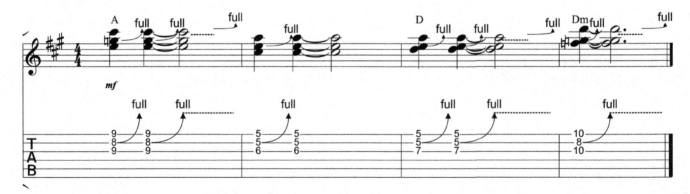

Here's an example that relies on bends found on the G string. Beginning with a bend from the 5th to the 6th on the G, the root and b7th are played against this on the B string. Note the pleasing tension as the F# and G ring into each other.

Measure four extends the idea by moving up to the 12th position and bending the b7 (G) up to the root (A), then playing the 3rd (C#) on the B string.

Example 8l:

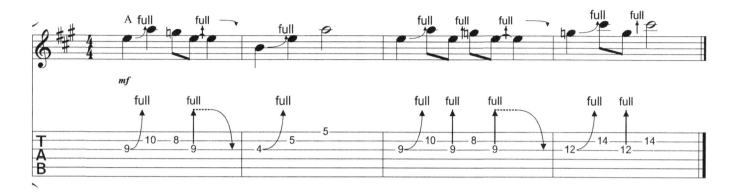

Next up is another idea on the B and E strings, moving down the neck.

Example 8m:

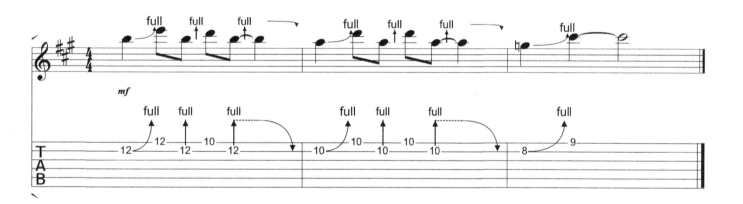

Now the bends are played on the G string, and the melody note is on the high E, allowing you to create some wider intervallic leaps.

Example 8n:

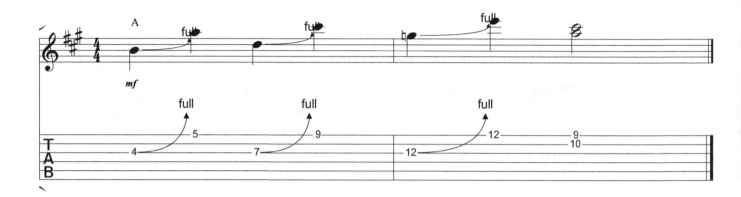

Finally, here's a lick that combines a bend on the G string with a static note on the D. The B (2nd) is bent to a C# (3rd) against a G (b7), creating an A7 sound. Using bends like this is common among the more 'high-tech' country players.

Example 8o:

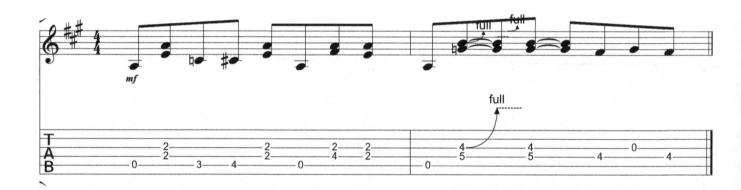

These licks aren't easy, but they illustrate the importance of context. At any given time the country soloist is always aware of the chord they're playing over, so their note choice will have the maximum impact. Nowhere is this truer than with bends.

To demonstrate awareness, here's a little idea played over the G7 - A7 - D7 - G7 progression we've covered previously.

The lick begins by playing over the G7 with a 9 to 3 bend on the B string, with a melody on the high E. This mirrors the idea in example 9e.

In order to outline the A7, we move down to bend the b7 to the root on the B string, as seen in example 9f.

For the D7 chord, we move up to the E shape and bent the 9th up to the 3rd as this position allows you to transition back to the G7 very smoothly.

Example 8p:

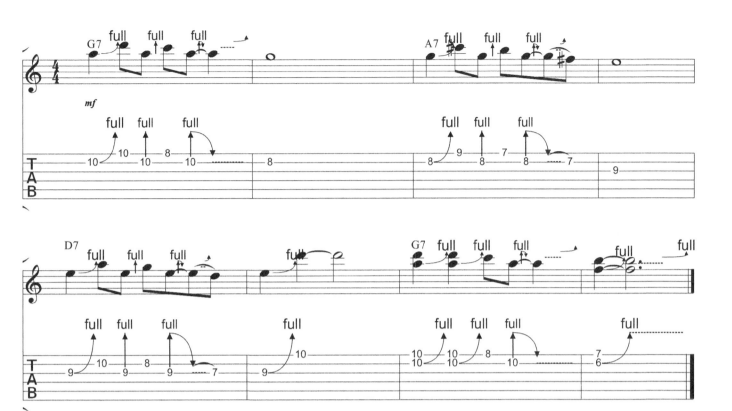

Chapter Nine - Pop Track

One of the true tests of a great country player (or any guitar player for that matter) is their ability to play the *right* part for the song. Often guitarists forget that they'll only be in the spotlight 5% of the time, the rest is about fitting in and adding creatively to the music.

To demonstrate this idea, I've composed a short track for you in the key of E Major, similar to the sort of thing you'd expect a modern country pop star like Miranda Lambert or Carrie Underwood to need guitar on. In this chapter, you'll learn the track one section at a time, and see how best to tackle playing it.

Session gigs are big earners for numerous country guitar players, from legends like Brent Mason and Dan Huff, to hot young players like Daniel Donato and Andy Wood. Understanding how best to fit in a band, and knowing your place is the secret to getting these gigs!

First up, you'll need to learn the chord progression for the intro section. As you can see, it features three chords E, A and B7 (the I, IV, and V7 respectively). I strum these chords on an acoustic to create the pleasing percussive effect you get from a thin pick on a bright guitar.

The only tricky part in this progression is bar eight as it's in 2/4 time, so while you'll be counting to four for the majority of the track, bar eight contains just two beats so (counting from bar 6) you'd count:

1, 2, 3, 4, **1**, 2, 3, 4, *1, 2*, **1**, 2, 3, 4.

This hasn't been done for any reason other than that I like the way it sounds. It has flavours of Alan Jackson's "I don't even know your name", from his 1994 album, Who I Am.

Example 9a:

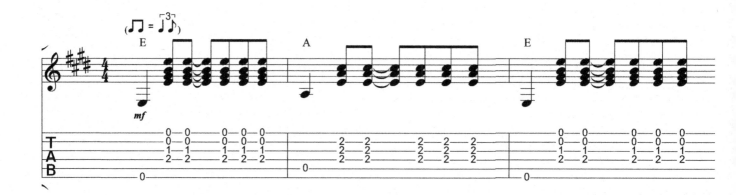

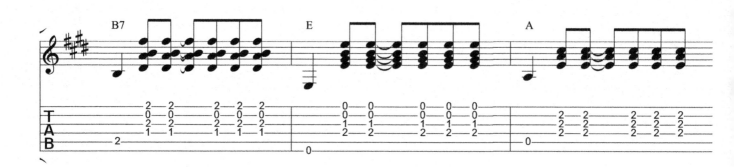

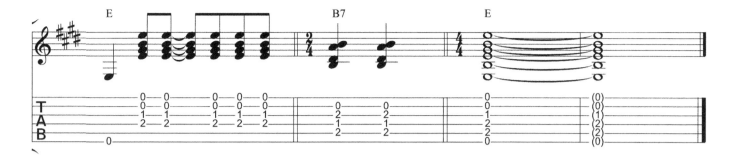

The intro solo features an "anacrusis" or a "pickup bar", this is a short phrase played before bar one to lead you into the song.

Each chord is addressed with pedal steel type bends, though the first three bars do also share a striking resemblance to the E Major Pentatonic scale.

To target the B chord, the soloing position moves down to the E shape at the 7th fret to play a similar bend on the E chord.

Example 9b:

The verse section uses the same three chords as the intro, but now with the IV chord (A) as "home". In order to support a singer, the guitar part is heavily stripped back; just playing chords on the off-beat.

Syncopated rhythms work great in shuffle settings like this.

Example 9c:

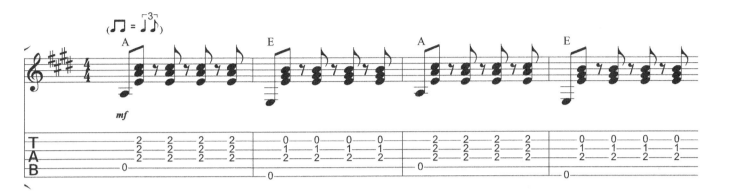

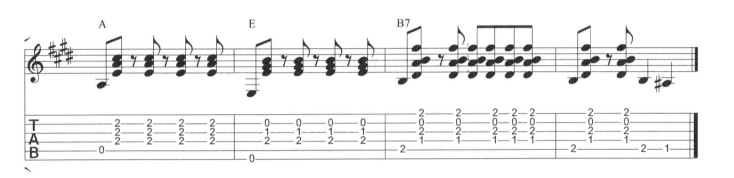

The next example shows an alternative way to play through the verse section, using double stops and bends to outline the chords.

The lick for the E Major chord in bar six is a tricky idea with a bend on the G string, a fretted note on the E string, and then the open E string.

This idea works best on a fixed bridge guitar like the iconic Telecaster. If you're a Stratocaster (or something similar), these bending ideas are often a little out of tune, but pushing on the bridge a little with the heel of the hand to compensate for the movement can help.

Example 9d:

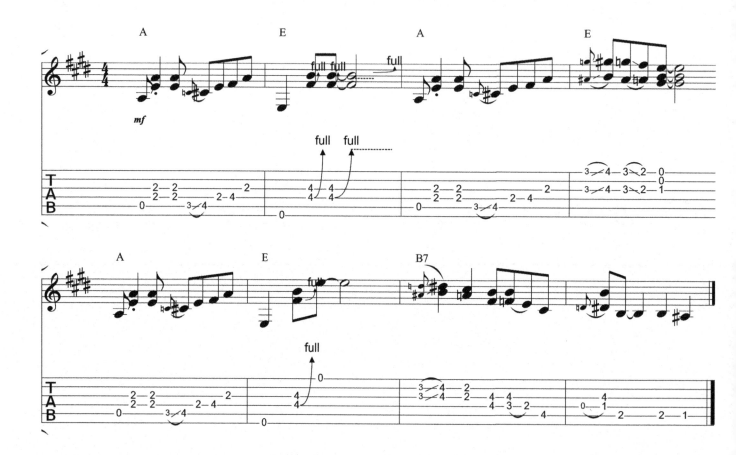

Here's another solo idea that fits over the intro chords (which are now acting as a chorus). The first two bars use the E Major Pentatonic scale, but end on the note A. Bar three features some descending 6ths for the E Major chord, moving to a bending idea to outline the B Major chord.

The next two measure use more 6ths, but this time with palm muted triplets on the D string, before ascending a classic bluegrass melody in the E Country scale. In the 2/4 measure there's a repeat of an earlier pedal steel bend that could be seen as an E Major chord but played against a B Major chord.

Example 9e:

The next example sits somewhere between the rhythm and lead role, mixing double stops based on 3rds that outline chords, with single-note phrases to add variation.

Working through ideas like these will teach you how each one fits into a bigger CAGED shape, and how those bigger forms are used to outline the chord changes.

Example 9f:

There are many ways to approach a track like this but these ideas will give you plenty to chew on. The most important thing is to listen to the greats and see how they tackle songs like this.

Country is still a huge part of the music scene across America, often incorporating many contemporary influences to keep it sounding fresh.

Chapter Ten - Rockabilly Track

As mentioned in Part One, early Country music incorporated a wide influence of styles that then became its own genre; Rockabilly. From Chet Atkins and to the great Scotty Moore, it was the blend of early Rock and Hillbilly music (hence; 'rockabilly') that would form the basis of Elvis Presley's career.

Musicians like Brian Setzer and Danny Gatton brought exciting twists to Rockabilly, but it never lost that early country influence. Players like James Burton kept the sound alive when Scotty Moore left Elvis.

An important part of Scotty's style was how his vocabulary revolved around the basic CAGED barre shapes, most often just the E, A and C shapes. Scotty also used a thumb pick, but there's no need for you to use one as all of these examples can be played easily with a pick (James Burton, Albert Lee, and Danny Gatton certainly don't need a thumb pick!). However, if you've not used a thumb pick, it's worth a try!

Aside from Scotty, other notable players who used thumb picks exclusively include Brent Mason, Jerry Reed, Scotty Anderson, and, of course, Chet Atkins.

This first example is a bare-bones introduction to Travis picking and, while this technique could easily fill a book by itself, the basic skills are relatively simple. As with the examples in Chapter Four, play the notes with downward stems using the pick (notes on the E, A, and D strings) and use the picking hand fingers to play the notes on the G, B, and E strings.

Example 10a:

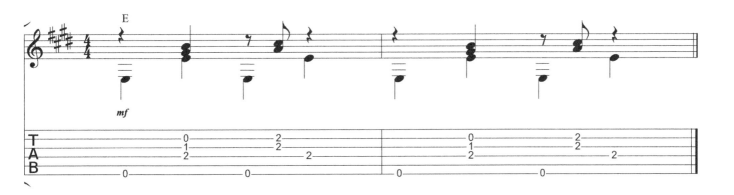

The next example presents an alternative picking pattern that you'll hear from players like Scotty Moore, or modern finger pickers like Buster B Jones.

It's worth learning the bass line separately until the picking motion is automatic, then add the melody.

Example 10b:

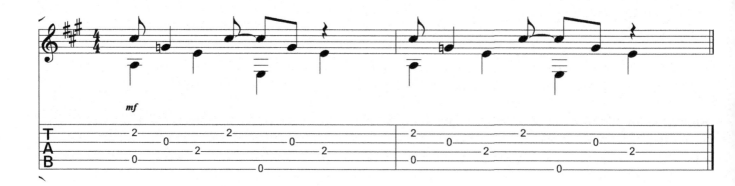

The following idea is a longer example of how to lay down a rhythm track over a twelve-bar blues using picking patterns. Here, however, I stretch the sequence out over twenty-four bars due to the faster tempo.

You'll notice a few tricks being used that help drive the piece forward, such as walking basslines that move between chord changes, but these shouldn't present any problem if learnt slowly. Add some slap-back delay and give it a try!

Example 10c:

When soloing in a setting like this, you may be the only guitar player in a small band, or may playing with a large group of musicians. Either way, using double stops can allow you to both dig in and be heard, while also defining the sound of the chords more effectively in your guitar part.

The following example covers the first eight bars of the tune and uses double stops on the G and B strings to create a nice melody.

Example 10d:

Example 10e features another common Rockabilly approach to lead guitar, which is to *arpeggiate* a ringing chord voicing. As with the previous example, this will add more power than playing single notes.

The voicing used is an extension of the C shape on the top four strings:

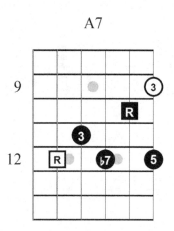

As the track resolves to E Major, I used some more melodic bends with the E Major Pentatonic scale to round it off nicely.

Example 10e:

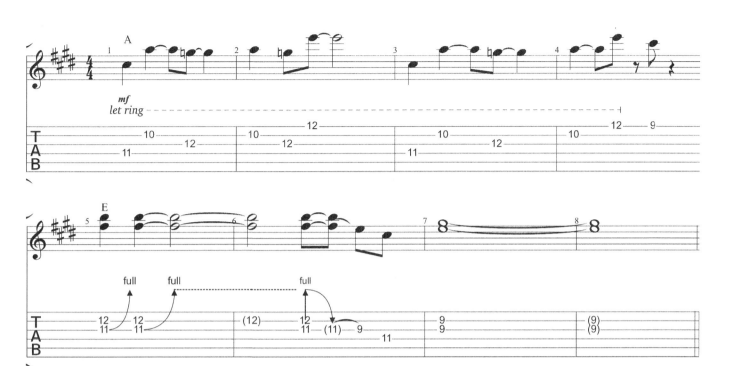

The next lick takes a cue from noted Elvis guitarist (and respected country picker), James Burton to outline the final part of the progression. The playing is visual; moving to the 7th fret for the B chord and then switching to the E Minor Pentatonic scale over the A chord.

Listen to the audio carefully here, as the bent note on the 10th fret is struck repeatedly while being gradually released. For authenticity, the notes should be played staccato (short), and this can be achieved by alternating between the pick and middle finger.

The second half of the lick shifts down the fretboard to the open position and descends the E Blues scale. with an added C# for a bit of colour.

Example 10f:

One the first repeat of the progression, the licks get a little trickier, with more notes and faster position shifts.

Lick 10g begins with some rock-inspired double stops that wouldn't sound out of place in a Chuck Berry solo. In the third bar I play the 6th (C#) and the b3rd (G) together before bending the B string slightly sharp.

The second half of the lick moves down the E Mixolydian scale (with added b3rd) and ends on the b7 (D) of the E Major chord.

Example 10g:

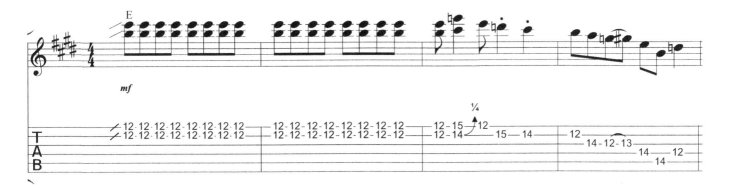

The next lick begins in the E Country scale, but towards the end of the second bar shifts to a series of descending 6ths before resolving with a bend against the open E string.

Example 10h:

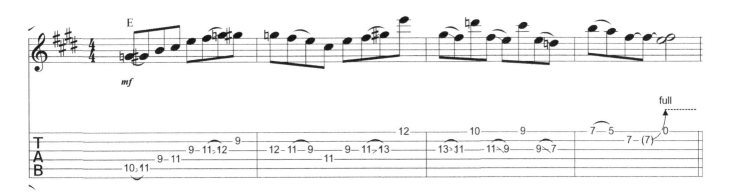

Over the A Major chord, there is a lick reminiscent of Albert Lee. The lick happens in three obvious sections, the descending A Mixolydian idea in the first bar, the open position lick in measure two, and the ascending 6ths towards the end. Albert's style is very position-based, but sounds anything but "boxed in".

Example 10i:

On returning to the E Major chord, you'll find a lick that begins on the low open E string and outlines the E Major Pentatonic scale. To add some spice to this idea, triplets are played on beats two and four, placing a chromatic passing tone between the two notes.

Example 10j:

Finally, over the B Major to A Major chords, I've demonstrated one way to add chromatic tension to a solo. Over the B Major, I approach the 3rd of the chord (D#) from a semitone below, before hitting the 5th (F#). This three-note fragment repeats five times with the note placement falling differently each time.

Over the A Major chord, we use the A Blues scale, before shifting up to end with some classic Mixolydian vocabulary around the E shape.

Example 10k:

Chapter Eleven - Outlaw Track

The final solo in this book is greatly influenced by the Outlaw, and Truck-Driving country traditions. Artists such as Waylon Jennings, Merle Haggard, and David Allen Coe were all well-known for their outlaw sound, so I've drawn on those influences here, along with the neo-traditional sound of artists like Alan Jackson and George Strait.

To mix things up, this track is in the key of G, meaning that the I, IV and V chords will be G Major, C Major, and D Major. First, however, here's the riff which forms the basis of the track. It requires hybrid picking on the double stops and uses notes from the G Mixolydian scale throughout.

Example 11a:

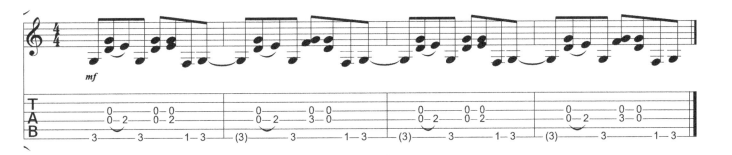

The verse can be played as both an electric and an acoustic part. First up, let's look at the acoustic part which gives you a good idea of the harmony and forms a twelve-bar blues pattern in G. The secret here is that the strumming pattern helps drive the music forward without getting in the way of the other instruments.

Example 11b:

Next, the electric part draws influence from the riff in the intro.

Over the C Major chord, the same basic idea is used, but this time one string set higher. The second half of the bar slides up to play around the G shape.

Over the D, I've played a Dadd11 chord (which is actually just an open C Major chord moved up two frets). An 'add 11' chord is where the (or 11th) is *added* to a Major chord (as opposed to a sus chord, where the 4th *replaces* the 3rd).

Example 11c:

There's a short bridge section before the solo starts. First up, take a look at the acoustic part and simply strum through the chords to get to grips with the changes.

Example 11d:

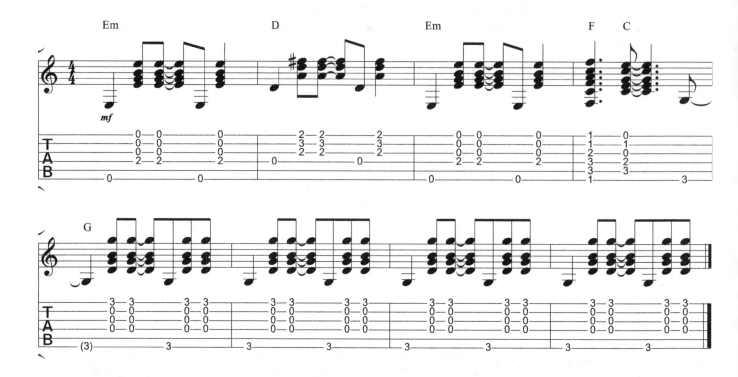

The electric guitar part is more reserved in this section, sticking tightly to the chords and using the Dadd11 from the previous section.

Example 11e:

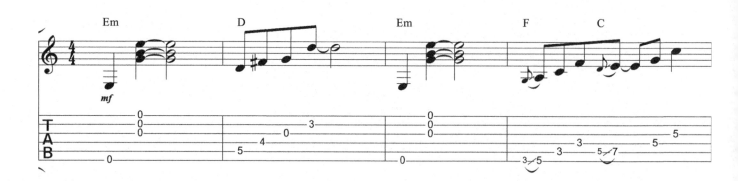

The first lick of the solo outlines a G Major chord, beginning with a pedal steel-inspired bend around the 10th fret, bending the 2nd up to the 3rd, and playing the 5th on the high E string.

The second half of the lick shifts down the neck using 3rds on the G and B strings to end the lick in the E shape. The lick here uses a typical blend of the Minor Pentatonic with an added Major 3rd.

Example 11f:

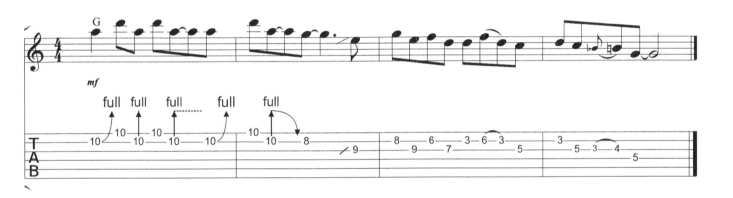

The second part of the solo moves to the C Major chord and back to the G Major. To outline the C Major, I've moved up to the 8th fret area (E shape) and hammered from the b3rd to the 3rd and used the C Mixolydian scale to outline the sound of the chord.

The second part of the lick moves back to G Major and is outlined with some descending 6ths from the G Mixolydian scale.

Example 11g:

The next two bars move from D Major to C Major. To highlight this change, I begin in the A shape, and slide from the b3rd (F) to the 3rd (F#) of D. The rest of this bar uses notes from the D Mixolydian scale before sliding up to the 3rd of C (E) and ascending the C Major Pentatonic scale.

The second half of the lick is typical of hot country players like Johnny Hiland, with 6ths played on the A and G strings while bending the higher note a scale tone.

Example 11h:

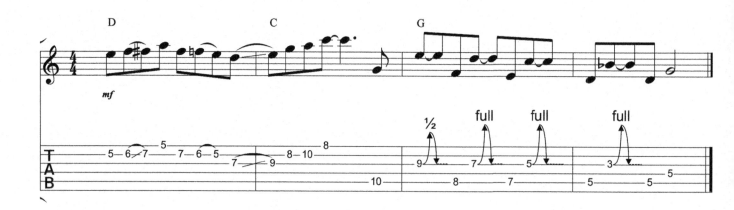

The repeat begins up at the 12th fret, with the G Major Pentatonic scale. The second half of the lick begins around the A shape with more b3rd to 3rd movements.

Example 11i:

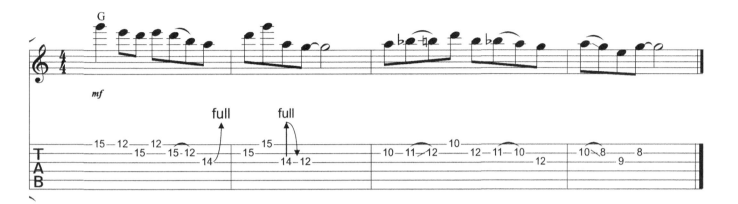

The next lick uses two positions in C Major, beginning with the D shape, before transitioning up to the C shape in the second bar.

The second half of the lick is over a G Major chord, and moves to the E shape high on the neck, bending from the b7 to the root and playing the 3rd on the high E string.

Example 11j:

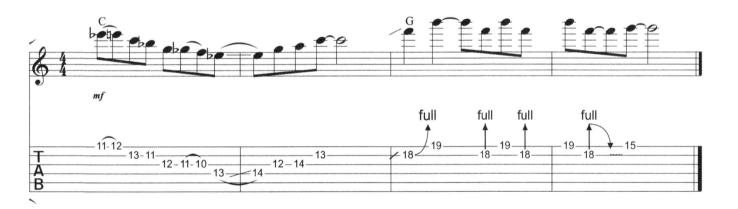

The following lick outlines the D Major and C Major chords before resolving to G Major to end. It begins in the same way as the idea on the C Major chord, is now played one tone higher to fit the D Major. The second bar ends with a classic bluegrass cliché played numerous times.

Example 11k:

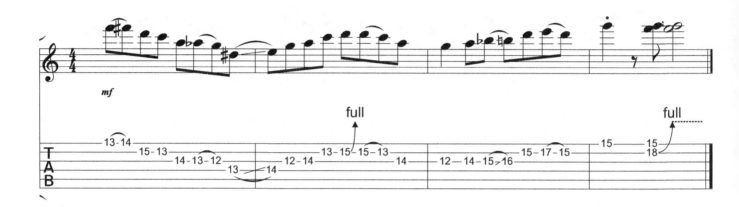

The final lick outlines the chords in the bridge with double stops and pedal steel-type bends. The last two bars require attention as you must hold notes on both the G and B strings while playing different notes on the high E string.

Example 11l:

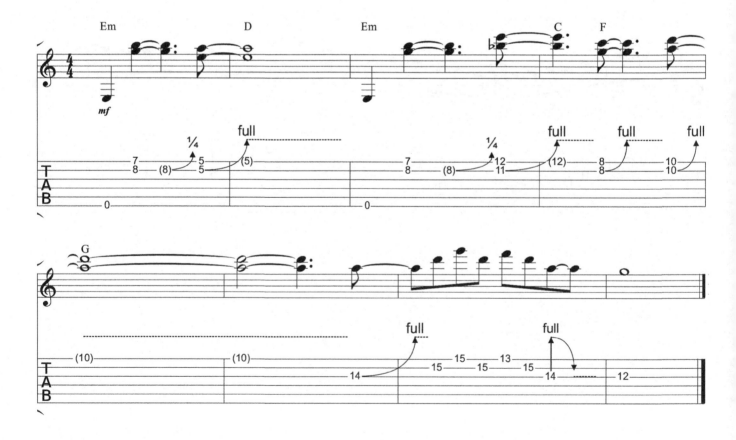

Conclusion

After working through the ideas in this book, you will be well on your way to playing great country guitar. Taking these concepts to the next level will require practice, so I'd like to offer you some tips to help you focus on the things that I feel matter the most in your playing life.

Music isn't about speed; it's about moving people. Sometimes this will require playing fast, perhaps to convey excitement... but *tone* is always king. Spend time listening to the notes you're playing and how they *sound*. Compare the projection heard by Gypsy guitarists, to picking lightly with the tip of the pick. Set a clean tone on your amp and experiment with different picks, dynamics, and picking directions. I find I can get a particularly strong tone by pushing the pick through the string, down towards the pickup.

Timing is also incredibly important. Outside of practicing to the tracks given, use a metronome and train *your foot* to tap on every beat will help your rhythm and phrasing tremendously in the long run.

Remember; the foot taps in time with the click and you *play to the foot*. You aren't tapping along to what you're playing! The pulse is the lifeblood of the music, and your foot will tell you where that is.

Also try practicing with the metronome clicking on beats 2 and 4, like a snare playing on the backbeat. This is especially useful when for faster tempos as your foot won't be moving like a Heavy Metal bass drummer! This feels awkward at first but will help your time keeping immeasurably.

Finally, Here's a suggested listening list of some essential country records for any collection. The beauty of a genre with so much history is that you'll find many 'best of' collections for a great price, so don't be afraid to give some of them a shot.

Alan Jackson - The Greatest Hits Collection

Albert Lee - Live at the Iridium

Andy Wood - Caught Between the Truth and a Lie

Brad Paisley - Time Well Wasted

Brent Mason - Hot Wired

Buck Owens - The Very Best of Buck Owens - Vol. 1

Buddy Emmons - Amazing Steel Guitar

Chet Atkins - The Essential Chet Atkins

Ernest Tubb - Texas Troubadour

Hank Williams - The Best of Hank Williams

The Hellecasters - The Return of The Hellecasters

The Hot Club of Cowtown - What Makes Bob Holler

Jerry Reed - The Unbelievable Guitar and Voice of Jerry Reed

Keith Urban - Days Go By

Maddie & Tae - Start Here

Merle Haggard - The Very Best of Merle Haggard

Merle Travis - Sixteen Tons

Pistol Annies - Annie Up

The Time Jumpers - The Time Jumpers

Good luck with your journey, I hope you've enjoyed these first steps, and I look forward to seeing you at the other end.

About Levi Clay

Since graduating from the University of East London with qualifications in both performance, and education, Levi Clay has been an unstoppable force on the international guitar scene.

Working as a writer, teacher, transcriber, journalist, and entertainer for various outlets, it only makes sense that Levi's musical passions are as varied as his skillset.

Having travelled the world as a writer, Levi is still a regular contributor for Guitar Interactive Magazine, both as an on-screen personality and ghost writer.

As a teacher, Levi is well known for his monthly Beyond Blues column for Premier Guitar Magazine, along with his selection of DVD releases for LickLibrary.com. He still maintains a select group of students from all over the world via Skype.

His work as a transcriber has kept him relevant and in demand, completing work for various magazines, publishers, artists, and websites.

Releasing two albums in 2015 ("Out of the Ashes", and "Into the Whisky") via a successful crowdfund initiative, Levi continues to connect directly with his fans and followers via Patreon and YouTube.

Be Social:

For over 250 Free Guitar Lessons with Videos Check out:

www.fundamental-changes.com

Fundamental Changes Twitter: **@guitar_joseph**

Levi Clay Twitter: **@LeviClay88**

Over 7500 fans on Facebook: **FundamentalChangesInGuitar**

Instagram: **FundamentalChanges**

COUNTRYGUITAR
SOLOINGTECHNIQUES

Learn Hot Country Hybrid-Picking, Banjo Rolls, Licks & Techniques

LEVI**CLAY**

FUNDAMENTAL**CHANGES**

Introduction

Few genres of music are as deceptively technical as country music.

Growing up as a fan of rock, metal, and shred, I was always aware of players like Albert Lee and when I saw his songs in guitar magazines, I would always think, "Wow... there's no way I could play that!". Fifteen years later, I can say that I might just be getting there.

The more I dug into the genre, the more appreciation I developed for the players. Not only do they generally possess a high level of technique, but it's also a style that's executed with ultra-bright, crystal-clean tones so there's nowhere to hide in the band.

From flat picking masters like Doc Watson, to electric guitar wizards like Albert Lee and Brent Mason, to talented singer/songwriters who spice up their songs with incredible picking like Brad Paisley and Keith Urban; there's a lot to master in this style.

Make no mistake about it, it takes a lot of devotion to be able to play in a guitar-driven country act, and to do it with the confidence you need to be successful.

This book teaches you the advanced techniques needed to play high-level country guitar. It's not for the complete beginner and for that I'd recommend my book, Country Guitar for Beginners.

It's also not about simple Pentatonic-based soloing. While that's an important part of any player's arsenal, this book is about the technique-driven 'Hot Country' style.

These concepts, however, aren't just presented from a technical angle, it's also important to learn the theoretical application of the techniques. All of the examples will be taught from a harmonic perspective. You'll learn both *where* and *why* the licks work.

After nine chapters exploring the core concepts of technical country guitar, I've written two full solos on an original tune composed for this book. These solos use all the techniques covered and can be played with the downloadable backing tracks.

The next logical step in your development is to learn as much stylistic vocabulary as possible, either by transcribing from records, or from a good book such as my best-selling title, Country Guitar Heroes: 100 Country Licks for Guitar.

Music is a language, and the licks we play are the words and vocabulary. This is something you can take on board immediately. Commit every single lick or idea you learn in this book to memory. Sing it, play it in different keys and use it over backing tracks.

Make. Music.

It's easy to get caught up in the practice room, always pushing for a few more beats per minute on the metronome (it's easy to track progress when it's something measurable). This is important, but don't lose sight of developing more musical ideas, your ears, and great phrasing.

My final tip is about tone. While country guitar can be played on any type of guitar, the Telecaster is king for a reason. No matter what guitar you choose, get comfortable hearing the bridge pickup with plenty of added treble on the amp. You won't always play with these settings, but they're often what you need. When you're comfortable with this tone, you'll be comfortable with anything.

There are no rules on amps, but a Fender-style, or even a Vox-style clean tone is a lot more common in the genre than a hot-rodded Marshall or Mesa Boogie! A simple compressor pedal is a subtle effect and hard for the listener to notice, but as a player you'll often rely on it for your sound.

For your reference, I recorded all the audio examples on a Mexican Fender Road Worn series Telecaster, with Joe Barden Danny Gatton pickups (The brightest pickups I've ever heard!). This was run through a rack-mounted Kemper profiling amp using an official Dr Z MAZ 18 NR profile with a splash of reverb and compression.

A lot of time went into getting the audio recordings right, so make sure you head to the www.Fundamental-Changes.com to download them. They're your guide to how you should sound, so listen carefully!

Good luck!

Levi

Get the Audio

The audio files for this book are available to download for free from **www.fundamental-changes.com**, and the link is in the top right corner. Simply select this book title from the drop-down menu and follow the instructions to get the audio.

We recommend that you download the files directly to your computer, not to your tablet, and extract them there before adding them to your media library. You can then put them on your tablet, iPod or burn them to CD. On the download page, there is a help PDF, and we also provide technical support via the contact form.

For over 250 Free Guitar Lessons with Videos Check out:

www.fundamental-changes.com

Twitter: **@guitar_joseph**

FB: **FundamentalChangesInGuitar**

Instagram: **FundamentalChanges**

Chapter One: Triads

The biggest difference between rock and country guitar is the emphasis placed on harmony.

In rock music, the musicians might take a song like Stairway to Heaven, see that the chords in the solo are A Minor, G Major, and F Major, and conclude that the progression is in the key of A Minor. At this point the details of the progression are often ignored in favour of a one-scale-fits-all approach, using just the A Minor Pentatonic (A, C, D, E, G) or the A Natural Minor scale (A, B, C, D, E, F, G).

While some country players may use a similar approach, taking a more considered approach to the chords will result in an instantly noticeable improvement to your country sound.

My approach is extremely simple. I don't see chords as being an incidental selection of notes taken from a scale I happen to be playing. To me, the chord tones come first, and then notes are added to make a scale. It's a subtle difference; but this perspective will have a significant impact on your playing.

In order that you can learn and understand this approach in a way that will be instantly useable, I'm going to use the CAGED system as a base.

I'll cover the basics here, but if you want a more detailed breakdown, check out The CAGED System & 100 Licks for Blues Guitar by Joseph Alexander.

Look at the following A Major barre chord. You will have played this many times, but probably overlooked the smaller, three-note triad voicings it contains.

A major (E shape)

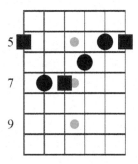

The notes on the top three strings contain all three notes (A, C#, E) of the triad. In this voicing, the root is on top, as indicated by the square. From low to high, the notes are arranged 3rd, 5th, root.

A major

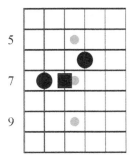

If you move across to the D, G, and B strings, you'll find that the same is true. All three notes of the triad are present, just in a different order. Here the root note is the lowest voice in the chord and gives the voicing R 3 5.

A major

You can also move this over to the A, D, and G strings for another three-note triad voicing. Now the root note is in the middle of the chord giving the voicing 5 R 3.

A major

I often warm up by playing these triad shapes as three-note groupings throughout the shape. In the following example, I've taken the A Major barre pattern and broken it down into three-note triads, then moved the whole idea up to the 10th fret to outline a D Major chord. The beauty of this system is that it becomes easy to move chords around the neck.

Example 1a:

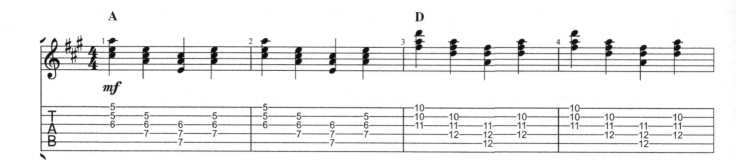

Here's the same idea, but now played as single notes across each grouping of three strings.

Example 1b:

These patterns can be picked in many ways, and I'll introduce those in later chapters. At this stage, play them however you feel comfortable.

Using just these simple three-note voicings, it's possible to create some simple, yet pleasing melodies without even considering scales.

The only thing I've added to the next example is a slide into the note C#. You can always play a note below a chord tone as long as it doesn't fall on a strong beat (and sometimes even if it does!). There's no theory needed, it's simple tension and release.

Example 1c:

The following example uses this barre form and moves it up and down the neck to outline a simple twelve-bar blues, a common progression in country music.

A two-bar melody is played around the 5th fret and then repeated with a slight variation to keep things interesting.

As the chord changes to D Major, the barre chord pattern shifts up the neck to the 10th fret to create a D Major sound. The original two-bar melody now outlines a D Major, rather than an A Major chord.

After two bars, this melody moves back down the neck to outline the A Major chord again before shifting up to the 12th fret to outline an E Major. It then moves down to the 10th for D Major and finally returns to A Major for the final two bars.

Example 1d:

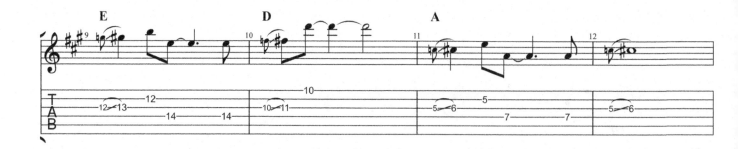

Another way to use these simple triad patterns is to explore the notes a semitone below each note of the triad. These are often called *chromatic neighbour tones*, and they're a way to create some melodic interest without having to worry about the 'correct' scales.

Example 1e:

It would be possible to fill an entire book with exercises and examples of melodies around just this one chord voicing, but to keep things moving, we'll now take a look at another major shape. There will be plenty of licks later.

Take a look at the C Major shape and the smaller triad groupings found within. The root of the C-shape chord is on the A string and played with the 4th finger. To play an A Major chord using this voicing, the chord must be moved so that root is played at the 12th fret on the A string.

A major (C shape)

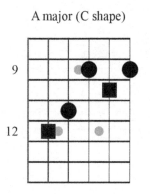

As with the E shape, the smaller triads are laid out quite clearly.

Example 1f:

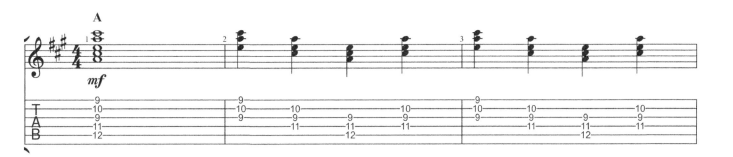

A great exercise is to cycle between both positions of the A Major chord. Visualise the bigger 5/6 string chord, but only play the smaller sections of it.

Example 1g:

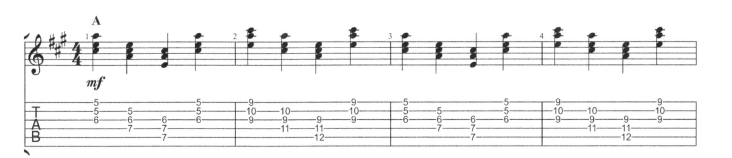

As a further exercise, here are the same two voicings, but now used to outline an A Major to D Major chord progression. For the A Major chord, use the C shape with the root on the 12th fret, then stay in this same area to use the E shape at the 10th fret to outline the D Major chord.

Example 1h:

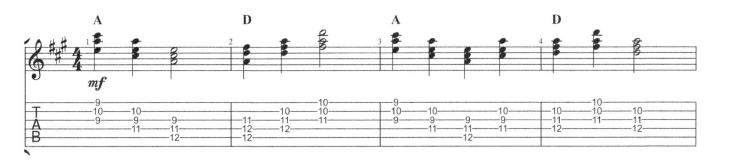

Here's a simple melody that outlines the chord change in this position. Notice how much more accurately this outlines the chords than just using the A Major scale, and it's a whole lot easier!

Example 1i:

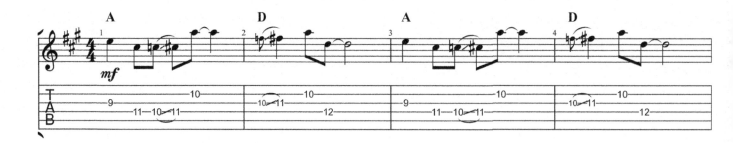

Using the same two shapes, I've written a lick that outlines A Major, D Major, and E Major. Beginning in bar one with the C shape, a simple descending triad connects into the D Major chord by landing on the F# on the G string.

The next shape outlines an ascending E Major triad using the E shape, before resolving back to the C shape on the A Major chord.

Example 1j:

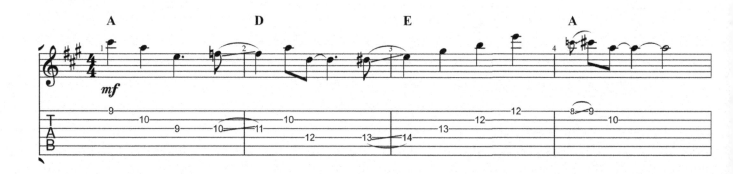

You can see how easy it is to make interesting melodies all over the neck, thinking of nothing more than the chords you're playing over. Scales are great when you need to play a lot of notes, but using chord shapes shows you where the strong and simple melodies are. Learn these first, and then add embellishments as you develop.

The final important triad position is built around the A-shape barre chord.

A major (A shape)

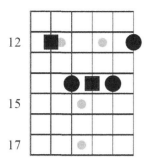

This can also be broken down into three-note voicings.

Example 1k:

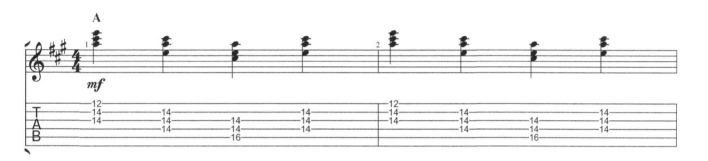

You'll notice that you have to break out of position for the C# (16th fret). This is actually in the G shape chord voicing. When playing country solos, you'll spend most of your time on the higher strings, but as you develop, you'll quickly find how elegantly these shapes connect.

Here's an eight-bar example that outlines the previous chord progression, but uses all three chord forms. As with the previous examples, notice anytime a note *below* a chord tone is played.

Bar one uses the E shape before shifting to the A shape in bar two, the C shape in bar three, and back to the E shape in bar four.

The second time through, the progression begins in the C shape, moves to the E shape for the D Major chord, then moves up a tone to the E shape for the E Major chord. The sequence finally resolves to the A shape for the A Major chord.

Example 1l:

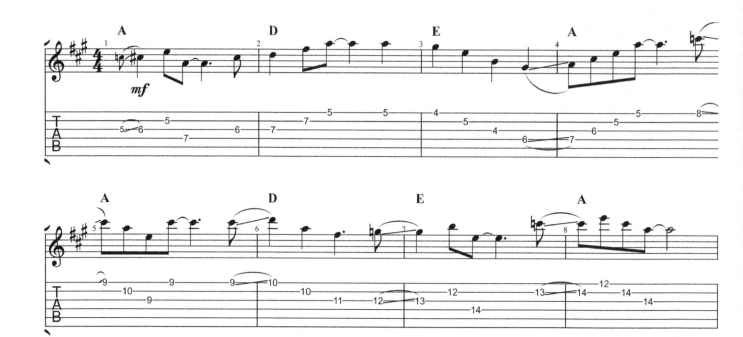

This approach can be used on absolutely any Major chord, regardless of style, but it's a great way to add a country sensibility to other genres.

Here's an example of this approach being used on a country gospel-type chord progression of A Major. A7, B7, D7, D/E. Almost every famous musician has played this progression, from Jimmy Herring (Bilgewater Blues) to Cee Lo Green (Forget You).

Example 1m:

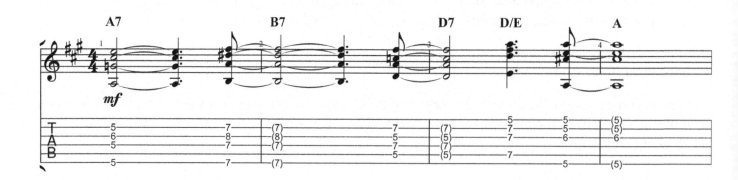

While these chords may contain more notes, at their core they're just Major chords.

A7 is an A Major triad with an added G.

B7 is a B Major triad with an added A.

D7 is a D Major chord with an added C.

D/E is a D Major chord with an E in the bass.

As such, it's possible to solo over this progression using the basic triads and approach notes shown above.

Example 1n:

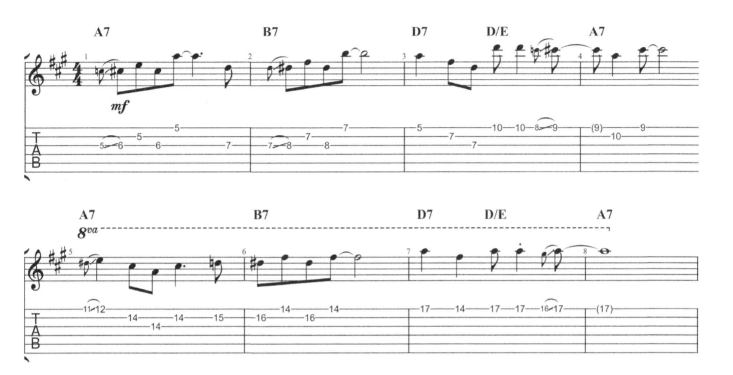

This approach will only take you so far, but it's a great way to dip your toe into the country guitar sound without needing to know a lot of theory or scales.

Don't underestimate the importance of triads, they're the basis on which everything else is built, and I'll refer to them repeatedly. Take your time with them and learn to visualise them in any key without hesitation. They hold the key that unlocks the door to playing like Brent Mason, Albert Lee, and many other legends.

Chapter Two: Major Pentatonic Scales

The Major Pentatonic scale is the country cousin of rock's ubiquitous Minor Pentatonic scale.

One approach that rock players often use with the C Major Pentatonic scale (C, D, E, F, G, A), is to see that it contains some of the same notes as the A Minor Pentatonic scale (A, C, D, E, G), and assume that the easiest thing to do is play their A Minor vocabulary over a C Major chord. While this works on paper, in practice it's a different story. An experienced player plays differently over A Minor than they do over C Major.

For example, here's a lick using the A Minor Pentatonic scale that I might play over an A Minor chord.

Example 2a:

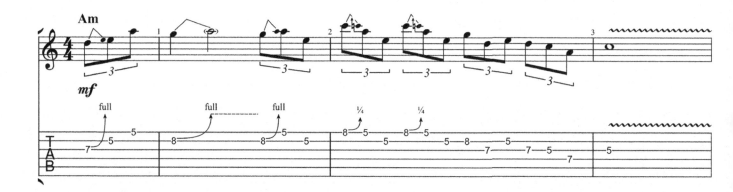

Now here's that same lick, but played over a C Major chord. Technically, I'm playing the same notes as the C Major Pentatonic scale, but it just doesn't sound right.

Example 2b:

It's not just about the notes you play, but *how* they're played. A common bend from G to A (b7 to Root) is perfect on an A Minor chord, but over a C Major chord the same bend has you landing on the 6th, and it's jarring.

It is more effective to learn the Major Pentatonic scale as notes added on top of the triads you've already learned.

For example, a C Major chord contains the notes C, E, and G, so you only need to add the notes D and an A to make a Major Pentatonic scale.

The following example shows a C Major triad in the E shape, before playing it again adding D and A as connecting 'Major Pentatonic' notes.

Example 2c:

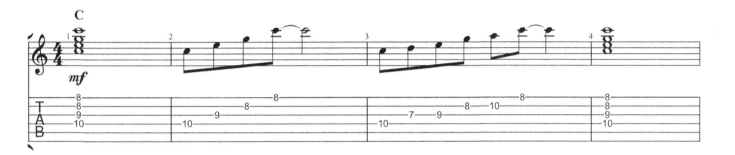

This isn't the quickest or easiest way to learn the scale, but it will help you keep track of the underlying chords and will be extremely useful in the long run.

Here's the full Major Pentatonic scale in the E shape. Make sure you distinguish between the chord tones (C, E, and G) and the Pentatonic notes (D and A).

Example 2d:

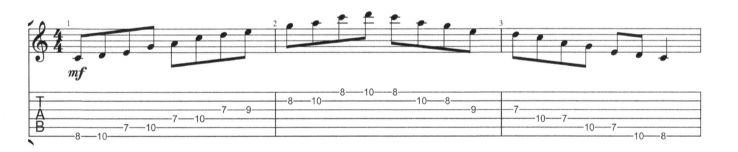

The following are a short series of licks played with this scale shape.

The first idea sticks strictly to the scale pattern. Note how the melody begins on the root (C) and the first half of the phrase ends on the 3rd (E) at the end of the second bar. The second half of the melody begins on that 3rd (E) and ends in the final bar on the root (C).

Example 2e:

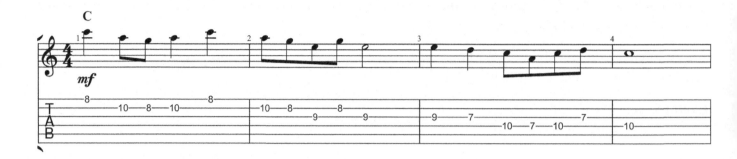

Next is another relatively simple idea that just uses the notes of the scale. You'll note that the first and last three notes are from the triad and helps the lick sound tightly tied to the chord.

Example 2f:

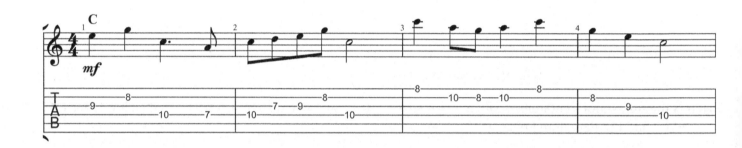

Here's another four-bar phrase to give you an idea of how many melodic ideas can be extracted from this simple scale. The possibilities are endless.

Example 2g:

Next, learn the Major Pentatonic scale around the C-shape chord. First, play the chord, then the triad, then the Major Pentatonic scale. This is an excellent, organised way of working on these scales to keep them tied to the underlying Major triad harmony.

Example 2h:

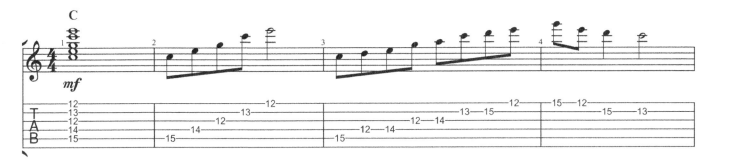

Here's the Major Pentatonic scale built around the A shape. As before, play the chord, the triad, and then the Pentatonic scale. It's important to see the scale around the chord form.

Example 2i:

Now you know three positions of the scale, here are some licks that use these notes in different positions to play simple melodies. When changing position, visualise the big chord form under what you're playing.

This first example uses the E shape for two bars before moving up to the C shape to extend the range of the melody.

Example 2j:

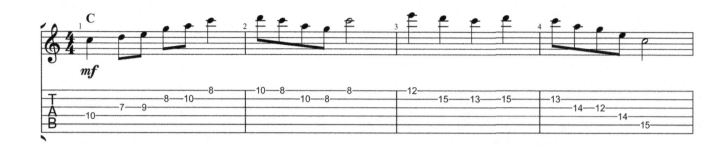

The next example moves through all three positions, playing simple melodic motifs on the top three strings before shifting up to develop the idea.

Example 2k:

This final idea begins high in the C shape and transitions down to the E shape in bar three.

Example 2l:

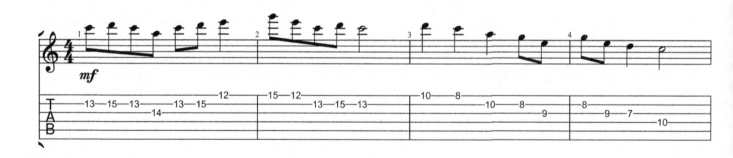

For the sake of completeness, there are two more Major Pentatonic shapes around the D and G shapes. These are often used, (especially when shifting through positions) so don't neglect them!

This is the G shape, both the chord and corresponding scale.

Example 2m:

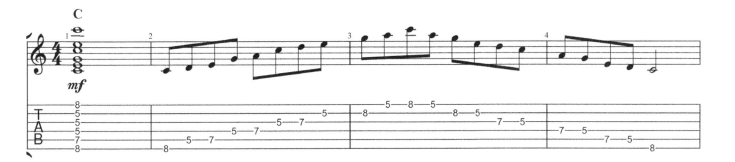

And here's the D shape.

Example 2n:

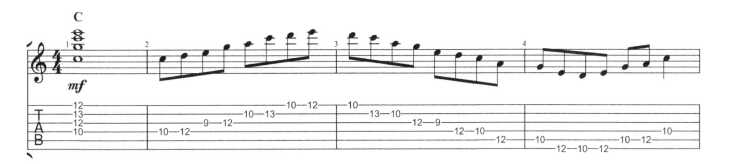

In the previous chapter, you learnt that it sounds great to play chromatic notes a semitone below a chord tone. This is still applicable in the Major Pentatonic scale. In fact, it's a key ingredient of what is known as *the Country scale*.

When playing the C Major Pentatonic scale (C, D, E, G, A), a common approach note to add is Eb (the b3rd which pulls up to E, the 3rd). This results in a smooth chromatic climb from D to Eb to E. The Major Pentatonic scale with an added b3 is often called the Country scale.

Here's the C Country scale played in the E shape. The Eb note is played on the A string 6th fret, and the G string 8th fret. To give it a more country sound, I've picked the Eb and slid into the E. This b3rd to 3rd movement will be heard repeatedly throughout the book as it is an important component of many country licks.

Example 2o:

This scale is often best fingered in a slightly different way when descending as it sounds best to slide or pull off from Eb to D. You'll notice the Eb is moved to the low E string at the end.

Example 2p:

Here's that scale played ascending and descending for the sake of completeness. Notice the different fingering in the tablature part.

Example 2q:

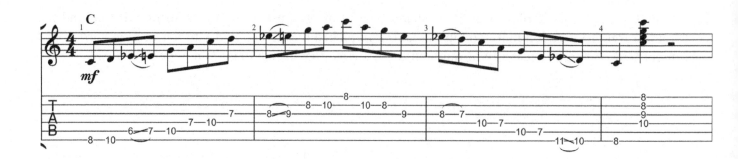

The following lick is often referred to as the "country cliché lick" as it's such a ubiquitous part of country music and is played several more times in the book. Here it's presented around the E shape. Remember that the triad can always be added in to punctuate solos.

Example 2r:

The following example shows the Country scale played ascending and descending around the C shape. This certainly isn't hugely practical at fast tempos, but remember that this scale is played in short fragments in the context of an actual solo, and rarely as a full ascending and descending scale.

Example 2s:

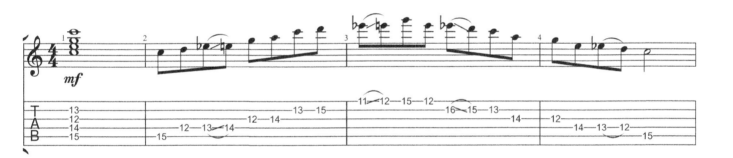

The following example shows the country cliché lick played in that same position.

Example 2t:

Finally, play the Country scale around the A shape. As with the previous shape, it's not ideal for playing quickly, but the phrasing concept is solid.

Example 2u:

Finally, play the cliché lick in the same position. You'll notice I've had to move up the neck to play the root note on the high E string to finish the lick.

Example 2v:

Another great way to practice and use the Country scale is to use the b3 to 3 movement as a way to shift position.

When playing the Country scale around the E shape, the b3rd was played on the A string despite it being easily accessible on the low E string. This is to allow you to *slide* from the b3rd to the 3rd. This can still be done when playing the b3rd on the E string, but it will result in shifting from the E shape to the D shape.

Example 2w:

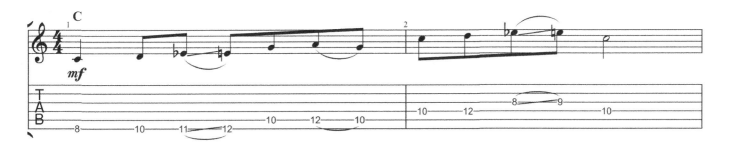

This next example works well in the A shape as a way of ascending to the G shape. It's an incredibly useful movement that facilitates quick position shifts up the neck.

Example 2x:

The next example begins in the A shape, transitioning up through the G shape to the E shape.

Example 2y:

Finally, it's possible to play other chromatic approach notes, but these are often used more sparingly.

This example features the Major Pentatonic scale, with an added Gb (a semitone below the 5th). It isn't a note I play too often, but it adds a great Western Swing flavour to the scale.

Example 2z:

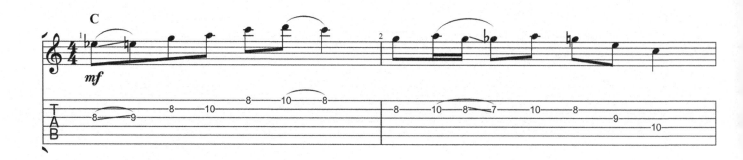

The possibilities are endless, and as you develop your country soloing techniques you'll see these concepts used time and time again. As you progress through this book, analyse each idea to see if it fits around a triad or Major Pentatonic scale.

Chapter Three: Together Again

Now you've got a couple of soloing tools under your belt, it's worthwhile to see how much music you can make with these important concepts before developing the other technical aspects of your playing.

The uncomplicated side of country guitar is often forgotten as we're wowed by stunning technical displays from the likes of Johnny Hiland and Albert Lee. However, for every technical player, there are 100 players who have entertained generations of fans with minimal technical ability. Playing fast is one thing, but paying tribute to the melodically-driven greats like Don Rich, Willie Nelson, Merle Haggard, Waylon Jennings, is important too.

To develop this side of your country playing, I've taken a simple I IV V chord progression, as you might find on Buck Owens' Together Again, and written some simple soloing ideas that use the concepts covered so far.

First, let's understand the chord progression.

The progression is a I IV V in the key of D Major (D, E, F#, G, A, B, C#), so the chords are D Major (I), G Major (IV), and A Major (V).

As the chords contain only notes from the D Major scale, it's possible to solo with just the D Major scale.

Having said that, unless you're either extremely lucky or have a highly developed ear, this approach is extremely risky as not all notes sound good over each chord. For example, C# sounds pretty 'out' on the D Major, and 'un-country' on the G, but great on the A Major chord.

Example 3a:

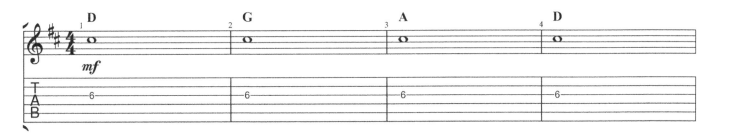

When looking to the D Major Pentatonic scale, you can end up in equally murky water, as any of these notes over the D Major sounds great, but the same ideas will sound a little off over the other two chords.

Example 3b:

The next example is a short solo that uses just the notes of the correct triad on each chord, along with a few chromatic approach notes for interest.

The solo begins up at the E shape at the 10th fret for the D Major, moving to the A shape when the chord changes to G Major, and then the C shape when the chord changes to A Major.

Example 3c:

Another way to outline this chord progression is to use Major Pentatonic scales built on each chord. In other words, play D Major Pentatonic (D, E, F#, A, B) over the D Major, G Major Pentatonic (G, A, B, D, E) over the G Major, and A Major Pentatonic (A, B, C#, E, F#) over the A Major.

It sounds obvious, but this application is more challenging, and very rewarding.

The next example shows how to play the Major Pentatonic scale ascending through each chord in a mixture of the E and C shapes. This sounds great because each melody sounds like it 'respects' and highlights the chord, and is common stylistically.

Example 3d:

Here's another solo that uses that basic roadmap around the neck, but doesn't use the same idea repeatedly. This is more musical, although it can be a bit tricky keep track of where you are. However, once you've spent the time developing the skills to see basic triads, you shouldn't have too many problems.

Example 3e:

Learn the following solo. It consists of just the country cliché lick played over the progression in several different ways. This is a fantastic way to develop fretboard knowledge while actually making music.

Example 3f:

Next is a trickier example that uses triads, the Country scale, and some simple bends.

Bar one begins with the cliché lick in the C shape moving up to the A shape. When the chord changes to G Major, a descending bending idea is played in the G Major Pentatonic scale. A slight variation of this is then played over the A Major chord before ending with a bending idea in the C shape over the D Major chord.

The second half of the solo features more notes but is still simple in concept. Playing first around the E-shape D Major chord, it shifts to a simple G Major triad over the G Major. Next, a busier idea using the C shape is played over the A Major chord before ending with the bending lick from the first part of the solo.

Example 3g:

You'll quickly notice that it's quite easy to play something enjoyable without trying to be too clever. Together Again is a classic country standard where the melodies and solo are traditionally played on the pedal steel guitar. These are formed from subtle variations of the vocal melody.

I recommend you check out Buck Owens' version on his Live at Carnegie Hall album, or even Vince Gill's version with Paul Franklin on the Bakersfield album.

Here's a final solo based on the vocal melody with simple embellishments from the triad shapes and the Country scale.

Example 3h:

Further to the ear training ideas in the previous chapter, spend time listening to each of these solos before moving on. When they're burned into your mind, try playing them again, but try to hear the notes you're about to play *before* you play them.

Remember, the ear is king!

Chapter Four: Alternate Picking Skills

While a technique-focussed approach isn't always a driving force in country guitar, that doesn't mean it shouldn't be studied or form a part of your sound. However, guitar technique in country isn't treated in the same methodical way it is in other genres like rock or metal.

There's still a huge following for players with high technical ability who often come from a more bluegrass background. Doc Watson lit this fire in the '60s, Tony Rice expanded on in the '70s, and the torch is still carried by incredible flat pickers like Carl Miner and David Grier. Check out the annual National Flatpicking Championship to see some seriously talented young players with technique to die for!

When it comes to alternate picking technique, some teachers will do everything in their power to finger scales with consistent amounts of notes per string. While there are obvious benefits to this (such as consistent string-crossing mechanics), there are some drawbacks.

First up, while it's easy to arrange a Major scale in a three-note-per-string fingering, or a Pentatonic scale in a two-note-per-string pattern, how about the Country scale? This six-note scale is extremely impractical when played as a strict three-note per string pattern.

Example 4a:

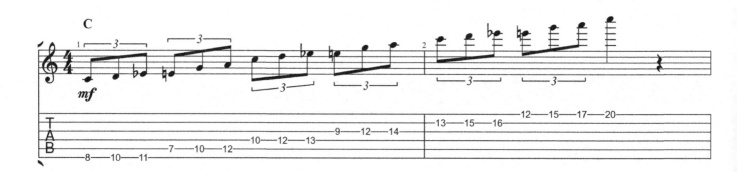

You may also have noticed that most music consists of more than just scales played up and down as fast as possible.

A great alternate picker doesn't look for shortcuts or excuses, and they don't need to arrange their scales into specific fingerings: they pick 'down, up, down, up,' whatever they see in front of them.

Let's look at an ascending and descending Country scale played with strict alternate picking. Play the first note with a down-stroke, the next with an up-stroke, and repeat all the way through.

I've included picking indications for all the following examples. This picking notation can be confusing as the symbol for an up-stroke seems to be an arrow pointing down. This system actually originates from violin notation and each marking symbolises the end of the bow that leads. A down-stroke leads with the square heel of the bow, and an up-stroke leads with the pointy head of the bow.

Example 4b:

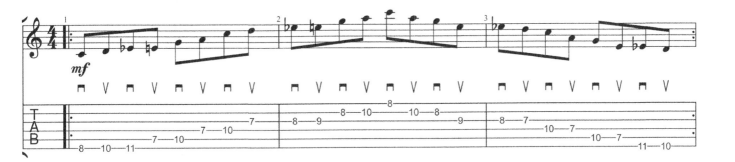

The troublesome aspect of alternate picking is crossing strings, and there are two mechanics that need to be mastered, *outside picking* and *inside picking*.

Outside picking occurs when a string is plucked, and the pick then travels past the next string to execute the next pick stroke. So down on the D string, and up on the G string. This creates a feeling of being outside the strings.

Example 4c:

This motion can be exaggerated by picking the A and B strings, which gives you a greater feeling of the 'outside' motion.

Example 4d:

In the following example, you'll notice that every string change requires outside picking. Some players favour this mechanic and structure their licks around it. There is nothing inherently wrong with this idea because taking one mechanic you're good at and exploiting it can be a great way to push your technique.

Example 4e:

While restricting their picking technique works for many players, I like to avoid any sort of self-imposed limitations as I never know what someone might want me to play tomorrow. It's for this reason I've spent a lot of time working on outside picking's less popular sister, *inside* picking.

Inside picking is the technique where you pick one string, then play the next string without first crossing it.

The following example begins with a down-stroke on the G string followed by an up-stroke on the D string. This time the pick feels stuck between the strings. It's very important to become comfortable and accurate with this motion.

Example 4f:

The next example exaggerates this motion between the B and A strings to highlight the mechanic. This often requires much work to make it comfortable. Your goal is to do this accurately at speed without looking at the strings.

Example 4g:

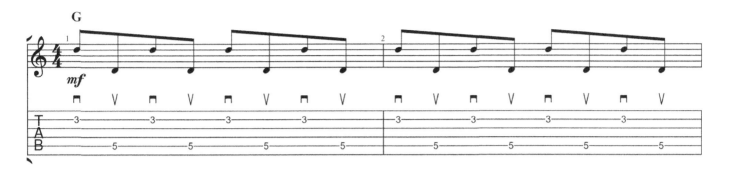

Next is an example based on the C Country scale (E shape) that uses both inside, and outside picking. It highlights why working on both mechanics is essential: every note of this lick must feel strong.

Example 4h:

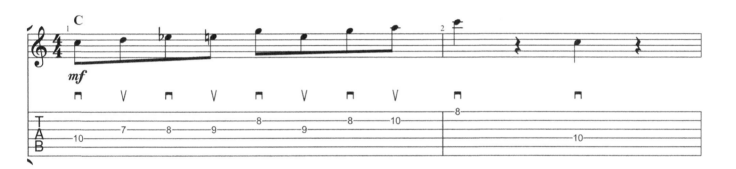

Now you understand these basic alternate picking mechanics, it's time to use these skills to introduce another important sound in the country guitarists' arsenal, the Mixolydian scale.

As with everything seen earlier, the new sound will build on what you already know.

The C Major Pentatonic scale (C, D, E, G, A) contains the intervals of the root, 2nd, 3rd, 5th, and 6th. The Mixolydian scale adds the 4th (F) and b7th (Bb).

Here's that b7 (Bb) added to a C Major triad in the E shape. The goal is to learn where this interval sits in the E shape so it can be used in conjunction with any other approaches you're using.

Example 4i:

Next, the full scale is played ascending and descending in the E shape. You'll notice that there's a mixture of inside and outside picking, but the picking pattern is consistent alternate picking!

Example 4j:

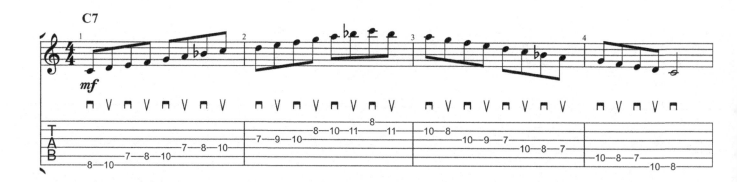

Here's a fun way to break up a scale to create a nice country flavour. First C is played, followed by the note a 6th higher (A). Then D is played, followed by the note a 6th higher (Bb). Then E followed by C, and so on. Essentially you are playing an ascending Mixolydian scale in 6ths. This exercise also gives your outside picking a solid workout.

Example 4k:

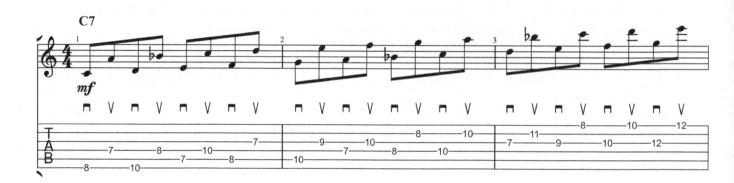

The notes in the C Major Pentatonic scale sound at home on a C6 chord (C, E, G, A), but the Mixolydian mode introduces a b7, which outlines a C7 sound (C, E, G, Bb)

An excellent way to practice this sound *and* develop a great alternate picking workout is to play the full C7 arpeggio.

Example 4l:

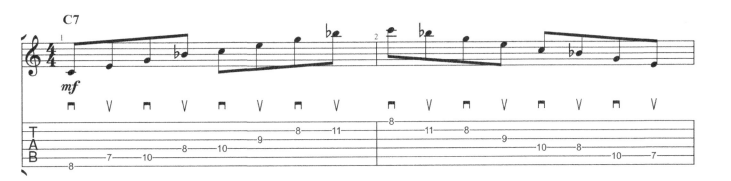

Here's an exciting line that combines ideas from the C Mixolydian scale and the C7 arpeggio. Notice how these help the lick outline a C7 chord. The line begins on a chord tone (G) and ends on a chord tone (E). In fact, anything that's not a chord tone is just a melodic way of connecting two chord tones.

Example 4m:

Often, players struggle with the descending part of the arpeggio in the previous example. The technique used is the pinnacle of high-level country picking: cross-picking.

Cross-picking is the name given to fast-picked parts that are played with just one note per string. These are the hardest picking ideas as they require absolute mastery of the inside and outside picking motions.

Here's a simple ascending idea that uses C Major and isolates this cross-picking concept.

Example 4n:

Now here's that concept applied to a C Major, G Major, F Major, and C Major triad on the D, G, and B strings.

Example 4o:

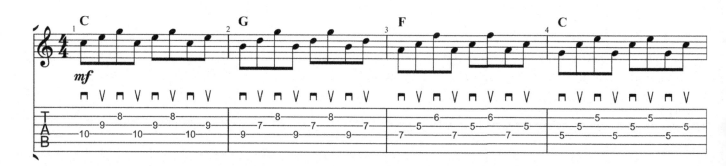

The next example takes the previous ascending (or forward) roll and reverses it.

Example 4p:

This next cross-picking pattern moves up and down a G triad and includes a string skip from the D to B string.

Take it slowly and build up speed over time.

Example 4q:

The same cross-picking idea can be used to outline chord progressions, too, like in the following example where I've increased the rhythmic subdivisions to 1/16th notes.

Example 4r:

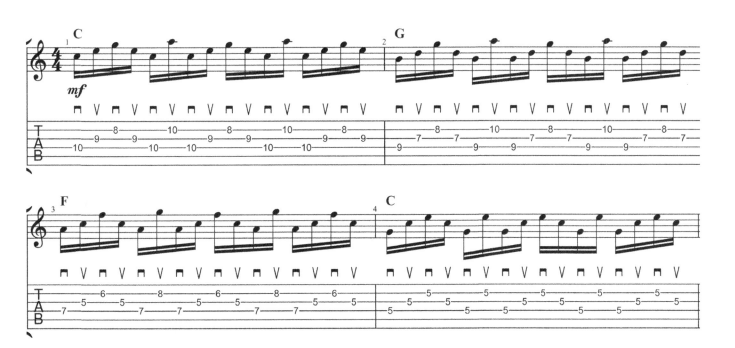

There are endless ways to use these cross-picking ideas effectively and a limitless amount of chord progressions to use them on. This is demonstrated by the following modern pop-type progression. It's played on a lower string set and uses palm muting throughout.

Example 4s:

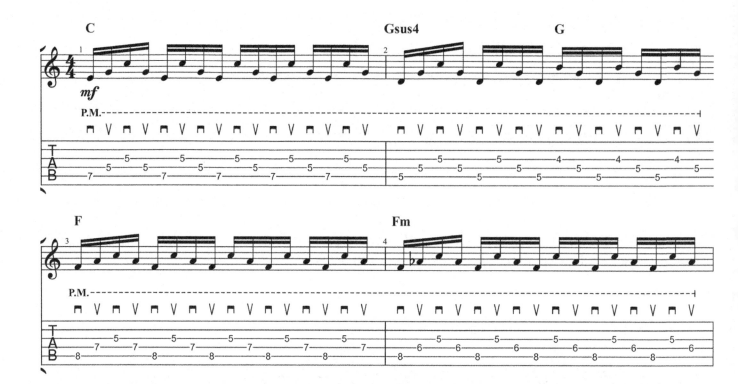

As your cross-picking skills develop, you'll be able to include rapid one-note-per-string ideas in your soloing. The following example outlines a C7 and D7 chord on the low four strings. Brent Mason plays something similar to this in his Pick It Apart solo, it's a real jaw-dropper!

Example 4t:

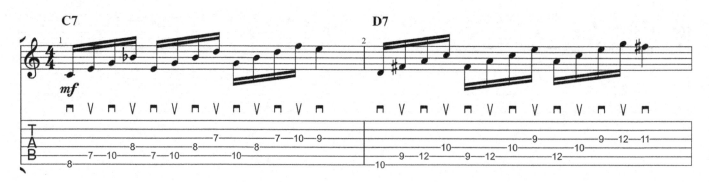

Here's one final lick that combines everything studied so far, and outlines a C7 chord in the E shape.

Example 4u:

As with every technique in this book, I could devote over a hundred pages to these ideas, but this should be more than enough to get the ball rolling and inspire you to develop the technique further.

Remember that there are four other CAGED positions to be explored and each of these has their own Pentatonic, Country, and Mixolydian scales, the arpeggio, and limitless licks and musical ideas. Devote some time to applying all the concepts in this chapter to a different position, like the C shape.

Don't expect quick results. World-class pickers develop these skills over many years of playing. While you'll be able to use these ideas right away, it will take time to develop speed and fluency. Make sure your picking hand is always relaxed because tension is the first step on the road to playing-related injuries.

Chapter Five: Slurs

One reason why players with bluegrass backgrounds need to be such good pickers is that in the world of unamplified music, not only do you need plenty of attack to be heard, but an acoustic guitar's sustain is insignificant compared to an amplified telecaster with some compression. Sustain and volume make it easy to use different methods of articulation, like hammer-ons, slides, and pull-offs when soloing.

Using these techniques gives you a wide variety of tonal options and also allows the picking hand a bit of breathing space as the fretting hand can pick up some of the slack.

Here's a simple exercise that puts hammer-ons in an ascending scalar idea. The secret to fluidity is to retain the sense of where alternate picking should occur.

Example 5a:

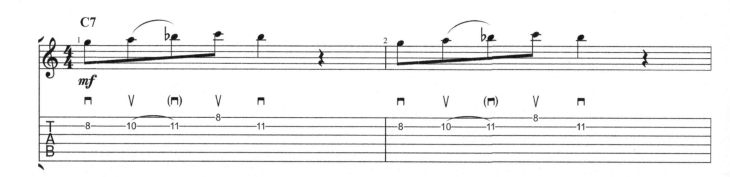

Look closely at the picking directions and you'll notice I've included a pick stroke in brackets. This is the stroke you would use *if* you were picking. The pick should still act like it's picking, so keep the movement, but don't pick the string. This will help you maintain good timing, and (in the long term) will stop you having to think about what you're doing while you're picking.

Here's a slightly longer idea using the C Mixolydian scale with an added b3.

Example 5b:

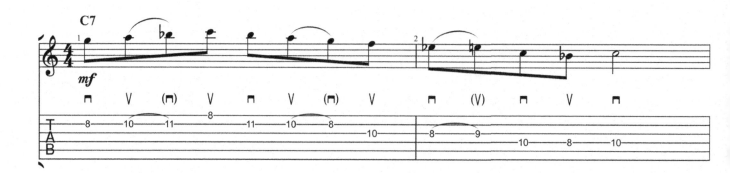

The next idea covers most of the neck and uses all five CAGED positions. It would be troublesome to pick so using slurs makes it easier to play and shift position.

Example 5c:

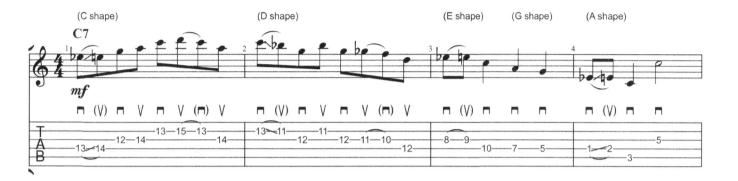

Next is another long idea covering several positions. The sky's the limit when it comes to using slurs to facilitate position shifts. You'll probably find a hundred licks like this on the average Albert Lee album.

Example 5d:

Here's an advanced lick using multiple position shifts to outline an A, D, E, A, chord progression. This line is trickier than the others because it uses triads, Major Pentatonics, *and* Mixolydian concepts on every chord! Your visualisation needs to be strong to improvise licks like this.

Example 5e:

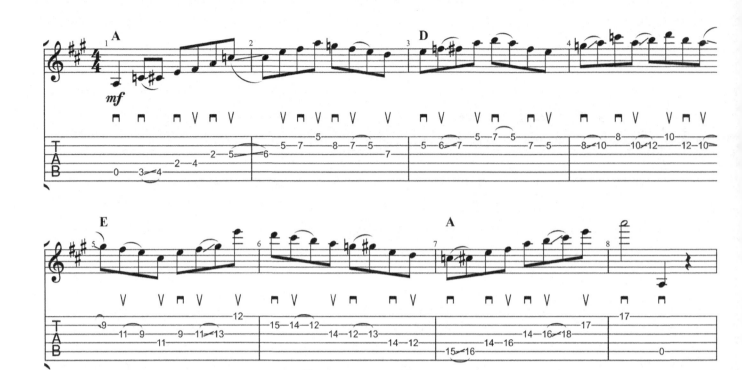

This next lick is a looping idea that shifts from the E shape down to the G and back up again. Ideas like this are great for building technique and speed.

Example 5f:

Example 5g begins with a common idea in the C shape and breaks out by moving up to the A shape.

Example 5g:

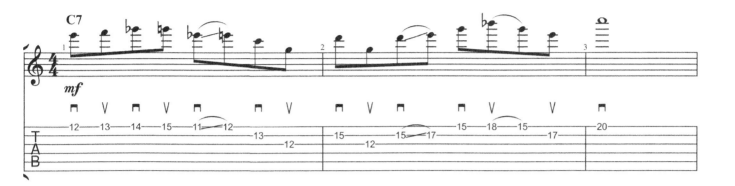

It's possible to combine slurs with complicated picking techniques like cross-picking, as demonstrated on this C7 chord using C Major, F Major, and Bb Major triads with slides to help facilitate the position shifts.

Example 5h:

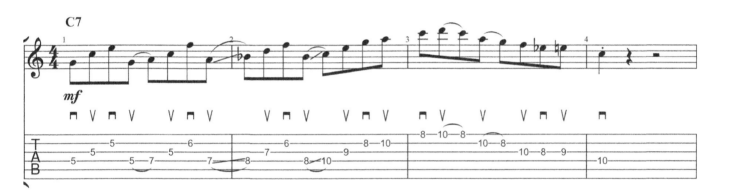

This next idea uses another mixture of the Country scale and Mixolydian mode. By now, the picking should be fairly automatic, but as your timing improves you may find yourself straying from the prescribed picking.

Example 5i:

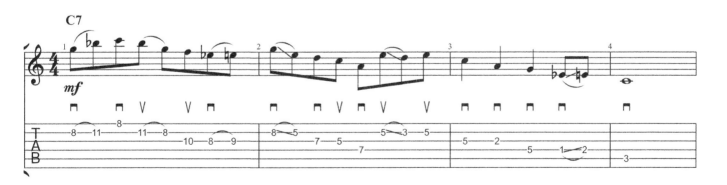

This Brent Mason-style, open-position chromatic idea in A is made much easier with slides, but try picking every note for a challenge and compare the sounds. Not only is it harder to play with every note picked, it also loses much of its charm.

Example 5j:

Slides and pull-offs in country music aren't a feature in the same way they might be in rock. You're unlikely to hear the long legato phrases in country that you might hear from players like Joe Satriani. Instead the technique is used to articulate and facilitate ideas, and the result is the signature hot picking sound.

All these techniques aren't just limited to 1/8th notes either. Here's a challenging idea that changes position and includes 1/16th-note hammer-ons and pull-offs for melodic excitement.

Example 5k:

Here's another idea that uses consecutive hammer-ons and pull-offs in a lick that moves from the C shape down to the E shape.

Example 5l:

Finally, this example uses sliding 6ths on an A Major chord and ends with some Country scale phrasing in the E shape.

Example 5m:

You may notice that these sliding 6ths feel easier when played with down-strokes on the A string and up-strokes on the G string. This breaks the continuous alternate picking rules studied earlier and we will address that in the next chapter!

Ultimately there are no unbreakable rules when playing music, but it doesn't hurt to have some technical guidelines when practicing. Work within them, then break them once you're in control.

Chapter Six: Hybrid Picking

An integral part of a top country players' vocabulary is the use of the picking-hand fingers to pluck strings in combination with the pick. This technique is known as hybrid picking, as it is a hybrid combination of regular picking and fingerstyle.

Hybrid picking has a unique sound that's synonymous with country twang and at first it may feel unnatural. However, with time it will become as natural as (if not even more relaxed than) alternate picking.

I keep the fingernails on my picking hand short, so I pluck with the flesh of the fingers. Many country players maintain fingernails, or wear false acrylic nails to give them a more pick-like attack. I do prefer the more pick-like sound, but I also play rock and often use tapping, so there's a degree of compromise. See how hybrid picking feels without nails, and then try developing a little nail and see if you like the sound.

This first example shows a repeating 6th on the G and E strings. Use the pick to play the notes on the G string with a down-stroke, then use the middle finger to pluck the high E string. The finger should pluck the string by pulling it away from the guitar to give the note an aggressive snappy sound as it slaps back against the neck.

I've indicated notes plucked with the pick in the normal way, and used a 'p' (pop) to indicate a note plucked with the finger.

Example 6a:

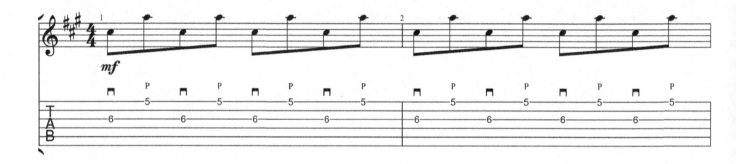

Next, play this idea with sliding 6ths. As before, use the pick to play down-strokes on the G string and the middle finger to pluck the high E string.

Example 6b:

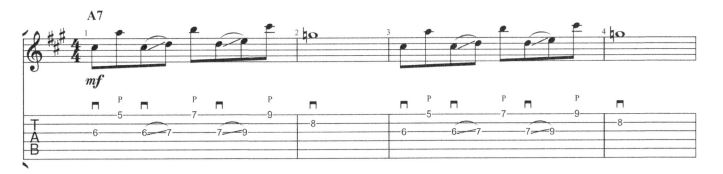

These examples highlight the idea that the picking hand won't always stick strictly to the alternate picking motion. This means you need to be careful with your timing when playing phrases like this, as it is often the alternate picking motion that helps us to keep time.

Make sure that the 1/8th notes are evenly spaced by practicing with a metronome or drum machine.

When hybrid picking, notes don't need to be played separately. You can use the pick and finger to pinch two notes at once, as shown in the following example.

Example 6c:

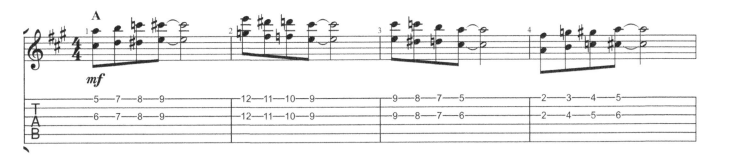

In the following example, play the first note with a down-stroke and instead of using an up-stroke to follow, use the middle finger to pluck the string and then repeat.

Example 6d:

Compare this technique to alternate picking and notice the difference in sound, and feel.

Here's a longer lick that uses lots of note pairs on adjacent strings. These could all be alternate picked, but hybrid picking is effortless at speed as your middle finger is ready to pick the string without having to cross it for an up-stroke.

Example 6e:

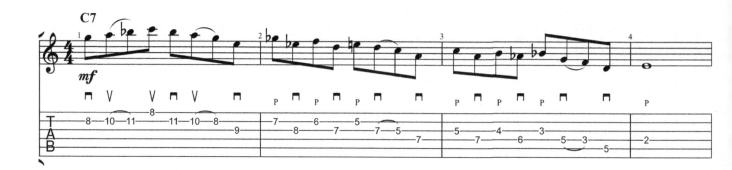

A common idea in the playing of Brent Mason is to use a triplet to add an exciting burst of speed. Pay careful attention to the picking directions and place the hybrid picked notes in the right place.

Example 6f:

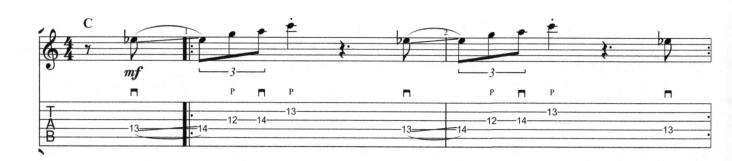

The next lick contains the same mechanic, but now it's used to play an exciting idea that ascends the neck over a C7 (or C Major) chord.

Example 6g:

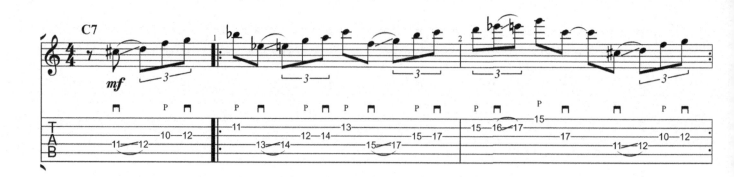

Here's a descending Pentatonic idea you might hear in a rock solo. I've notated it with a hybrid picked note followed by two down-strokes. There are many ways this could be played, so go with what feels comfortable. Personally, when I go into hybrid picking mode, I rarely play up-strokes with the pick. Instead, I use the picking hand finger.

Example 6h:

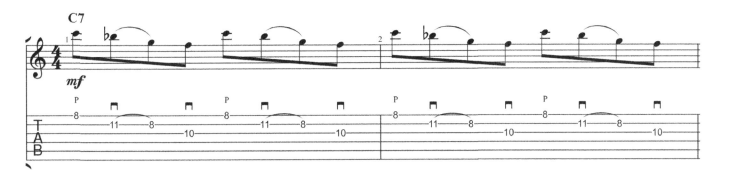

The following lick uses the same descending mechanic but is now developed into a more typical hot-country phrase that includes position shifts.

Example 6i:

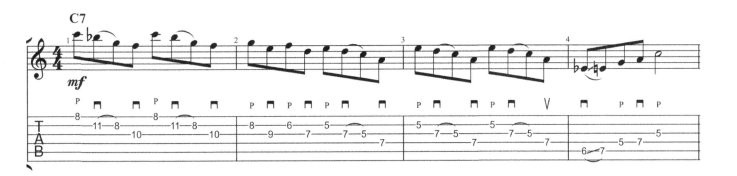

Hybrid picking should gradually start to feel more natural and developing this technique will allow you to play wider interval licks effortlessly. You'll have access to a whole vocabulary that would be difficult to play with just the pick alone.

Example 6j:

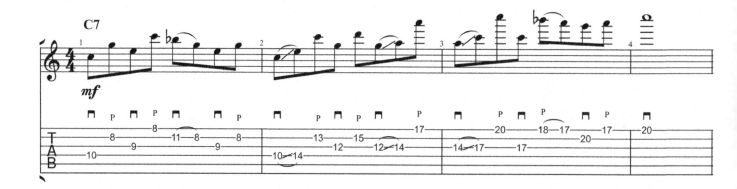

You'll hear these licks in the playing of virtuosos like Carl Verheyen, players who aren't afraid to try something new in their country phrasing. Once hybrid picking feels natural, the sky is the limit.

One liberating aspect of hybrid picking is that it frees up more than one finger to pick with. This opens the door to the exciting world of double-stops. A double-stop is simply the name for playing two notes at the same time. In country guitar, these are common as they create a richer sound and help you to imply the harmony a little better.

It's possible to play a double-stop in several ways. In the following example, I've taken a triad pattern from Chapter One and played it two notes at a time.

The first time through I strum the two notes with the pick. This is how Jimi Hendrix might have played it.

The second time, I pick the lowest note while plucking the higher note in a pinching motion with the middle finger. I use this approach when I solo using just double-stops.

The final way is to use the second and third fingers. This results in the most 'spank', and is the best way to combine double-stops with picked notes.

Example 6k:

This approach can also be applied to each *position* of the triad and is applied to a G Major chord below. On the recording I've played this with the pick and finger, but you should feel comfortable playing it in any way.

Example 6l:

Ideas like this are fun and are used to great effect by players such as Scotty Anderson.

The easiest way to start using the concept in a musical way is to combine single notes and double-stops together.

For example, here's a C Major triad with the low note on the D string, and the double-stop on the G and B strings.

Play the lowest note with the pick, before plucking the G and B strings together with the second and third fingers simultaneously.

Example 6m:

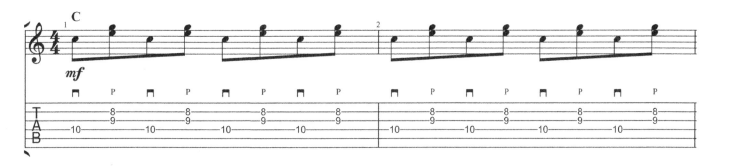

The next idea is based on the previous example, but now includes a double-stop on the B and E strings. The first double-stop includes a hammer-on from the b3 (Eb) to the 3 (G).

Example 6n:

The following lick combines a triplet idea from earlier with double-stops on the high string for an exciting phrase that outlines an A7 chord in multiple positions.

Example 6o:

A common trick in country music is to play the triad of the chord you're playing and then play a triad one tone lower. So, over an A Major chord, you can play an A Major triad followed by a G Major triad. The next example uses this technique.

Example 6p:

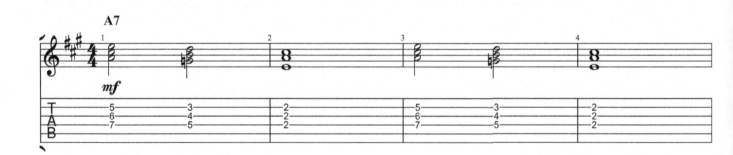

Using this 'roadmap' as a guide, I've split it so that double-stops are played on the G and B strings, with picked notes on the D string.

Example 6q:

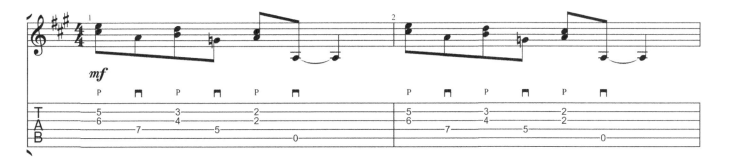

Here's the same basic pattern but now connected with chromatic passing double-stops. Don't worry about the theory, this sounds great so just learn it and apply it to your own solos.

Example 6r:

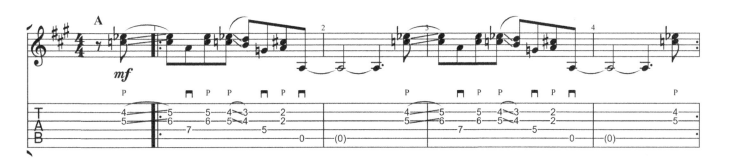

Now that you're getting comfortable using two fingers, it's only logical that you learn to pick with two fingers and the pick together to create triple-stops.

A great way to practice these triple-stop ideas is to take influence from pedal steel players like Buddy Emmons, Speedy West, or Paul Franklin.

Here's a triple-stop idea based around the E shape that outlines a C6 chord (C, E, G, A) instead of the plainer-sounding C Major. These triads are actually A minor triads (A, C, E), but played over a C bass note you'll hit all of the important notes of a C6 chord.

Example 6s:

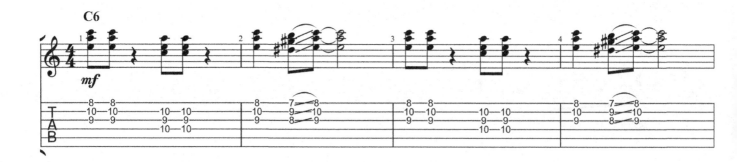

You can make a great deal of music by simply combining these minor triads with chromatic approach chords, as you can see in the following example.

Example 6t:

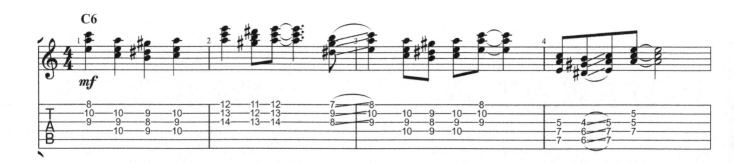

The following is an exciting lick in C Major that combines, single notes, double-stops, and triple-stops over the entire neck. Keep track of the underlying CAGED chords as you move up the neck as these will help you move around the neck fluidly.

Example 6u:

It's also possible to use these concepts to outline chord changes. The following example shows this on a blues in C.

Example 6v:

There are many chord voicings here, and the key to remembering them is to see them as simple embellishments on the basic CAGED positions discussed previously.

Take your time with these examples because carefully developed dexterity in the picking fingers will help to elevate your country playing to new heights. You'll need to have a good command of hybrid picking as you move into the challenging world of banjo rolls.

Chapter Seven: Banjo Rolls

So far, our exploration of hybrid picking with multiple fingers has been limited to chordal ideas. As your dexterity improves, it's possible to start using these fingers independently to pick individual notes on different strings.

The banjo roll seeks to imitate the rapid 1/8th note arpeggios played by banjo players. Banjo players wear metal picks on each finger which results in a smooth and consistent tone no matter which finger is used. This 'Scruggs' style of playing (named after banjo maestro Earl Scruggs) traditionally utilises the thumb and two fingers, and it's possible to begin imitating these ideas with the pick and fingers.

The easiest way to work on this idea is with a *forward roll*. Use the pick to play the D string, the second finger to play the G string, and the third finger to play the B string.

To execute these accurately, you need to work on what I call a 'pre-placement' technique. This means that the pick and fingers begin the roll *already* placed on their respective strings (as opposed to having the fingers float in the air and attacking the strings when needed).

Example 7a:

Example 7b shows a simple forward roll that changes string sets. Play the first roll as before, then after plucking the G string with the third finger, move the pick and fingers over and pre-place them ready to begin the next roll.

Example 7b:

Play the following example in the key of G that moves from the open position up to the 12th fret. You may not play this in a solo, but it's a great way to get the fingers warmed up.

Example 7c:

It's possible to play the forward roll backwards which results in the aptly named *reverse roll*. In the following example, I begin with the pick on the low string, then move over to the B string and descend. This may feel difficult at first but stick with it as it is an extremely useful skill to develop as a country player.

Example 7d:

So far, each example has been played using triplets. A more challenging way to practice is to play straight 1/8th (or 1/16th notes), so you have to abandon those accents of three, and accent in fours instead.

This example takes the reverse roll pattern and places it in the middle of a straight 1/8th note lick.

Example 7e:

To give you an example of how you might use an idea like this, here's a descending pattern in E that uses 6ths on the G and E strings. The open B string helps to tie the lick together nicely too, almost like the repeating high G note often heard on the banjo.

Example 7f:

Now play this similar 1/8th note idea, but this time with a forward roll in the middle.

Example 7g:

Here's that same mechanic, but this time on the higher strings, and moving through some double-stop positions. I've kept the high E string open to create an interesting drone.

Example 7h:

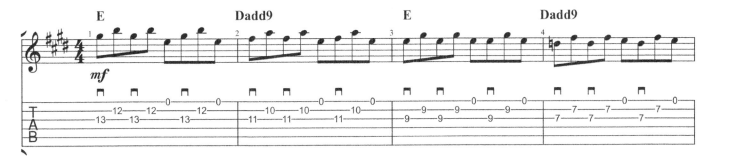

Next up is a reverse roll idea similar to example 7e, but here the pick moves between the D and G string. This will create more melodic possibilities when you expand your knowledge chord voicings.

Example 7i:

The same idea can be applied to any chord. The next example demonstrates this using F Major and G Major triads. With the high E left to ring, you also create some more colourful chords.

Example 7j:

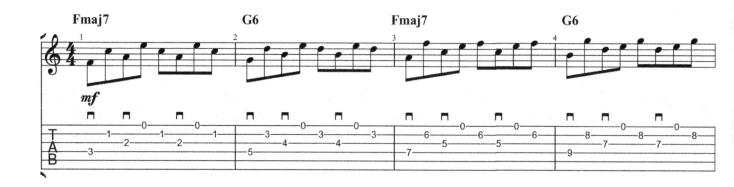

Here's another reverse roll idea, but this time with a hammer-on on the G string to offset the rolling motion.

Example 7k:

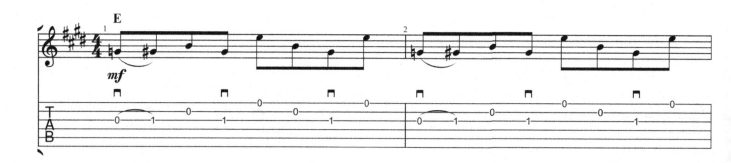

Rolls like this can be used in extremely creative ways, as demonstrated in the following example. I've outlined an E7 chord in the A, C, and E shapes, and allowed them to ring as much as possible.

Example 7l:

An excellent way to improve your speed with rolls is with an accelerating exercise. Here, a three-note forward roll is played four times across two bars, followed by two more rolls played as triplets. This creates a cool accelerating feel.

Example 7m:

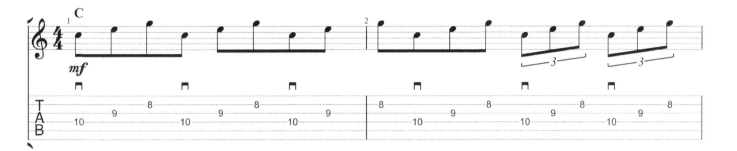

The same concept can be applied to a reverse roll to create another fun technical workout.

Example 7n:

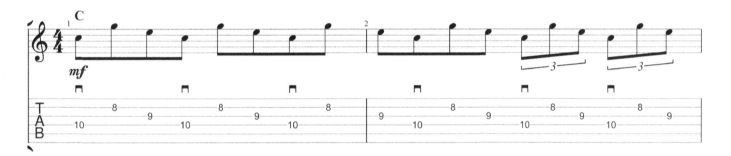

The next example is a trickier lick inspired by the playing of Danny Gatton and Jerry Reed.

Example 7o:

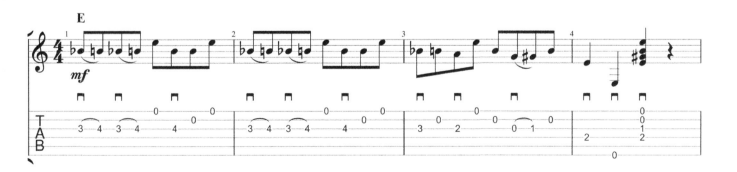

This next roll is inspired by the great Albert Lee, and outlines a G Major, D Major, and C Major chord.

Example 7p:

This is a much trickier roll taken from Danny Gatton. It uses a forward roll over three strings before the pick moves to the high E string to create an ascending four-string roll.

Example 7q:

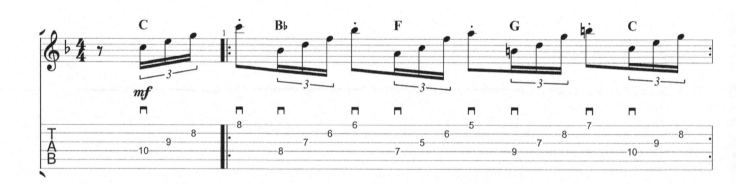

This final roll is an awkward concept to play at speed. It uses two consecutive forward rolls over all six strings. The first is on the E, A, and D strings, and the second is on the G, B, and E strings. The trick here is to work on the transition from the first roll to the second. The pick must keep moving across the strings as the fingers pluck the second and third notes.

Example 7r:

Rolls can become a unique part of your country hybrid picking style, but they must be developed with a high degree of accuracy. However, it needn't be limiting. If you've developed your alternate picking skills to incorporate fast and fluid cross-picking ideas, it is worth going back through this chapter and seeing if you can achieve similar effects using just the pick.

Remember that the techniques you learn are to help you execute musical ideas. There are no rules on how to play notes, and your main focus should always be on how those notes sound. If they sound good you're on the right path.

Chapter Eight: Open Strings

One of the obvious staples of the country guitar style is the use of open strings to create dynamic ideas with ringing notes.

Open strings work well because country players don't use much overdrive or gain, so the ringing open notes don't create as much sonic clash as they might if they were to be played through an overdriven amp.

There are two distinct approaches to using open strings, and it helps to start with the trickier, more academic approach.

If you're like most people and play in standard tuning (E, A, D, G, B, E), open string licks will only work in certain keys.

For example, in the key of C (C, D, E, F, G, A, B), all of the open strings will work.

In the key of G (G, A, B, C, D, E, F#), all the open strings work.

In the key of D (D, E, F#, G, A, B, C#), all the open strings work.

When you move to the key of A, however, problems start to arise. The key of A contains the notes A, B, C#, D, E, F#, and G#. The open G string will always clash with the G# note in the key. This makes the G string one to avoid in the key of A.

The more accidentals a key has, the harder it is to use open strings. This is one of the main reasons that country guitar players love keys like G, D, A, and even E, but often avoid keys like F, Bb, and Eb as they contain many alterations to notes that exist on the open strings.

This means that open-string licks are normally key specific and virtually impossible to transpose. Ultimately, you'll need to build an arsenal of open-string licks in many keys.

Now, with all the theory out of the way, let's look how to use open strings in licks.

One of the first scales most people learn on guitar is an open-string idea: The C Major scale. Say the names of the notes as you play through them and you'll quickly realise that the notes D, G, and B can all be played on open string.

Example 8a:

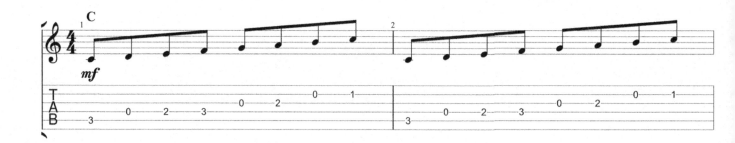

Here's the G Major scale. As before, say the names of the notes you're playing out loud, and observe where the new accidental (F#) appears.

Example 8b:

When you are aware of note names in scales, rather than simply patterns, the fingering possibilities are endless, as the following alternate pattern for G Major shows.

Example 8c:

Here's another way you might arrange the notes of G Major to make the most of the ringing strings.

Example 8d:

One of the most important aspects to consider when playing open strings is to create a consistent tone and dynamic between the fretted and open notes. It's possible to make open-string notes that stand out like a sore thumb, so your goal is to make the previous three G Major scale examples sound as homogenous as possible.

An age-old trick to help the notes blend is to use a compressor pedal. This will level-out your dynamics, raising the volume of notes that are too quiet, and compressing notes that are too loud. This can result in a 'squashed' sound depending on much compression you use.

Compressors also increase the sustain of each note by pushing up the volume of notes as they decay. There are lots of great compressors on the market, but you can't top the Wampler Ego compressor in my book. If you're only going to have one pedal as country guitarist, make it a good compressor!

The next lick is played around an E-shape A Major triad and outlines the A Major scale. When I create phrases like this, I think of the note names and place anything I can on an open string. You can also descend the phrase to create a unique-sounding lick.

Example 8e:

Here's an idea that descends the A Mixolydian scale and has an ending similar to earlier ideas. In this phrase, the open strings ring out a little, which sounds very country.

Example 8f:

Compare the sound of the previous example to the same phrase played with fretted notes. It's still cool, but it doesn't have quite the same charm compared to the open string variant.

Example 8g:

These concepts become even more exciting when you start adding chromatic passing notes. In the following example, I've added the b5 (Eb) and the b3 (C) to create something a little less academic, and a little more musical.

Example 8h:

Here's a similar line that places the Eb note on the 4th fret of the B string. You'll hear licks like this going back decades in the hot bluegrass style of Doc Watson. If you become familiar with this style, the movement of 4th fret B string to open E string will become habit.

Example 8i:

The next lick is similar, this time in the style of Brent Mason.

Example 8j:

Another excellent way to use open strings is to help facilitate position shifts, especially during licks with a large range. This next lick moves from the 12th fret to the open position, and the open strings allow the large position shift to be played smoothly by giving the fretting hand time to move.

Example 8k:

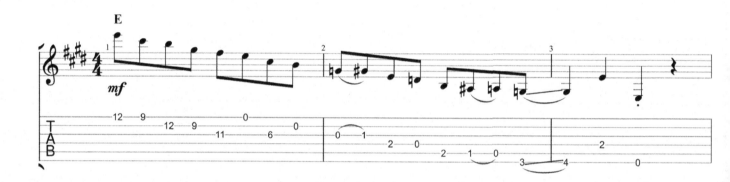

The following example uses open strings to help with position shifts, and also contains hybrid-picked forward rolls on the G, B, and E strings. These rolling ideas are common in the style of Danny Gatton who often used an open string to tie many ideas together.

Example 8l:

The following *common-tone* approach is often exploited to the extreme during repeating pull-off-to-open-string licks. Not only does this technique sound impressive, it's a great way to shift positions on the neck.

This idea takes a series of diatonic 6ths on the A and G strings and adds pull-offs to the open G string. The repeating common-tone *pedal* note helps to tie the line together. Note that the lower note of each 6th is palm muted, this helps to keep the tone consistent.

Example 8m:

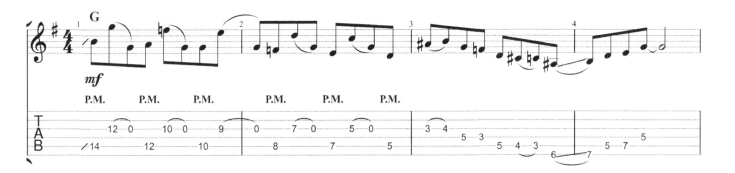

Players like Brad Paisley use open strings like to create fast, chaotic lines with wide interval leaps that would otherwise be impossible to fret.

This example is inspired by the up-tempo track Mr Policeman, and uses a G Minor Pentatonic scale in the first position, along with open strings for a bit of extra fun.

Example 8n:

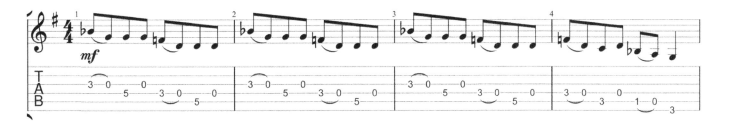

The above lick works so well because it's diatonic (all the notes are in one key), but the concept can be extended to include all manner of chromatic chaos.

Here's an idea that uses a similar technique but with different notes. Essentially, I'm thinking G Minor Pentatonic and moving down the neck as I play. You'll quickly notice that the pattern features a 3rd interval between the D and G strings which descends chromatically.

Example 8o:

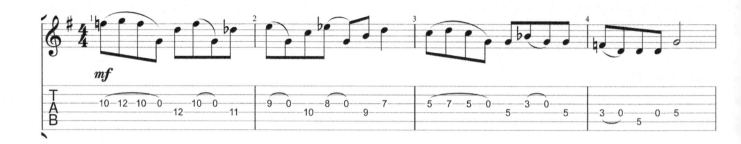

This next lick has a uniquely 'guitary' sound because it uses almost as many open strings as fretted notes. This has all the reckless abandon of rock players like Van Halen but won't sound out of place in a modern up-tempo country solo.

Example 8p:

As with everything in this book, these examples should be a springboard for your own exploration. There are limitless ways to use open strings in your playing, and everyone approaches the technique differently.

Check out players like Doyle Dykes, and YouTube acoustic picking wizards like Martin Tallstrom, and Lars Schurse for a wealth of inspiration on the subject. Pay attention to how they use these ideas in unique ways.

Wide intervals aren't unique to the guitar, but it's certainly easier to execute them on the guitar than many other instruments. Becoming a great country player is about celebrating the unique aspects of your instrument.

Chapter Nine: Bending Tricks

The final technique needed for solid country guitar soloing is the bend. Bends are fairly unique to string instruments and used for their vocal, expressive qualities. While possible to play bends on certain wind and reed instruments, these are not nearly as extensive.

Bending became more prominent among country guitar players when amplification and lighter gauge strings became common, with James Burton being an early adopter. He even used banjo strings on his Telecaster.

The most important aspect of bending (aside from actually hitting the target note accurately) is having an awareness of the note you're bending from, and the note you're bending to. In this book, I'll always describe bends as 2nd to 3rd, or b7th to Root, etc. This means that the 2nd interval of the scale is bent up to the 3rd, or that the b7th note of the scale is bent up to the root.

The terminology places emphasis on which scale tone is being bent, and where it's being bent to.

To clarify, here's an example in the key of A. The note G (the b7th) is then picked and bent up to A (the Root). This is a b7th to Root bend.

Example 9a:

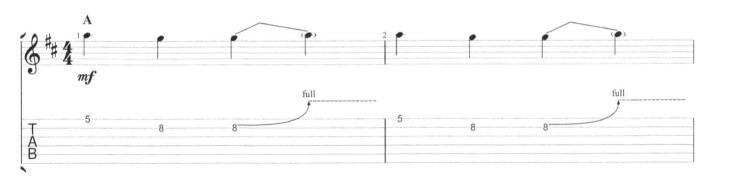

Here's a descending A Major Pentatonic scale that ends with a bend from B (the 2nd) up to C# (the 3rd). This is a 2nd to 3rd bend.

Example 9b:

What you'll quickly hear is that accuracy is everything in this style. There's no use just bending wildly and hoping for the best. It's important to focus on accuracy and make sure your bends are intonated correctly.

The following exercise is based around the A Mixolydian scale and requires you to first play a note, then play the note you intend to bend to, then bend the original note up to the second one. Using this method, you're able to accurately check that the note you're bending to is in tune.

Example 9c:

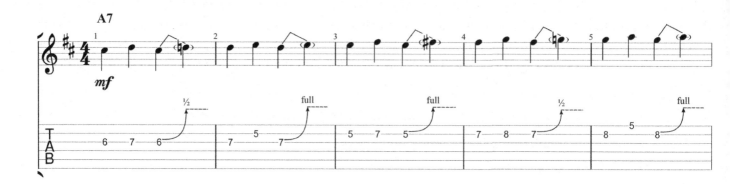

You may have struggled with fingerings when playing that last example, especially with the 5th fret B whole tone (two-fret) bend. You'll eventually develop the skill to play this with the first finger, but while you're developing your skills, these bends can be executed with the second or third finger until you're comfortable.

In the following example, you'll see why bending in tune is so important when done in conjunction with chords. First, two notes of an A Major triad are played, and then the 2nd (B) is bent up to the 3rd (C#). The same idea is then played with a full three-note triad voicing.

Example 9d:

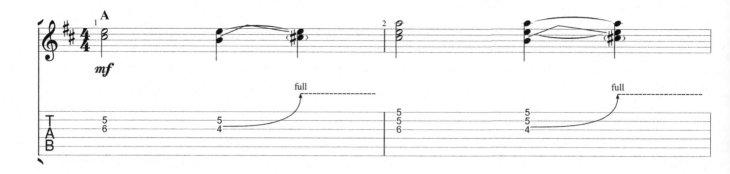

The tricky part of this bend is that just one note is bent, while the others stay at a consistent pitch. This means the power behind the bend has to come from the fingers rather than the wrist rotating (which is the more traditional technique).

For this reason, lighter gauge strings are recommended. Gauge 9 strings on a Fender scale-length guitar will do the trick. While this is more than possible on 10s, or maybe even 11s, you're putting unnecessary strain on your hands, and that could lead to problems later on.

Combining bends and held notes is integral to the country style and often you will bend one note and hold it while playing a series of changing notes. This technique is taken from pedal steel guitar players, who can do this by using pedals to change the pitch of the strings.

Here's a lick based around the 2nd to 3rd bend, with a note that changes on the B string.

Example 9e:

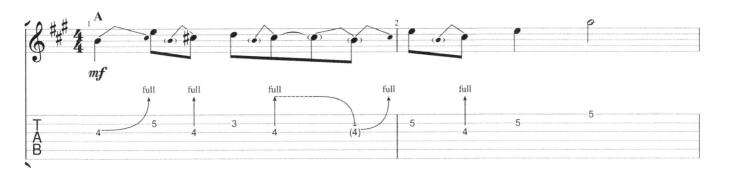

The position of this lick may present problems early on, as being closer to the nut makes strings harder to bend. You can try the same idea transposed up the neck to the key of E.

Example 9f:

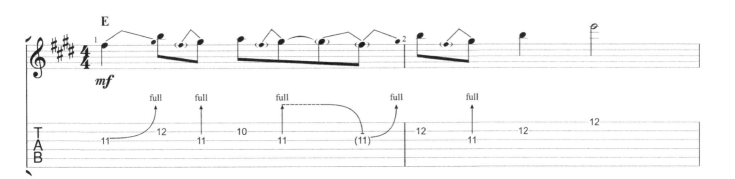

The next lick features a bend using a similar contour, but now in the C shape. To keep things interesting, I've ended the idea with a little sliding double-stop. Try to incorporate these lines musically into your solos as soon as possible.

Example 9g:

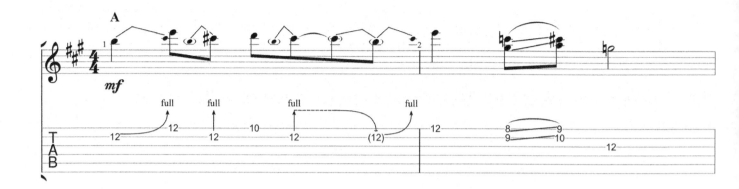

The following example features both bends, but they're now connected together with a single-note melody. As with all licks, keep track of the underlying triads and CAGED positions as you transition.

Example 9h:

Here's another idea, this time over an E7 chord.

The lick begins in bar one with a 2nd to 3rd bend, moving to a b7th to Root bend in bar two. There's a 5th to 6th in bar three, and an open position E lick in the final bar.

Notice which pitches are played against the bent strings. In the second bar of this lick, the b7th is bent to the root before the 3rd (G#) is played on the B string. This means you play two notes of the triad which is a great way to outline the chord.

Example 9i:

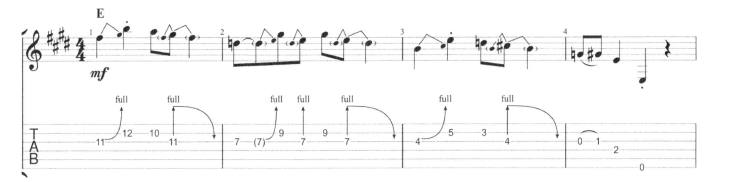

Another challenging way to explore the 2nd to 3rd bend is as the highest note on a triad.

Example 9j:

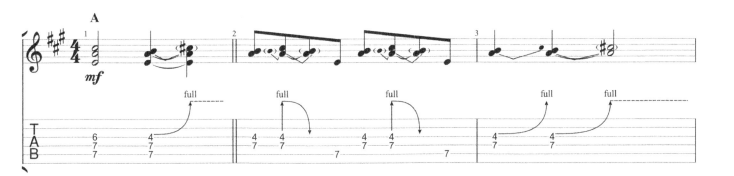

The above chord is a great way to end a lick and this is demonstrated below.

Example 9k:

It's possible to take any interval bend and explore it in different places on the neck. Here's the b7th to Root bend, played in three different places, first around the C shape, then the E shape, then the A shape.

Example 9l:

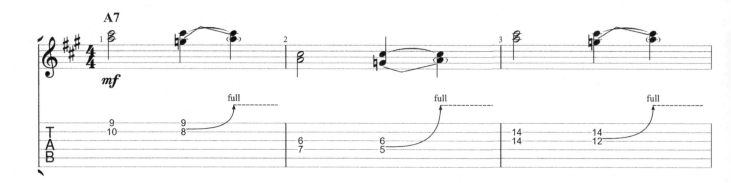

This bend can be used in limitless ways, just as with the last. Here's a lick that begins with the b7th to Root bend, and ends with the 2nd to 3rd.

Example 9m:

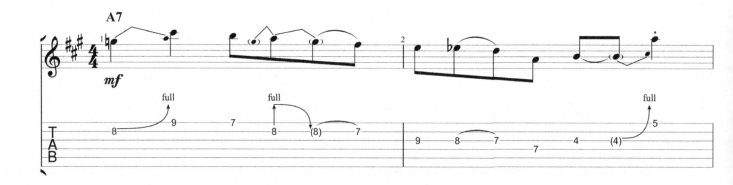

Here's another way to use both bends. I've added an open string to help with a shift to the open position using an idea similar to those you saw in the last chapter.

Example 9n:

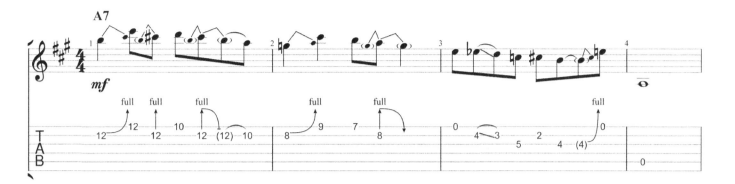

Combining these techniques and concepts is a great way to start developing your vocabulary. Here's a Brent Mason style open-string phrase that ends with a 2nd to 3rd bending lick.

Example 9o:

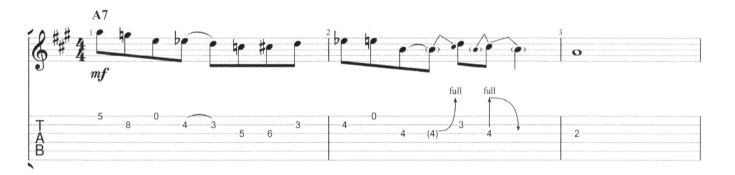

Here's another way to play the 2nd to 3rd bend, this time on the lower stings. This one may be hard to get in tune, so make sure that D string bend is pitched from the B to C# accurately.

Example 9p:

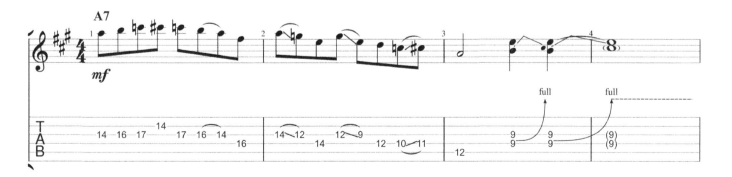

You're not limited to just the b7th to root, or 2nd to 3rd bends. Any note can be bent as long as you know where you're bending it to.

The following lick begins by bending the 6th (F#) up to the b7th (G) and ends with a bend from the 4th (D) to the 5th (E). Ideas like this are a little less like a pedal steel in nature, but they're still exciting tricks to have at your disposal.

Example 9q:

When you start to understand the concepts behind these bends, you can experiment to find new ideas. For example, here's a C6 voicing you played in the triple-stop section. It makes sense to bend the 5th (G) up to the 6th (A) in the double-stop.

Example 9r:

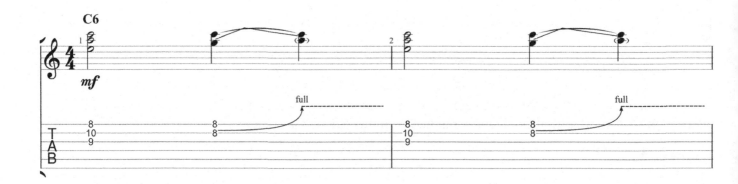

Next, use this idea over a C6 chord to create an interesting lick with just two strings. Note that each double-stop has a C on top, so it's all about the notes played underneath. Before moving on, make sure you can name what intervals these are in relation to C.

Example 9s:

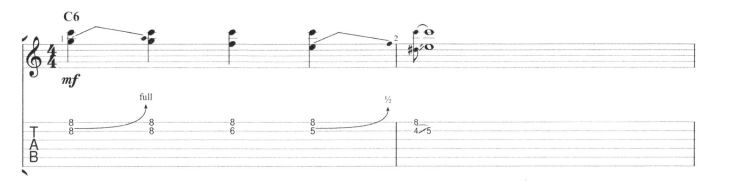

In time, you'll find a few places where it's possible to bend *two* notes at once.

In the following example, I hold a C and E note with the third and fourth finger, bend the C up to D, and the E up to F. These bends are rarely perfectly pitched, but Jerry Donahue comes close!

Example 9t:

Here's a C Major triad with the top voice (the 5th) ascending from the 5th to the #5th (G#), then bending up to the 6th (A). In the second bar, the root note moves down to the b7th creating a great voicing of a C13 chord.

Example 9u:

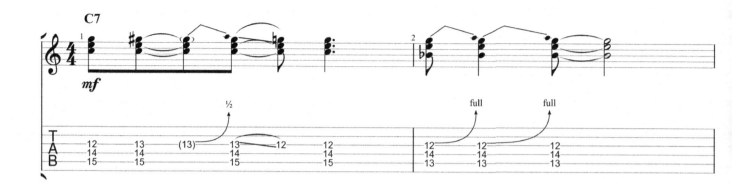

Another exciting and flashy technique is the *behind the nut* bend. Playing an open note, and pushing the string down behind the nut will increase the tension and raise the pitch of the string.

This only works with guitars that have a decent clearance under the string behind the nut, such as a Telecaster or Stratocaster. Gibson guitars tend to have far too little clearance in this area (especially with truss rod covers), and don't get me started on headless guitars!

In the following example, place two or three fingers on the string behind the nut to push it up without hurting yourself.

Example 9v:

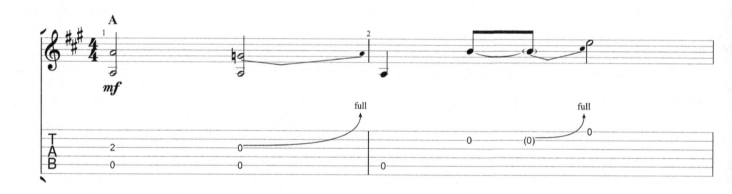

The next lick combines fretted and open-string behind the nut bends, to outline an A7 chord.

Example 9w:

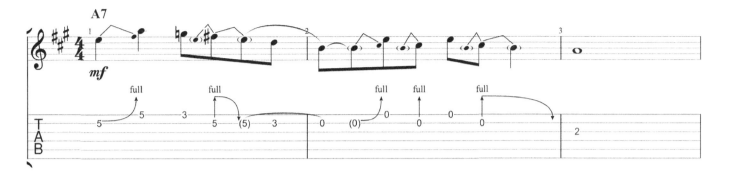

Here's one last example that manipulates harmonics at the 5th fret via a bend behind the nut on the A string. It implies a G Major chord and is an excellent way to end a solo.

Example 9x:

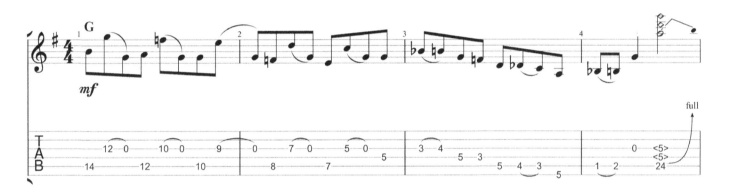

This chapter just scratches the surface of what's possible using open strings, so pay attention when listening to your favourite soloists to see how they use these ideas in unique ways. Often these techniques are used to help them play things they couldn't with standard techniques.

Wider intervals aren't unique to the guitar, but it's certainly easier to execute them on the guitar than many other instruments. Becoming a great country player is about celebrating the unique aspects of your instrument.

Chapter Ten: Hot Dang Twang

Now you're armed with all the techniques you need to play modern hot country solos, it's time to learn a complete track that shows you how these concepts come together in the real world.

I wanted to write something that had the vibe of Jerry Reed barrelling down the back roads in his truck in the Smoky and the Bandit movies. The result is a three-minute tour de force of country picking with a main riff, a bridge, and an extended soloing section.

Composed in the key of A, each chord can be treated as an individual dominant chord, meaning any combination of Major Pentatonic, Blues scale, and Mixolydian modes will work perfectly.

First, I'll break down each section/lick individually along with the theory behind them, before giving you the transcription of the song in its entirety.

The main riff is based around an open A power-chord that combines the pick and hybrid-picked double-stops.

As with every example in the book, pay careful attention to the articulation. For example, after playing the first open A note, the 2nd fret double-stop is played staccato, before lowering the E to and Eb, re-picking, and pulling-off to the open D string.

Rhythmically there's nothing too challenging, just be careful not to rush or drag the triplet in bar four.

Example 10a:

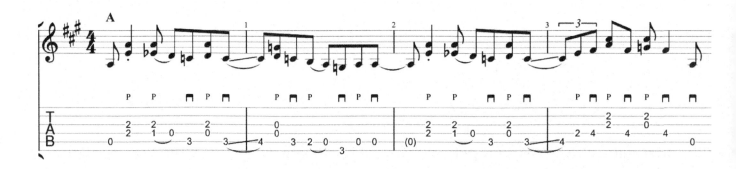

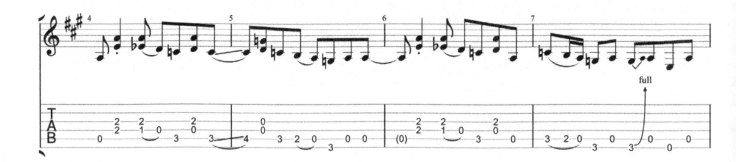

The first section is 16 bars long which is a long time to sit on a single chord (A), so in the B section, I've added a few more chords which help to keep the audience's attention.

In essence, the progression is D/F#, G Major, A Major, played four times and ending on an E Major. This E functions as the V chord of A, and helps to pull the section back to the main riff.

The guitar part is spiced up with some simple licks on each A chord. When I play this live, I'll improvise those licks. It's just about playing something in A to keep the section moving along, but the double-stop ideas on the recording are a great place to start your own explorations.

Example 10b:

After the B section, the track returns to the main riff for 8 bars before entering the solo section.

The solo section begins with 16 bars of A Major (or A7), which is an opportunity to show off some of your chops without having to worry about playing over any chord changes.

The first lick begins with an open string idea that starts in the E shape and moves down to the G shape for a pedal steel style bend. This is a good example of a lick that uses an open string, a triplet idea, and a bending phrase. As always, it's about playing something interesting, not just cycling through impressive techniques.

Example 10c:

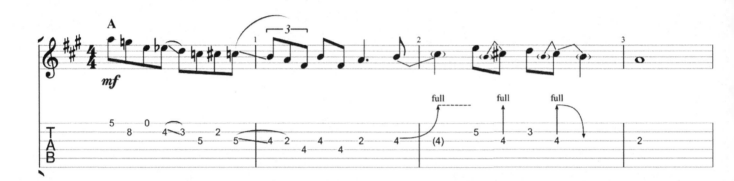

The second four-bar lick increases the excitement with some fast-paced ascending triplets and double-stops that move from the G shape to the E shape, then up to the C shape before descending back down to the E shape again.

The use of multiple positions is another hallmark of an experienced player. Music is about playing what you want to hear, and trying to limit your ideas to just one position may be possible, but restrictions like that can inhibit musical freedom.

As with the intro, the best way to execute an idea like this is with hybrid picking. Pick the note that slides into the triplet with the second finger.

Example 10d:

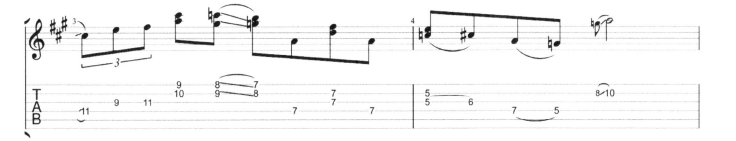

Next is a pedal steel lick on the top two strings that moves through multiple positions.

The first bar uses a 2nd to 3rd bend in the C shape. The second bar features a b7 to Root bend in the D shape, and the third bar contains a 5th to 6th bend in the G shape, before moving up to the E shape to finish.

Example 10e:

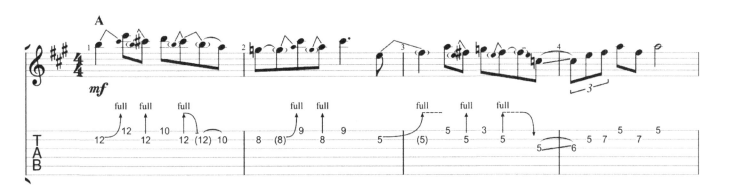

The lick over the final A chord begins with some 1/8th notes phrased around the C shape which transitions down the neck into the E shape.

The most challenging part is in the second two bars, with a series of rapid-fire, forward-roll hybrid-picked triads. While each of these fragments is played over the A chord, the three-note triad sequence could be identified as C#Dim, B Minor, A Major, G Major, D Major, G Major, and A Major.

Take this one slowly, and stick to the pick, second finger, third finger hybrid picked roll.

Example 10f:

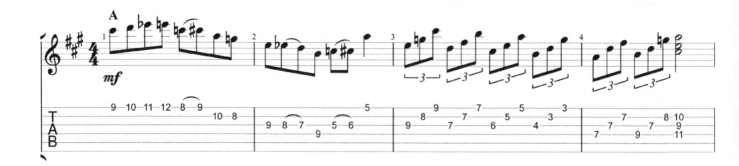

The second part of the solo section features more chord changes, each played for two bars. Each chord can also be played as a dominant 7 voicing.

The next three licks outline a D Major chord for two bars, then an A Major for two bars. This is challenging, but the key is to try and create one flowing melodic idea that moves seamlessly through both chords, rather than two individual, generic licks that you play over each.

Beginning in the E shape over the D Major chord, you'll notice that the triplet rhythm has been used again. This use of repeating rhythms helps to tie the solo together and make it seem like one cohesive unit. This is all based on a Mixolydian scale with an added b3.

The second bar continues the Mixolydian-with-added-b3rd vibe, but shifts down the neck to the A shape. When in the 5th fret area, the easiest approach is to use the E shape. The line I've opted for uses a selection of 6ths played melodically. As with the familiar rhythms, 6ths are an approach I'll often use to help tie the solo together.

Example 10g:

The second D Major to A Major lick begins around the A shape at the 5th fret, and transitions down to the C shape. Note-wise, this is simply dressing up the triad in a melodic way, using an F (b3) as a way to approach the F# (3rd) of D Major. It's used again as a passing note when descending from F# down to E.

The second half of the lick moves back to playing 6ths over the A chord, and this time begins in the E shape and transitions up to the C shape. Again, this helps to tie the solo together but is also a big part of the country vernacular.

Example 10h:

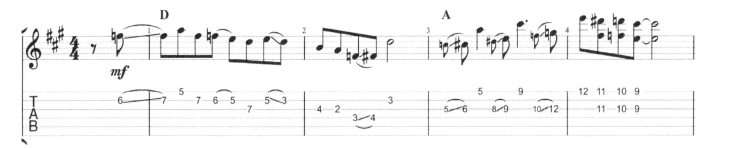

The final D Major to A Major chord change again features the triplet and 6ths idea. First, the triplets are used to help the melody transition from the G shape to the E shape over the D Major chord, and then the 6ths are used over the A Major, but this time on adjacent strings.

Most often you'll see 6ths fretted with a string between them (as in the previous example), but 6ths played on adjacent strings are a useful trick to have up your sleeve. They're often used by rockier country players like Carl Verheyen and Michael Lee Firkins.

Example 10i:

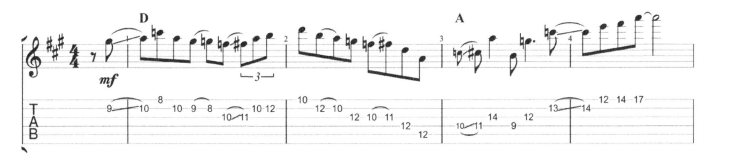

The final two bars in the solo progression conjure up images of Brent Mason's Hot Wired, as this F to G to A movement is something Brent plays there.

Over the F Major chord, we move from the D shape down to the E shape, and then transition from the G shape to A shape over the G Major chord. That's four positions of the CAGED system in one lick! Remember, these licks can be easily transposed to any key when your visualisation skills are strong.

Example 10j:

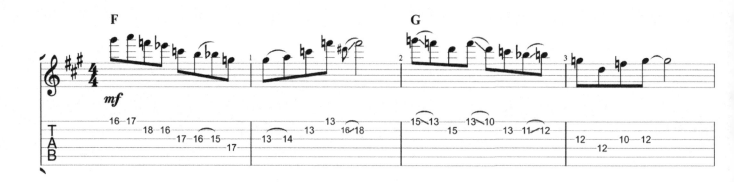

The next example is something I might play when the main riff returns before the next solo.

The goal is to move from the end of the previous lick down to the open position so I can play the riff, or rhythm guitar part to support another soloist.

This line is a fluid blend of the A Mixolydian and Blues scales. Although these nine notes could descend into a chromatic mess, it's not too hard to sound good if you know how to combine them like the pros!

Example 10k:

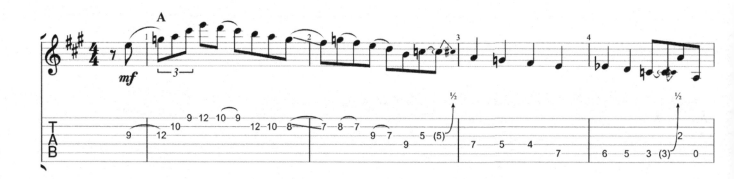

In a real gig situation, another player would now take a solo, but just for fun, here is a second solo I've written to fit the tune.

The first lick begins with a collection of double-stops that descend the neck and transition to a dynamic open-string lick which should ring out as much as possible.

Example 10l:

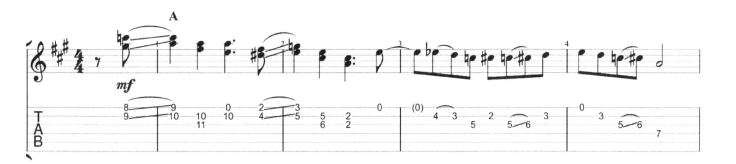

It felt like the solo wouldn't be complete without this country lick! This moves up the neck before hitting a classic James Burton style bend in the G-Shape Major Pentatonic pattern.

Example 10m:

Next, I play a six-note lick around an A Major triad and repeat it one tone lower to outline a G Major triad (a great example of that 'triad-a-tone-lower' trick). This is used as a way to move from the 9th fret area down to the 5th fret and ends with more 6ths on the G and high E strings.

Example 10n:

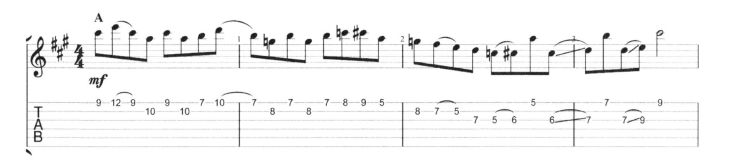

This lick mimics the second part of example 10g, but an octave higher. Repetition of phrases and quoting previous ideas is another excellent way to give your solo some continuity.

The second part of the lick features another held pedal steel-type 2nd to 3rd bend on the B string. However, rather than playing the E and D on the E string, the F# and E are played instead. This is much easier to play with a B bender (a mechanical bending system built into some specialist country guitars) but is certainly playable without.

Example 10o:

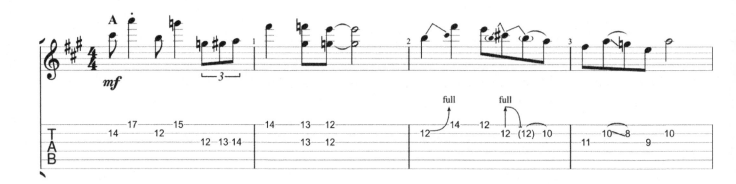

When the chord changes to D Major, I've played some trickier ideas that combine arpeggios and descending scalar licks. These require attentive alternate picking as the consecutive single notes on one string aren't easy to play quickly.

This D Major lick takes place around the 10th fret (E shape). When the chord changes to A Major, it's easiest to think of the C shape. Obviously, you don't need to impose this type of restrictions on yourself, but it can help you to keep your ideas flowing smoothly into each other.

Example 10p:

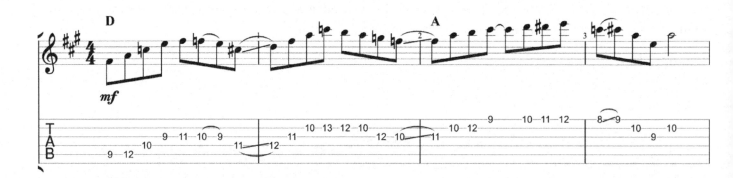

When the D Major chord returns, I've played a lick that contains a chromatic shift. After sliding from the D note down to C note and playing the note A (on the B string), this two-note pattern shifts down chromatically from to target G# and B. G# isn't an obvious note choice but sounds great to me!

The second half of the lick introduces a 1/16th note rhythm that adds excitement in the middle of a scalar run. You'll hear this approach all the time among western swing and bebop players.

Example 10q:

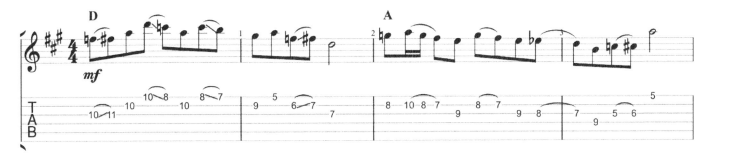

For the final D Major to A Major movement, I've stuck to double-stops. These are played around the A shape over the D Major chord and mimic the descending note from the main riff. The final section moves from the E shape up to the C shape on the A Major chord.

This approach of playing around the basic chord is always the most effective way to outline chord changes.

Example 10r:

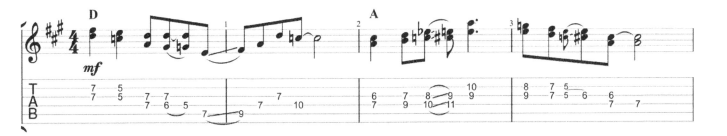

The final lick (over the F Major, G Major, A Major movement) begins around the C shape on the F Major chord and ascends (using triplets) to the G Major chord. Next, it moves down the neck and shifts into the C shape for the final A Major chord.

Example 10s:

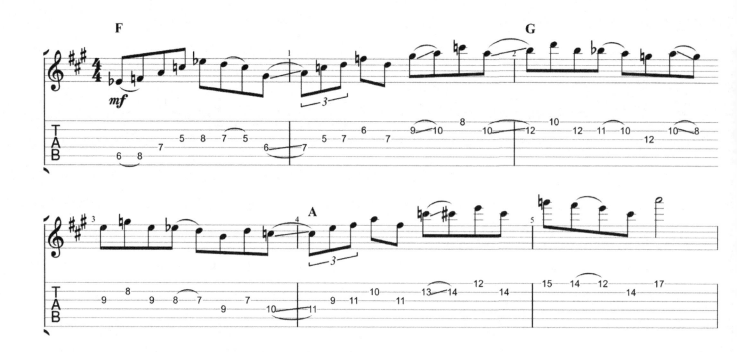

I have compiled all of the previous licks into one long transcription. Not only will this give you a better chance of reading it while playing, but it also gives you a better idea of how the licks fit together. Check out the recording to hear this song as a continuous whole.

Occasionally I have syncopated the occasional lick naturally on the final recording. This makes sense in context but would have made the previous breakdown much more complicated to explain.

Example 10t:

This isn't an easy thing to learn, so to preserve your sanity I've included two backing tracks, one at the full speed of 180bpm, and a slower one at 135bpm to give you a fighting chance!

Remember, it's not just about playing the licks I've composed, try some of your own ideas, or even just rework and transpose the licks from elsewhere in the book (or from your own studies).

Conclusion

If you've made it this far, then it's safe to say that you've armed yourself with everything you'll need to play most high-level country guitar soloing ideas.

Moving forward, you should focus on both speed and accuracy, but remember that these are always inhibited by tension in your body. Introducing tension into your technique might yield short-term results, but in the long run, it can produce more serious issues relating to the physiology of your playing. It's not easy to undo carpel tunnel syndrome, so go easy and stay relaxed.

As with any musical journey, it's important to listen to the music you want to play.

When I was going through this part of my technical development, I was heavily into Brent Mason, and while there's a wealth of knowledge to be found on his Hot Wired album, you'll find even more in his session work. Check out www.allmusic.com to see the 1200+ credits he has on records and take a listen. His work with Alan Jackson and Mark O'Connor (in particular, the solo on Pick It Apart) will blow you away!

There's no shortage of exciting players to check out and dig into. Johnny Hiland is an obvious name, with songs like Barnyard Breakdown providing a huge amount of melodic information to be harvested. And don't overlook the young players coming up and making waves too, such as Andy Wood, Guthrie Trapp, and Daniel Donato.

Often, the best place to experience these incredible players to watch them on YouTube. You'll quickly find an incredible collection of videos showcasing them in both the studio and live settings. There's no better way to develop your own playing than seeing great players tackle all the songs you're likely to play in a country band.

Next, get out there and meet like-minded people who love the music you do, and get playing. If you can't find country musicians, find blues guys and put a country twist on things. You'll always become a better player by making music with real people.

You could also consider digging deeper into the world of Western swing, jazz, or even rock and roll. These are all genres that compliment country as a style. Be it the chords you'll find in jazz, or the driving rhythms found in rock and roll (a genre popularised by country musicians playing rhythm and blues), you'll find exciting new influences to bring into your country playing, and bring a country twist to these exciting genres.

Good luck, and keep me posted with your progress!

Levi

Country Guitar Heroes:

100**COUNTRY**LICKS
FOR**GUITAR**

Master 100 Country Guitar Licks in the Style of the World's 20 Greatest Players

LEVI**CLAY**

FUNDAMENTAL**CHANGES**

Introduction

Music is many things to many people. It's an escape, it's art, it's a passion, it's work, it's frustration, it's culture, and many more things too.

There are also many facets to learning music and as players, it's easy to get caught up in the technical aspect. While technique is hugely important to your development as a player, it only *prepares* you for playing music, but isn't actually music in itself. Playing a chromatic scale up and down the neck isn't music, but there are several technical benefits to doing it. There are many great books out there that cover the technical side of playing guitar. That's not what this book is about, but developing technique will be an important part of mastering the content here.

Many players get caught up in the theoretical aspect of playing music. Depending on your goals as a player, it may be useful to memorise scales, keys, chords, arpeggios, etc. But you're still not talking about real music, just the building blocks. Knowing arpeggio substitution options on dominant 7 chords isn't music, but may result in a more informed note choice when soloing.

I like to think of music as a language. You can't learn to speak a language if you've never heard it spoken. You may be a great picker and you may know the right scale to play over a song in G – but that's not enough to pass as a country player! You can't just invent words or ignore things like sentence structure.

Playing music is about understanding the language. There are only twelve notes in music, but every genre treats those notes differently.

This book is presents you with an authentic vocabulary as performed by 20 of the greatest country players the genre has seen. It's about learning how real country players use the techniques and theory you may already know (ideally from my best-selling book: Country Guitar for Beginners!). It's about making you sound like a real country player.

On the other hand, I've seen many books that just throw licks at you like that's the answer to making you a good player. I didn't want to do that here. I want this to be more than a book of 100 licks that you learn and never use.

The solution is to understand where these licks come from and how you can use them in any key and any setting. Before learning the licks, I'm going to teach you how to memorise this vocabulary the way I do. Then, when you've got all these licks under your fingers, learn some solos that adapt them into new and fresh sounds. 100 licks may seem like a lot, but once you start connecting licks and mutating them to your desires, you'll find them almost infinite.

Playing music isn't just about playing licks. As I sit here and write this sentence, I'm not just using combinations of words that I know work. I'm expressing my thoughts freely because I understand the language. The more you develop as a player, the less you'll rely on things you've learned. You'll be free to play what's in your head, but you'll look back and appreciate how great your phrasing is because you learned the language from the masters.

There are twenty players showcased here, with five licks given in the style of each. That's not a lot to tell you about a player, but every single one of these musicians has a wealth of recorded music that's essential to check out. After all, that's how I developed all these licks!

If you're familiar with a few names on the list, then take the chance to check out some of the others. You never know... you might find 100 more licks you want to learn! The artists have been presented alphabetically as there's no clear ramp in difficulty, some artists play things that are incredibly simple and then play something that could rip your head from your shoulders – so dig in where your interest takes you.

The final piece of advice I'll give you is to internalise the sounds of these licks. It's not just about playing the notes on the page to sound like the recording. Listen to the recording 50 times till you know the lick inside out. Try singing it before playing it. As you learn the idea, focus on the notes you're expecting to hear before you play them.

This is a subject that feels a little esoteric as it's quite challenging to demonstrate. Developing the ear is always our number one goal. When that ear is well developed, you'll be able to put on any guitar solo, hear a lick, sing it… and then play it! I know that goal seems a million miles away but a journey of 1000 miles begins with a single step!

Keep at it, and you'll reach your goals in time.

Good luck!

A Note on Guitar Tone

Rather than spending hours creating unique tones for each artist, my intention was to have one basic sound that's attainable by anyone. This way, you get an idea of how you can bring the sound of each artist to your own rig and make it your own.

Aside from the Jerry Reed examples which were recorded on my Godin Multiac Nylon String, every example was recorded using a relatively cheap Mexican Fender Road-Worn Telecaster (with Joe Barden's Danny Gatton pickup set).

Amp-wise, I used a profile of a Dr Z MAZ 18NR on my Kemper Power Rack. While that's not a cheap piece of kit, the idea was to replicate a really great clean-sounding amp that would drive just a little bit when hit hard. Any Vox-style amp will to get you in the ballpark. However, if you want my exact tone, it's available on the official Dr website. Recording the audio for this book wasn't about having a million-dollar tone, it was about creating something that could be accessible to anyone.

I've recorded the slower examples at the intended speed. Anything a little pacier is played slowly before being repeated at full speed.

Get the Audio

The audio files for this book are available to download for free from **www.fundamental-changes.com**, and the link is in the top right corner. Simply select this book title from the drop-down menu and follow the instructions to get the audio.

We recommend that you download the files directly to your computer, not to your tablet, and extract them there before adding them to your media library. You can then put them on your tablet, iPod or burn them to CD. On the download page, there is a help PDF, and we also provide technical support via the contact form.

For over 350 Free Guitar Lessons with Videos Check out:

www.fundamental-changes.com

Twitter: @guitar_joseph

FB: FundamentalChangesInGuitar

Instagram: FundamentalChanges

Chapter One: How to Learn These Licks

As mentioned in the introduction, the most important aspect of learning licks to make sure you can play them whenever you need them.

The problem with the guitar is that it's easy just to put your fingers where the tab tells you to and be done with it. This approach is great if you want to play covers songs as you get results quickly. If you want to take things you learn to the next level, you need to understand the *context* of these licks and how you can call upon them at will.

The following lick is something you'll quickly be able to get under your fingers. The question is, how fast could you play it in Bb? Or Eb?

Example 1a:

This may seem like a daunting task, but once you know how, it's actually incredibly easy to do.

For me, the fastest way to achieve this is a solid understanding of the CAGED system. There are many great resources to learn this in detail, but you'll learn what you need to know here.

My system is very simple, Root note > Chord > Arpeggio > Scale > Vocabulary.

Meaning, if I can see a root note, I can see a chord. If I can see a chord, I can see an arpeggio. If I can see an arpeggio, I can see a scale. If I can see that scale… well… I can play anything.

The lick you learned previously fits in the 'A shape' of the system, meaning it's around the following chord.

G7 (A shape)

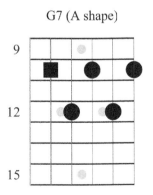

This shape is an open A chord (A7 in this case) moved up the neck to the 10th fret with a barre added.

I can find this chord in any key because I know the root note is right there on the A string. So, if I need a C7 chord, I move it down to the 3rd fret (as the 3rd fret of the A string is the note C). If I need to play an E7, I move to the 7th fret (as the 7th fret A string is the note E).

This is how you can learn to play this lick anywhere. The lick begins by approaching the note on the B string (the 3rd of the chord) from a semitone below.

Here's the same lick, but before playing it I've played the chord as a reference point of where this lick sits in relation to a shape I can easily keep track of.

Example 1b:

Here's the same thing, but transposed down to a C7 chord.

Example 1c:

Here's the same lick, but transposed down to be played on an E7 chord.

Example 1d:

Here's another lick around that chord form, now over the G7 chord.

Example 1e:

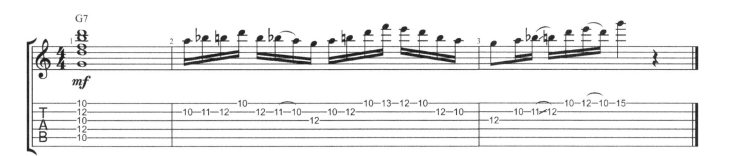

And here's that same lick, but transposed down to fit a D7 chord.

Example 1f:

Now, you may be looking at this lick and thinking, 'but this starts on a note not in, or next to, a note in the chord!', and this is where arpeggios and scale visualisation comes in.

An arpeggio is the notes of a chord, played melodically. The notes of a G7 chord are G, B, D, and F, and these can be played in order around this chord form, they look like this.

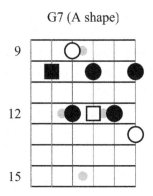

G7 (A shape)

Here's the same idea played as a musical example, preceded by the chord form it's based around.

Example 1g:

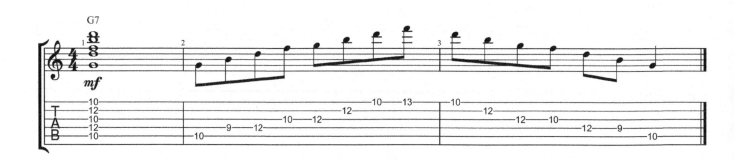

The arpeggio is the melodic sound of the chord in its most direct form. It's possible to play melodies that will sound great over the chord using just these notes.

A scale takes other notes and adds them in between these arpeggio notes, so G7 (G, B, D, F) becomes G Mixolydian (G, A, B, C, D, E, F). Here's that scale shown as a diagram.

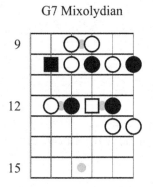

G7 Mixolydian

236

Here's the same thing played as a musical example, preceded by the chord form it's based around.

Example 1h:

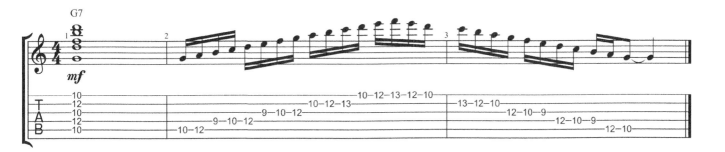

From here, it's up to you to decide how you'd visualise the lick shown before. You could see it as starting on the 9th degree of the scale, or a tone below the 3rd.

Spend some time getting to grips with this chord, arpeggio and scale relationship, and then add some licks before moving on to the next stage.

From here it's about learning the five other positions of the CAGED system.

Here's a G7 chord you may have played before It's based on the C shape. The root note is on the A string (as with the previous shape) but played with the third finger.

G7 (C shape)

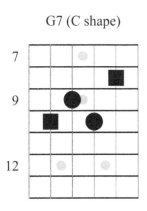

Once you're comfortable playing that chord, learn the arpeggio below.

G7 (C shape)

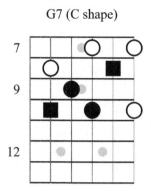

And here's the scale that fits around that same area of the neck

G7 Mixolydian

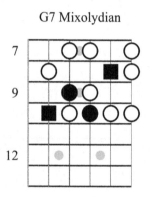

Finally, here's a lick you might play in that area of the neck.

Example 1i:

Here's that same lick, but played over a Bb7 chord

Example 1j:

Given below are the chord diagrams for the D, E, and G shapes. These are your primary forms for visualisation. If you want to dig deeper into this concept, my Country Guitar for Beginners is a great place to go as you'll learn this and a whole lot more.

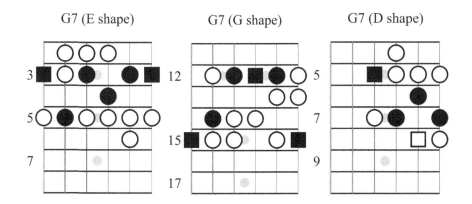

Chapter Two: Albert Lee

Considered to be one of the fathers of modern country guitar playing, Albert Lee's influence cannot be overstated. His style is part of the DNA of almost every hot picker that's come since, which is all the more amusing when you consider one of the biggest influencers to modern country playing wasn't born to a life of rodeos and ten-gallon hats, he was actually from Herefordshire, England!

Born in 1943, Lee grew up in a time when rock and roll was all the rage among the youth. Any country fan will tell you that you just need to look at the players who were influential during this time and you'll find some of the top names in country guitar. Just looking at guitarists Elvis worked with, you'll see Scotty Moore, and two other guitarists covered in this book, James Burton and Jerry Reed. All of them were major influences on the young Albert Lee.

After some success in the UK, he moved to LA where he worked as a session musician until he was asked to join Emmylou Harris' band as the replacement for none other than James Burton. From here, his career went from strength to strength, with a five-year stint working in Eric Clapton's band, almost two decades with the Everly Brothers, and many, many more.

As a solo artist, Albert has 15 studio albums to his name, with numerous live albums, and instructional videos. It's very easy to dig in and become familiar with his ferocious style, but 1982's self-titled album is a great place to start.

Unlike most country players, Albert's signature sound has become more associated with the 'quacky' Strat pickup configuration of the bridge and middle pickup position on his signature Music Man guitar. His playing is full of blistering, alternate picking runs that cover the entire neck, hybrid picked banjo rolls, and slick open string licks.

There is no better introduction to playing country guitar than Albert Lee!

The first lick works over an E or E7 chord. The theory books will tell you that the scale of choice for this chord should be E Mixolydian (E, F#, G#, A, B, C#, D). A seasoned country player will add both the b5 (Bb) as a passing note between the 5th and 4th, along with the b3 (G) as an approach note to the 3rd (G#).

Bar one of this lick sits around the A shape at the 7th fret and transitions down the neck to the C shape in bar two. It ends in the open position in bar three.

Example 2a:

The second lick uses the same note choices over the E chord as the previous lick.

Beginning with a bend from the 2nd (F#) to the 3rd (G#) in the C shape, the lick then moves over to the high E string and plays chromatically from A to B before moving back down to the G (b3) and sliding to the G# (3). This minor to major third move is an integral part of the country sound.

Bar three shifts up to the A shape around the 7th fret. The position shift from the 5th to the 8th fret isn't easy at speed, so aim to hit the 5th fret B with the first finger, then slide from the 8th to the 9th fret with the third.

The lick then ends on the root note (E) on the 12th fret, meaning this short four-bar lick has covered the neck from the 3rd to the 12th fret. This sort of coverage is an integral part of Albert's style.

Example 2b:

The third Albert Lee lick begins by using notes of the 'Country scale' (E, F#, G, G#, B, C#) which may be familiar to you as the C# Blues scale.

Bar one starts on the root (E), with a run of 1/8th notes before using some sliding 3rds to move from the G shape, down to the A shape, and then straight down to the C shape.

The lick ends with the biggest country cliché in the book; a pedal steel-inspired bend where the note on the B string is bent, while the note on the high E stays static.

Example 2c:

Lick four feels like it's drawn from the E Blues scale (E, G, A, Bb, B, D) for the first three bars, though it doesn't actually play that crucial G note, so the notes also fit in the E Mixolydian framework.

The final bar showcases Albert's seamlessly integrated double-stop technique. Use the pick to strike the note on the D string, then with the second and fourth fingers simultaneously pluck the G and B strings. Double-stops are a staple of good country guitar playing, so spend some time getting comfortable with this technique.

Example 2d:

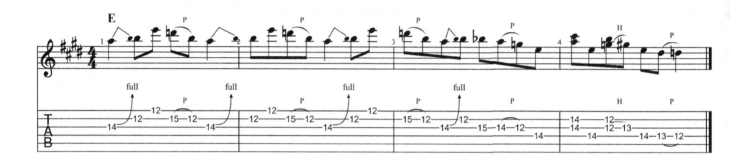

The final lick moves to the key of G to allow the use of the open G string in the middle of these descending banjo rolls.

Albert's ability to play these reverse rolls at speed is really incredible (especially when you consider that he uses the fourth finger to pluck the high note!). I would encourage you to pluck the B string with the third finger, the G string with the second, the D string with the pick, and then repeat.

From here it's about familiarising yourself with the position shifts as you're going to be moving pretty quickly between then. Take it slow and build up speed over time.

Example 2e:

Chapter Three: Brad Paisley

It's almost impossible to ignore the meteoric rise of Brad Paisley. Since releasing his first album in 1999, he's gone on to become one of the key figures in modern country music, with the full package of song writing skills, good looks, beautiful voice, and outrageous guitar picking skills!

Born in West Virginia in 1972, Brad picked up the guitar early in life after being inspired by his guitar-playing grandfather. His influences were exactly what you'd expect from a young country picker, though he's always been particularly vocal about Buck Owens, Don Rich, and Redd Volkaert.

It was Brad's voice that brought him attention from the music industry, but it quickly became apparent that he had a talent for writing songs, and before he knew it he had scored a publishing deal with EMI.

When Who Needs Pictures was released in 1999, it showcased his trademark ability to write a combination of touching, and funny songs, punctuated with a fiery modern take on country guitar. Brad sounds like someone who had just as much love for Eddie Van Halen and the Eagles, as he did for Buck Owens and Hank Williams.

To date, Brad has released 12 studio albums, and every one of them is worth a spin. As the years have passed, he's embraced more modern pop elements compared to the country and western sounds of earlier records. 2005's Time Well Wasted is widely considered to be the perfect middle ground and is worth a listen. If you want to focus on his playing, 2008's largely instrumental Play is also worth a listen.

Brad's sound is 99% Telecaster into various Dr Z amps, with his axes of choice being Crook Custom Guitars in a variety of finishes with McVay G bender systems installed (a huge part of his playing style). He's also extremely fond of his 1968 pink paisley-finished Tele, aptly named 'Old Pink', which is fitted with a Lindy Fralin pickup, and the G bender he can't live without. It's warming to know Brad isn't afraid to play (and modify) a guitar with that level of historical significance.

The first lick showcases some of Brad's melodic pedal steel inspired bends. This sort of thing can be hard work on the fingers, so try to avoid this on guitars with strings heavier than 10s (9s are ideal).

Begin by taking the b7 (F) and 3rd (B) of G (in the A shape) and bend the b7 up to the root (G). It's important to keep that note on the B string where it is, though. With the G string held, the notes are then repicked three times with a gradual release on the final time.

From here, the lick is relatively straight forward; just make sure you're holding those bent notes up at their intended pitch as it's important that everything is in tune.

Example 3a:

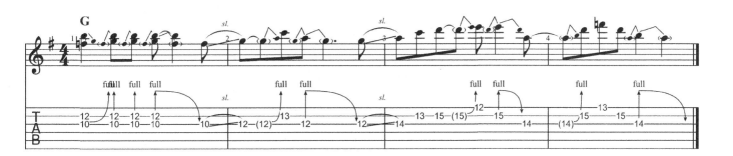

The next lick shows Brad's wild use of open strings, which is done with almost reckless abandon. Licks like this are often played fast, meaning it's possible to get away with notes that might not work at slower speeds, in fact, it's one of Brad's trademarks.

Bar one feels a lot like a shape 1 A Minor Pentatonic/Blues scale, but with pull offs to the open B, G, and D strings. The Eb really shouldn't work, but it adds some spice to the lick. The lick descends down the neck to the 3rd position and the perspective changes a little with a shift to hybrid picked rolls using notes of the G Minor Pentatonic scale (G, Bb, C, D, F), again the Bb here creates a pleasing clash with the open B string.

You'll hear ideas like this all over Brad's more up-tempo numbers, like Mr Policeman from 5th Gear.

Example 3b:

The next lick adopts a Van Halen-like approach to chromatic playing on a D chord, beginning with a classic lick using the D Major Pentatonic scale (D, E, F#, A, B) before taking the notes on the G and D strings with an open string pull-off and moving it down the neck chromatically to get to the open position.

The use of triplets helps to create a chaotic tumbling feel, but that just makes the resolution to the D note all the more rewarding.

The final chord is another pedal steel idea that Brad might execute with the G bender but it's more than possible to do it without. Take the notes indicated, and while holding the third and fourth fingers still, pull down and bend with the first finger to shift the note from an E to an F#, creating a beautiful D triad.

Example 3c:

This next lick moves the descending chromatic concept away from the rock influence and towards jazz.

Beginning in what looks like E Minor Pentatonic, you quickly descend an Am triad (A, C, E) and then move down chromatically to an Abm (Ab, Cb, Eb) and then G. This gives you a melody line on top that moves E, Eb, D, which ties the idea nicely together.

Once resolved, there's more chromatic playing around the (A shape) G Mixolydian scale, which then moves down to a lovely G triad in the C shape.

There are a lot of notes to consider here, but you should pay close attention to how they sound over the underlying G chord.

Example 3d:

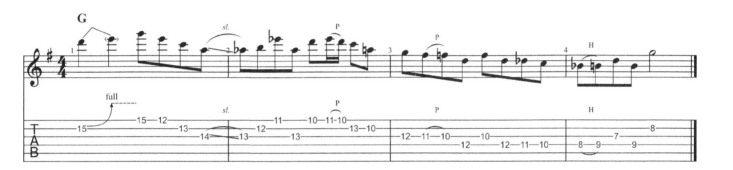

The final lick is virtually impossible to play without the right kit, but I can't talk about Brad and not include a G bender lick.

A bender system is a mechanical device whereby pulling on the strap operates a series of levers that pulls a string up a tone. It's definitely more common to see this on the B string, and production models have been released with this modification, and the G bender is a much rarer beast. The Gibson Music City Jr (which I use on the recording) comes fitted with a Joe Glaser-designed bender that can be switched from a B to a G, but another option is retrofitting a Hipshot palm bender.

Begin by sliding from the 2nd to the 3rd fret, then play the G string and use your bender to pull the G up to the 3rd of F (A). It's also possible to achieve this with a behind-the-nut bend, but more on that in the Jerry Donahue chapter.

With the note held, play the notes on the B and E string before releasing the bent note.

The second half of the lick uses the bender on double-stops. These can be played without a bender, but the bender adds a unique, mechanical, pedal steel sound.

Example 3e:

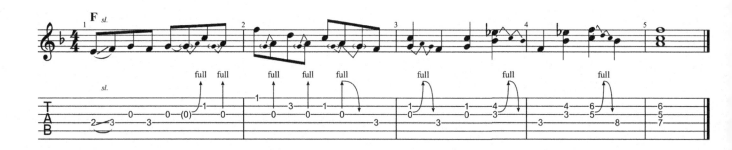

Chapter Four: Brent Mason

Considered as one of the pinnacles of class in country guitar, Brent Mason is also one of the world's most successful session musicians to boot, having won numerous Country Music Awards (CMAs) and Grammys.

Born in Ohio in 1959, Brent relocated to Nashville as soon he could to pursue a career in music. He would gain a following as the guitarist in the Don Kelley Band (a proving ground for many up-and-coming players over the years, including Guthrie Trapp and Daniel Donato), Brent ended up catching the attention of Chet Atkins and recording on his 1985 album Stay Tuned.

Over the years, Brent has gone on to be *the* guy to call for session guitar work in Nashville. His voice as a player has helped to shape the sound of country guitar, having worked with legends such as Alan Jackson, Shania Twain, Waylon Jennings, Dolly Parton, Olivia Newton-John, Toby Keith, Willie Nelson, and many more.

As a featured artist, Brent's recordings are limited to Hot Wired (1997), The Players (1999), and Smokin' Section (2006). Each of these is a great listen and will result in you picking out Brent's style on many other recordings, from albums to the big screen.

As a session player, Brent's job requires him to be versatile and to wear many hats, but his use of a thumb pick (like his hero Jerry Reed) is a big part of his personal style, allowing him to dig in and get that snappy hybrid-picked sound. His grey 1968 Fender Telecaster (three pickups, fitted with a Joe Glaser B Bender) is almost as iconic as his playing, despite having a signature model with PRS it's hard to get Brent to put down that Telecaster. After all, there's very little that says country quite like a Telecaster bridge pickup played through a clean amp.

The first lick brings up shades of Albert Lee (a common theme in Brent's faster licks), using notes of the A Mixolydian scale (A, B, C#, D, E, F#, G), again, with that added b3 (C) and b5 (Eb).

This particular lick uses an open E to aid in the position shift from the 5th fret (E shape) down to the open position (A shape).

Once in that open position, open stings are heavily utilised before moving back up the neck to the E shape. This use of the Mixolydian scale with added b3 and b5 is an integral part of any hot country player's vocabulary. It's all about using the notes in an authentic way.

Example 4a:

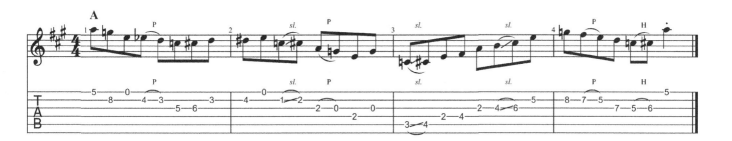

The next lick uses pull-offs to open strings and triads to descend the neck. Play the first note with the pick, then hybrid pick the double-stop and pull off to the open G. The fretted notes consist of an A triad (A, C#, E), this pattern then moves down a tone to G (G, B, D), and then to an open A chord.

Bar two begins with an A5 chord where the lower note (E) walks down chromatically to Eb then D, then ascends with one of Brent's trademark triplet patterns.

The final bar quickly moves up the neck, playing an open A, then up to the E shape (5th fret) then the C shape (9th fret).

Example 4b:

The next lick would probably be played with a B bender (it certainly makes it easier), but I've recorded it without.

Begin up in the C shape by bending the B up to C#, reach over to the high E string to play the F# (with the fourth finger) then re-pick the bent note before playing the 12th fret high E, picking and releasing the bent note. This then shifts down to the D shape, bending the b7th (G) up to the root (A) and then playing the 3rd (C#) on the E string.

The second part of the lick features another ascending triplet and some double-stops to move from the C shape, down to the E. As with the last lick, you may notice Brent plays the A triad and then moves the idea down one tone to G (in the second half of bar three) before resolving down to A again in the lower position (E).

Example 4c:

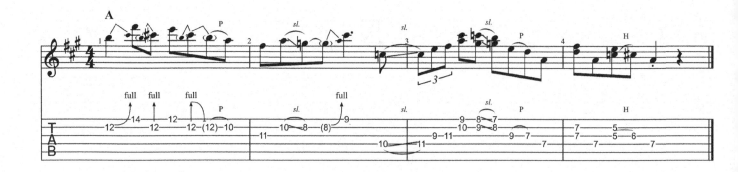

248

The next lick demonstrates how much mileage you can get from playing the same idea in different octaves. Begin by playing a classic Brent idea in the D shape, approach the 3rd from below, then descend down using the b5th (Eb) for that country flavour. This same idea is then repeated, but an octave lower in the E shape.

The second part of the lick sits around the G shape and uses the open G string to help transition back up the neck to the E shape.

These ideas rely heavily on being able to move up and down the neck, so mastery of those basic CAGED positions is essential for your future development. Both Brent and Albert Lee have demonstrated this idea on their instructional videos, and while they never expressly use the term 'CAGED', their method of seeing licks as tied to chord positions is undeniable.

Example 4d:

The final lick explores more of Brent's great bending ideas, this time on the B and G strings. The aim with a lick like this is to have it sound as mechanical as possible (like a pedal steel guitar) so each time you bend a string, do it quickly, and accurately.

The lick begins by bending the b7 up to the root, then playing the 3rd and 2nd on the high E string. After descending down the neck to the E shape, a similar bending lick is played in the G shape. Bend the 2nd (B) up to the 3rd (C#) then play the 5th fret B and 3rd fret high E. This creates an A7 chord, so it's important you keep that bend in tune.

Example 4e:

Chapter Five: Buck Owens/Don Rich

Buck Owens was born in Texas in 1929 and would become one of the true pioneers of country music and the Bakersfield sound with his group, the Buckaroos. Buck Owens met Don Rich in 1958 and they played together in Tacoma before Buck moved to Bakersfield the following year. In 1960 Don dropped out of college to become the guitarist in the Buckaroos.

As a guitar player, Buck could hold his own, but he would often sit back and let Don take the spotlight. This allowed him to let his personality shine through.

Developing as a rejection to the slick productions and string-heavy arrangements coming out of Nashville at the time, the Bakersfield sound took things back to country roots. Many consider Budd Hobbs' 1954 recording, Louisiana Swing, to be the first song in this new style (which featured Buck on lead guitar), but it wasn't until Buck and Merle Haggard brought the sound to the masses in the '60s, that it really took off.

Buck's music had a sound that was more at home in honky-tonk bars, than what was coming out of Nashville. There was a something a bit rock and roll to the sound, with the harsh twangy electric guitars and sweet vocal harmonies.

As players, Don and Buck took a lot of influence from depression-era country musicians and western swing pickers. Their playing was about melody rather than flash. Getting their sound is about turning your Telecaster bridge pickup loud, and playing things you'd want to sing.

Sadly, Don Rich was killed in a motorcycle accident in 1974, robbing the world of his potential, but Buck kept recording albums right up to 1991, with 39 albums to his name.

A great place to start to get into this iconic guitar duo is the 1966 live album, Carnegie Hall Concert.

This first example showcases Buck's picking prowess with a run of fast alternate-picked 1/16th notes.

You don't need to worry about crossing strings here, so just make sure you're playing the fretted notes in the first two bars with downstrokes. Over the E major chord you're simply using notes of the E Major scale.

Example 5a:

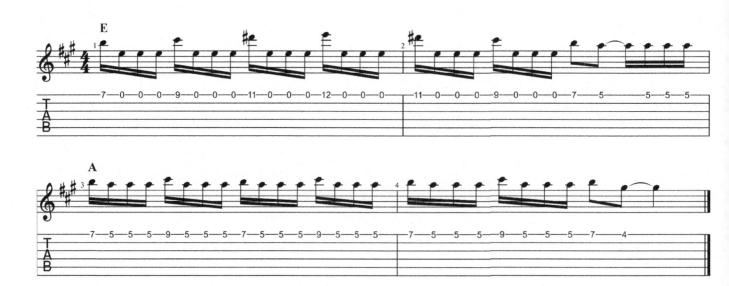

The following example is a lower register lead guitar idea over an A chord, using the notes of the A Major Pentatonic scale.

The key here is getting a swinging feel and hitting the syncopated notes with good rhythm. Keep a constant picking motion with the picking hand to keep you on track.

Example 5b:

The next example is a faster Don Rich type lick over a D and G chord.

You'll notice the same phrase in the C shape is played over the D chord, and then moved up the neck to outline the G chord. It's a simple, yet effective method of outlining the chord change.

Use alternate picking for the 1/16th notes, and downstrokes for the rest.

Example 5c:

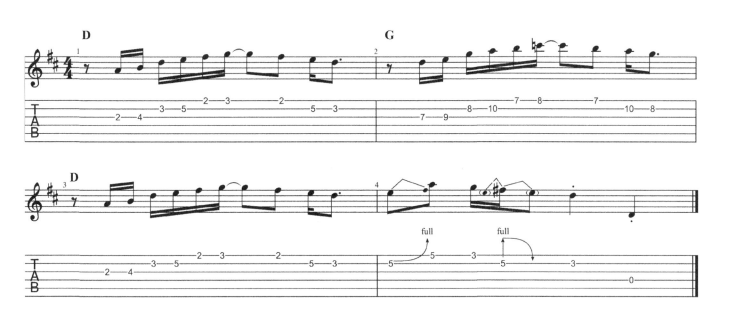

Here's a slippery little lick that fits primarily around the C shape with some small position shifts.

Don is drawing largely from the G Major Pentatonic scale (G, A, B, D, E) here. There's also the added b3 (Bb) for some spice, giving it the G Country scale vibe.

Ideas like this are less rock or blues in nature, they don't fit in tidy little shapes, the hand moves where it needs to in order to play the melody the ear wants to hear.

Example 5d:

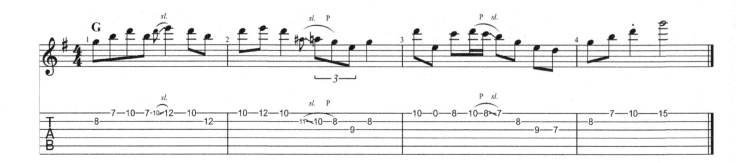

The final lick moves between a G and D chord.

Over the G chord the lick appears very much like a G Major Pentatonic idea in the A shape, and when the chord changes to the D, the melody moves down to the D Major Pentatonic scale, but moves quickly back to the G Major Pentatonic scale in the final bar.

The tricky part here is hitting that position shift, but seeing the G and D chord in barre forms is a great way to not get lost.

Example 5e:

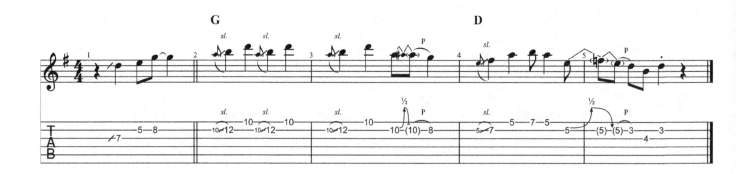

Chapter Six: Chet Atkins

Often referred to as 'Mister Guitar', there are few who have done as much for the instrument, or indeed country music, as Chet Atkins.

Born in Tennessee in 1924, Chet played the fiddle and ukulele before picking up the guitar at the tender age of nine. It was around the age of fifteen that Chet first heard the great Merle Travis and began to work out how to play Merle's trademark thumb picking style.

Over the next fifty years, Chet would build a rich legacy in the music industry, eventually making his way up to the position of A&R Director of Country Music at RCA. This put him in the position of finding new talent and helping to produce their records, a role he held for many years while simultaneously releasing his own recordings.

At the time of his death in 2001, Chet had recorded an astonishing 87 studio albums as a solo artist, and collaborated or guested on countless other. He had also helped launch the careers of many household names, including Brent Mason and Jerry Reed, worked with everyone in the business from Dolly Parton, to Elvis, and won no fewer than 14 Grammy awards.

To this day, fans the world over gather every year for the Chet Atkins Appreciation Society (CAAS) convention, it's the premier place to go to see the cutting edge of fingerstyle players, from country to jazz.

His style on the guitar was broad, taking influence from country, classical, jazz, blues, and rock n' roll players. Though probably best known for his Travis Picking style (as covered in my Country Fingerstyle book), he was quite the soloist, and even classical guitarist. Other than Merle Travis, his influences included Django Reinhardt, Les Paul, and even Jerry Reed.

Due to the wide range of his recordings, it's difficult to recommend one, but 1959's Mister Guitar is a good starting point, or the 1970 collaborative effort with Jerry Reed; Me & Jerry.

As mentioned previously, Chet's sound is dominated by his use of the thumb pick which enables fluid fingerpicking ideas. Guitar-wise he had signature models with both Gibson and Gretsch so imitating his sound is simply a case of using any decent semi-hollowbody instrument, perhaps with a Bigsby tremolo arm and some slapback delay.

The first lick is a classic open-string lick outlining the G Major scale.

The idea is very simple. Start on the G root note and move down the scale using the open strings where possible. You'll also note that the scale has been fingered in a way that allows as many of the notes as possible to ring out.

It's possible to do this for any scale that contains a combination of open strings and fretted notes, although C, D, G, A, and E are probably the most common.

Example 6a:

This next example features small chord strums to create a big sound.

Hold down the chord (A major in the C shape) and palm mute the lower part. Next, strum the A, D, and G strings and stop them from ringing out. Then, move over to the G, B, and E strings and repeat. This is all then punctuated with a melody on the B and E string using thirds.

As the chord changes to D, the picking stays the same while the left hand changes. Now you're holding down a D chord in the E shape.

Example 6b:

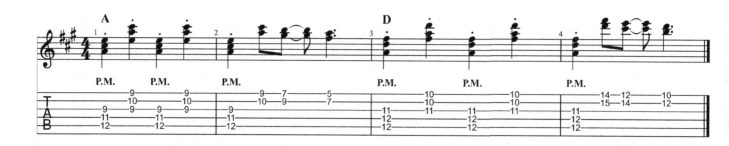

This lick is a classic country string-skipping lick using sixths. The idea is that you play a diatonic sixth on the G and E strings (for example, the 16th fret G and 16th fret E), and move into the lower note chromatically from a tone below.

This idea then moves down the neck, keeping the basic sixths diatonic to the E Mixolydian scale.

To execute this lick, alternate between the pick, first finger, pick, and second finger. This may take a while to get used to, but it's essential for playing quickly with a thumb pick.

Example 6c:

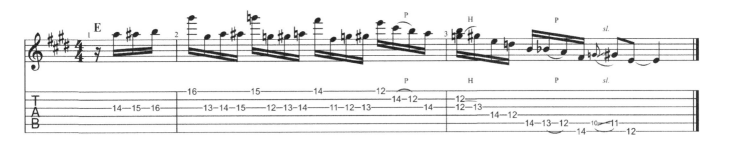

The next lick sees Chet hold down four-note chords and sweep through them to create exciting melodic ideas.

The secret to mastering the sweep-picking technique relies on the rest stroke. You don't pluck the D string, instead you push the pick through the string so it comes to rest on the G string. Now you're ready to push through the G string and land on the B, etc.

Try not to let the strings ring into each other, and keep the rhythm defined.

Example 6d:

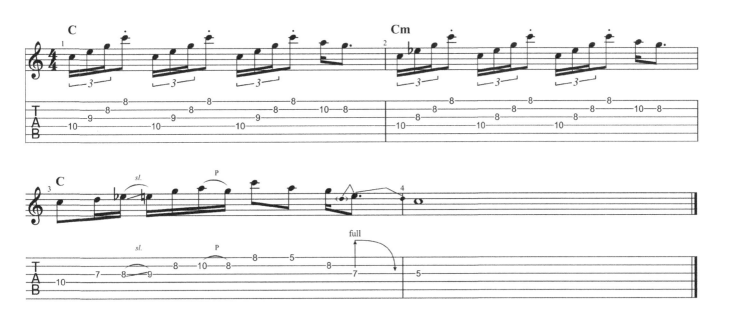

The final lick (often referred to as the 'super lick') demonstrates just how far ahead of the curve Chet was.

Sweep-picked arpeggios are often claimed by metal players as their technique, but in a post-YouTube world it's become easier for us to see and hear things from years before. One of the more popular videos in the last few years is a classic appearance of Chet and Jerry Reed where Chet plays some incredible 5-string ascending and descending sweep-picked arpeggios… almost a decade before players like Yngwie Malmsteen or Frank Gambale would hit the scene.

As with the previous example it's essential that you use the same picking technique when descending. The best way to do this is turn the pick so it's angled the opposite way to when playing the ascending idea.

Example 6e:

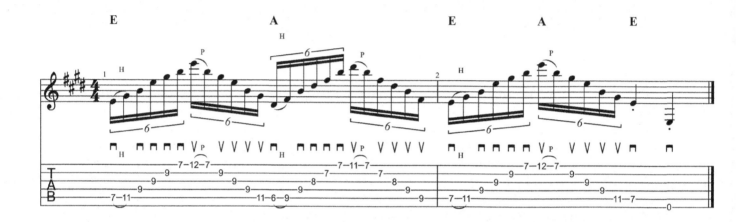

Chapter Seven: Danny Gatton

Born in Washington D.C. in 1945, Danny Gatton would build a cult following on the underground music scene as one of the greatest unknown guitar players. Danny's skill on the instrument was so legendary that he earned himself the nickname of 'The Humbler'.

Danny may seem an odd choice for a book like this, as he wasn't really a country player at all. He's often assumed to be by people who are less familiar with his playing (probably due to the fact he played a beat-up Telecaster!), but the truth is Danny's playing falls much more in line with the rockabilly and jazz genre than straight ahead country.

Having said that, he's clearly come from that country sensibility, with incredible hybrid picking technique at his disposal for playing banjo rolls at speed. He's also no slouch at Travis picking, though he would execute that technique with a flat pick and fingers.

Danny committed suicide in 1994. At that time he had nine albums available and, since his passing, eleven more records have seen an official release. As his recordings are so diverse, every album has a slightly different vibe, his 1991 major label debut, 88 Elmira St, or the 1993 follow-up, Cruisin' Deuces, are good places to start.

My personal favourite is his 1978 record, Redneck Jazz, or the two Redneck Jazz Explosion live albums which feature Danny playing with Buddy Emmons on pedal steel.

1994's Relentless is another highlight, seeing Danny really open up over nine tracks with Joey DeFrancesco handling organ duties.

As mentioned previously, most of Danny's career was dominated by his use of the Telecaster (in particular, his 1953 Fender Telecaster), and a signature model was released for him. He also used a Les Paul with home-built effects mounted to the body of the guitar (the dingus box), but he stopped using this when he started getting the nickname of 'Danny Gadget'. Getting Danny's sound is all about being confident with the high end on a Telecaster bridge pickup, especially as Danny used a signature set of Joe Barden pickups that are well known for their 'ice-pick' qualities.

The first lick showcases Danny's use of hybrid picking to execute banjo rolls.

Pick the first note and hammer on to the second. This process then repeated before plucking the high E string with the second finger. Next, use the pick, second, and fourth finger to execute a forward roll on the G, B, and E strings.

Danny would also often pluck the E string as he hammered on the G, but that's really next level stuff and I'll leave that to The Humbler!

Example 7a:

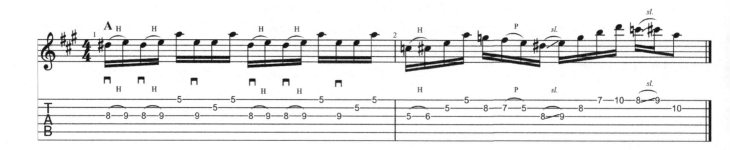

Here's another example of Danny's hybrid picking, this time used to execute the kind of idea that Chet Atkins would sweep.

Pluck the note on the D string, then forward roll with the second and fourth fingers on the G and B string. Then come over and pluck the E string with the pick.

Doing it this way is definitely harder and requires a high level of dexterity in the picking hand fingers. The reason Danny would do it this way is for the more percussive snappy sound. You're able to really dig in with the pick on the high E string to get a sharp chicken pickin' sound.

Example 7b:

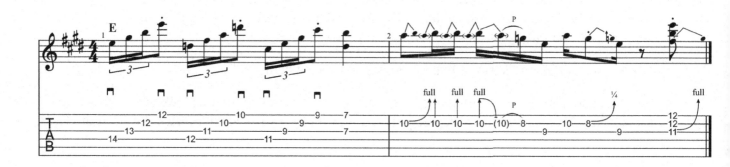

This lick moves down to the open position for a more rockabilly inspired sound, not too distant from something Albert Lee might play.

The tricky part here is making sure you put the pull-offs in the right places, as they help to give the lick that snappy sound.

The second part of the lick moves from the open position up to the C shape. By this stage you should be getting pretty comfortable with these CAGED patterns.

Example 7c:

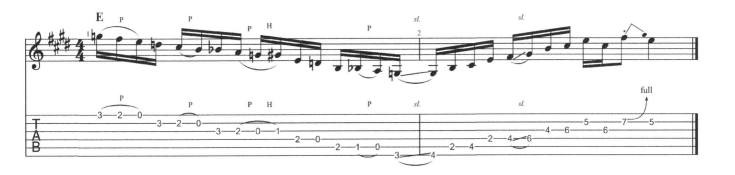

The fourth lick demonstrates Danny's amazing double-stop licks, mainly around the C shape A chord. To play these I'd suggest a combination of the pick and second finger, rather than trying to strum them.

Begin by moving chromatically into the root and 3rd. From here, the first bar is full of notes that really sound more like a D chord, though the notes are still from the A Mixolydian scale (A, B, C#, D, E, F#, G).

The second bar requires you to hold down an A7 chord (fingered as an A/G), and play through it two notes at a time.

Example 7d:

The final lick features more double-stops, but this time they are played with the pick.

Use the first finger for the double-stop on the 12th fret, the fourth finger for the 17th fret, and the second finger for the 14th fret. Take this one slowly and make sure the hammer-on is in time as things can quickly fall apart at speed.

The second part of the lick slides into the 12th fret and moves down chromatically, pedalling against the open E. Ideas like this are supposed to sound wild, and were a big part of Danny's style and were similar to other names on the scene, like Roy Buchanan.

Example 7e:

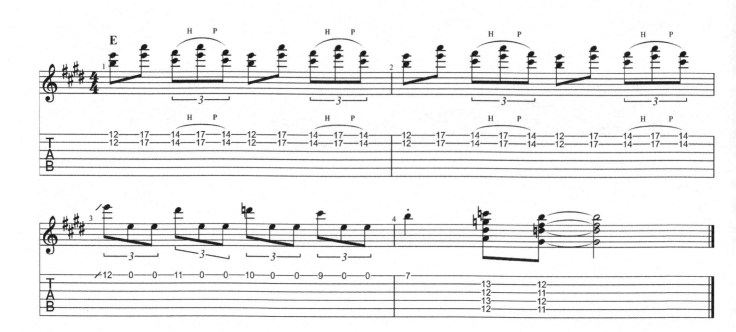

Chapter Eight: Eldon Shamblin

Born in Oklahoma in 1916, Eldon Shamblin would go on to be one of the biggest names in the western swing movement.

Eldon learned to play in a time before rock n' roll or tab, and his learning experience was more formal in nature. He developed the ability read and arrange music, taking his cues from jazz players like Eddie Lang. He was definitely a jazz player who was thrown into a country setting, and this helped to define the western swing sound.

Eldon spent his days working in radio as this was the popular media of the time. Eventually he would begin working with Bob Wills as part of the Texas Playboys, and from 1938 to 1954 he made over 300 recordings with the band. It's sometimes hard to distinguish which parts he's playing, so you need to listen out for Bob calling Eldon's name to be sure.

He would also play on many recordings with the outlaw Merle Haggard, which saw him gain an even bigger cult following.

Like his hometown peer Charlie Christian, Eldon was also ahead of the curve. He became well known for adopting the electric guitar long before his peers moved away from the archtop guitars synonymous with the genre. In 1954, Eldon was presented with one of the first Fender Stratocasters ever made (in a beautiful custom gold colour), and it became his main guitar for many years, helping to define his sound.

As you might predict, Eldon's style is more rooted in the jazz genre than country, but playing his licks and ideas in country can bring a very sophisticated edge to your music. He was also a pioneer of the twin guitar harmony, often alongside a pedal steel guitar.

The first lick fits over an Emaj7 chord. The obvious scale choice to solo on an Emaj7 chord is the E Major scale.

This lick fits nicely over the chord by sticking to the G shape.

Example 8a:

Example 8b fits into the same setting, but this time comes from a more arpeggio-based perspective.

The musical part here is the three-note ascending E major idea with a G# on the G string, the B on the B string, and then a note that changes on the high E each time.

Alternate picking here will help with the timing.

Example 8b:

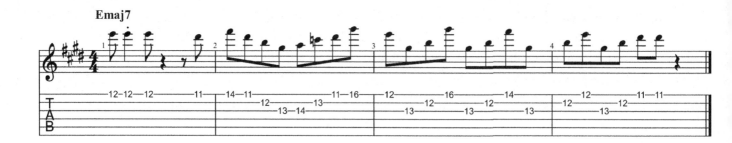

The next two licks take place over the ending or turnaround of a song. The use of non-diatonic chords (like the C6) help give it a jazzy sound, and require careful attention when soloing.

The first bar is treated as being an E7, so the E Mixolydian scale works well, in this case using the A shape. Over the A/C#, I've played an A triad before landing on the C of the C6 chord.

The final two bars contain chords from the key of E, so notes of the E Major scale are used again.

Example 8c:

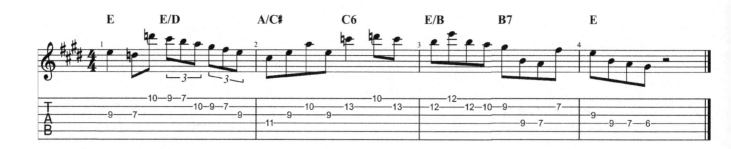

The second lick over this progression takes almost the same path as the last, using the E Major Pentatonic scale in bar one and playing notes of the C Major Pentatonic scale over the C6 chord.

The final two bars target the B chord by approaching the triad from a semitone below; these little chromatic neighbour tones are a big part of that country-jazz influence.

Example 8d:

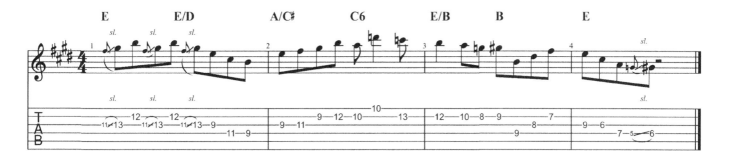

The final lick showcases a simplified version of Eldon's amazing rhythm playing.

It's hard to miss the connection to gypsy jazz here, it's very close to the 'le pompe' sound, with small strokes on beat 1 and 3 and heavy accents on beats 2 and 4. For the sake of reading, I've written the chords as complete voicings, so listen to the recording to hear how it should be played.

The secret here is the application of inversions to create melodic interest in the rhythm playing. Playing the same A chord voicing for two bars could be considered boring.

The first chord is an A chord in the E shape, this walks up to an A/C# in the second bar, then up to A/E.

When the chord moves to D, the D triad is held on the D, G, and B strings, while the bass note moves between the D, A, and F# notes.

Example 8e:

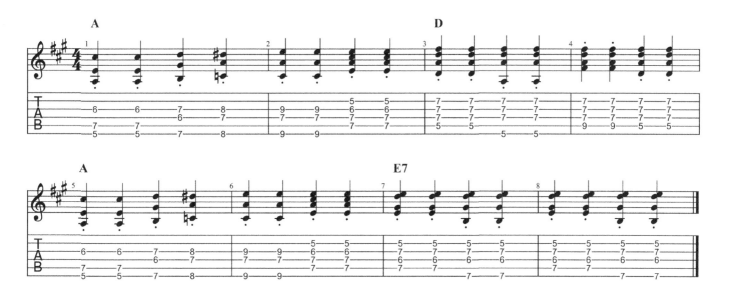

Chapter Nine: Glen Campbell

Born in Arkansas in 1936, Glen Campbell was one of the 'full package' country musicians since his career began in 1956, right up until his death in 2017.

Very much like Brent Mason and Brad Paisley, Glen left his home to make a career in music using his skills as a session player, and song writer. He would very quickly find real success in these areas, playing a key part of The Wrecking Crew (A group of LA session musicians who were in high demand during the '60s and '70s). Glen would do session work for countless names that included Ricky Nelson, Nat King Cole, The Monkees, Frank Sinatra, Elvis Presley, and many more.

As a player, Glen always displayed phenomenal technical ability on the instrument, playing fast alternate-picked runs at speeds his contemporaries couldn't touch, though his career was much deeper than just his playing.

Glen was an amazing on-camera personality and made lots of comedy appearances on TV shows alongside people like Jerry Reed. He also had a decent run of success in Hollywood, appearing in cult classics like True Grit (alongside western icon John Wayne).

As a composer, Glen's work is timeless, with songs like Gentle on my Mind and Wichita Lineman being masterpieces. That's before considering the signature touch he brought to the compositions of other people, such as Rhinestone Cowboy and Southern Nights.

Glen was diagnosed with Alzheimer's disease in 2011, and in 2014 was the subject of the documentary I'll Be Me, which saw him on tour in the throes of the disease. It's amazing to see someone unable to recognize his daughter each day, but then be able to get up every night and sing all of his hits and play some amazing guitar still, all while not really knowing where he is from moment to moment. Sadly, Glen passed away between the writing and publishing of this book.

Glen's sound is all about the notes he chooses rather than the instruments he uses as he's played everything over the years. Probably seen most with a Strat in later years, he's just as likely to be seen with his Ovation acoustic where his picking is just as scary!

The first lick shows off some of Glen's picking skills with this great line over an A7 – Dm chord change.

Minor keys are definitely less common that major in country music, but it's still important to get to grips with them as they do come up.

While the notes could be seen as coming from the D Harmonic Minor scale (D, E, F, G, A, Bb, C#), I find it easier to see it as an embellishment of an A7 arpeggio, adding the b6 (F) on the B string, and the b9 (Bb) on the high E string. This tells me that it implies an A7b9 chord.

Example 9a:

The second lick fits over a C major chord, using the G shape.

There are some great chromatic notes used here, including the Eb at the start (approaching the 3rd of the chord). This suggests the C Country scale (C, D, Eb, E, F, G, A, B) meaning the Bb and F# are just chromatic passing tones to help connect notes. This is common in Glen's faster playing and has the added benefit of adding a jazzier edge to his soloing.

Example 9b:

This next lick is more country/blues/rock in nature, and a tricky one to play at speed!

Outlining a D chord in the G shape, the notes hint at the D Major Pentatonic scale, but there's more going on here.

The first two bars require you to keep the D note on the high E string while the B string walks chromatically up from the 3rd (F#) to the 5th (B), and down again hitting the b3rd to 3rd before ending on the octave.

The final bar uses the D Country scale with a classic country/pop cliché.

Example 9c:

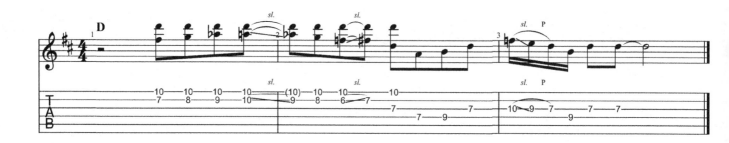

The next idea warms you up to some of Glen's faster alternate picking, outlining a D chord with lots of chromatic passing tones.

The idea still fits loosely around the G shape D Major Pentatonic scale from the previous lick. Take this slow as you learn the fingering and build up speed over time.

The last bar should all be played with the first finger, shifting down the neck.

Example 9d:

The final lick is played in the style of Paul Gilbert and Al Di Meola... but nearly ten years before they would become associated with this sound.

The secret to playing this one fast is making sure you hit the last note on the B string with a down, and the note on the E with an up. This is often described as 'outside picking' as the pick stays on the outside of the strings (try playing up on the B and down on the E to see what inside picking sounds like).

266

The ending is a classic open position country lick in E to bring it back from the chaos of this shred-like alternate picking.

Example 9e:

Chapter Ten: Hank Garland

Born in South Carolina in 1930, Walter Louis 'Hank' Garland is one of the great sophisticated players of the genre.

Hank began at an early age, inspired by the guitar playing he would hear on local radio stations, and worked hard learning to play. At just 15 he scored a gig with the Cotton Pickers after a chance encounter in a guitar store. He moved to Nashville at the tender age of 16 to pursue a career in music as a session player and artist. Two years later he would sell over a million copies of the single Sugarfoot Rag, securing his demand on the session scene.

Well known as one of Elvis's session guitarists from 1958 to 1961, Hank also appeared on recordings by Patsy Cline, Roy Orbison, and many more. His ability, and willingness to play different sounds kept him in demand as rock and roll took hold in the '50s.

He was also a respected jazz player, playing with legends like Charlie Parker and influencing the design of the Gibson Byrdland.

In 1961, Hank was involved in a serious car accident which left him in a coma for a week. Due to some of the treatments at the time (like electroconvulsive therapy), it's speculated that Hank suffered additional damage to his brain, effectively ending his music career.

Hank's playing is a treasure trove of ideas, especially in a country setting, as his voice as a player was so influenced by the swing jazz he grew up on. These outside influences add a twist on the genre not heard from many of his peers. Hank's playing has influenced many people, but none have been more vocal than Chet Atkins, who regularly cited Hank as the greatest guitarist he ever heard.

Getting Hank's sound is really about a good neck humbucker and a punchy clean tone, I access that with the neck pickup on my Gibson Howard Roberts Fusion, with the tone rolled back to about 7.

The first Hank lick can be split into two sections, the first two bars, and the last.

Taking place over an A chord, an idea like this works great on a country blues jam. Beginning in the G shape, the A root note is played on the G and high E string, with as ascending chromatic scale being played on the B string. Note the repeated use of the b5 (Eb), which adds a bluesy edge to the lick.

The second part sits around the E shape, using a wide stretch on the high E string to reach from the root (A) to the 4th (D), and then sliding down a semitone to the 3rd. It would be possible to see this entire lick as being A Mixolydian but with that added b5 for that blues sound.

Example 10a:

The next lick uses triads over an A chord to create melodic interest.

Bar one consists of an A triad (A, C#, E) over the A chord in the C shape, this then moves down a tone giving a G triad (G, B, D). This technique is called an 'arpeggio substitution' - playing one arpeggio over another note to create a different sound. Over a G chord, G, B, and D, are the root, 3rd, and 5th. In the context of that A chord, G is the b7, B is the 9th, and D is the 11th. These notes aren't as strong over the A chord, but they help to create some jazzy colours before resolving back to the A triad in the next bar.

Arpeggio substitutions can be written as slash chords, or as their implied harmony. G/A tells you that it's a G triad, over an A bass note. A11sus tells you it's a dominant 11 chord without the 3rd. While either works, G/A is a little more specific.

Example 10b:

The next lick combines double-stops with alternate picked single note ideas.

As the lick takes place over an A chord, the double-stop nots are the 3rd, and 5th (C#, and E), and are approached from a semitone below.

The melody in bar two actually looks a little more like the A Dorian scale (A, B, C, D, E, F#, G), not the cleanest choice over an A chord as the C in the scale clashes with the C# in the chord.

The second half of the lick repeats the first bar, then moves down to the G shape and picks notes out of the A Major Pentatonic scale.

Example 10c:

The fourth lick begins in the lower register and uses notes of the A Major Pentatonic scale in the open position (G shape).

The second part of the lick features another wider stretch as you're playing four notes spanning five frets on the high E string. By now, the movement should make sense, you're adding a chromatic passing tone between the 2nd (B) and 3rd (C#).

The last note requires that you slide up the neck to the 17th fret to play the root note (A). This can feel difficult at first, but generally this is because you're looking at where your hand *is*, rather than where it's *going*. The solution is to be looking at the 17th fret as early as possible, I look at it while I play hammer-on and pull-off in bar three.

Example 10d:

The final lick uses the A Major scale (A, B, C#, D, E, F#, G#) on the high E string, moving down with some fast hammer-ons and pull-offs.

Pick the first two notes with a down and up stroke, and then repick the first note before hammering and pulling to the second. This process is repeated on each note of the scale as you descend the neck. Use the first and second fingers for notes that are a fret apart, and the first and third for two fret gaps.

The beauty of this type of lick is that it can be adapted to fit any scale in any key, as long as you know the notes of the scale.

Example 10e:

Chapter Eleven: James Burton

Born in Louisiana in 1939, James Burton would become one of the key names in the development of electric guitar in country music, inspiring millions with his iconic flat-picked chicken pickin' licks.

Primarily self-taught, James took influence from guitarists on the radio, Chuck Berry, Elmore James, Lightnin' Hopkins, and (of course), Chet Atkins. Listening to these players and spending endless hours trying to imitate their playing was a quick method to gain proficiency, resulting in James playing professional gigs as early as age 14.

James would quickly develop a reputation on the session scene, his unique pedal steel inspired lead work was in demand in the '50s, playing with Bob Luman, Ricky Nelson, and the Dale Hawkins band. James would often replace electric strings with lighter banjo strings to help him bend further. Standard 9 gauge strings give a .009, .011, .016, and .024, James was known to use .009, .010, .012, and .024, giving a lot more room for bending the B and G.

James also had success playing dobro guitar, working with Glen Campbell, and Johnny Cash. This would lead him to hit the session stratosphere, sometimes recording as many as six sessions a day! The tragic part of this is that much of the work at the time was undocumented, so it's a case of listening and guessing which records he might have been on.

In 1969 James took the gig with Elvis (a gig he'd turned down in '68), and this would result in super stardom levels for James and his playing. He held this gig until Elvis died in 1977.

During this period, he would record two solo albums, 1969's Corn Pickin' and Slick Slidin' and 1971's The Guitar Sounds of James Burton. Both are fascinating listens as you get the rare chance to hear James come to the fore.

In terms of sound, James' voice comes from his combination of a Telecaster and the snappy attack from the flat pick and first finger (on which he usually used a finger pick). James also took the Paisley Telecaster and made it cool. The originals were released in 1968 but didn't do well, people often ended up buying them cheap and repainting them. When James started using one with Elvis, everybody wanted one, and those original '68-'69 Paisley Telecasters are now extremely sought after.

The first lick fits nicely over the last four bars of a 12-bar blues in E, and showcases James' choppy staccato chicken pickin' sound. The concept behind this sound is that it imitates the 'clucky' sound of a chicken.

Pluck the G string and bend, then use the pick to pluck the B string, then re-pluck the B string with the second finger of the picking hand. When doing this, place the pick and fingers on the strings as soon as the notes are played to keep them as short as possible.

Bar two contains a pre-bent note which is repeatedly picked as the bend is released. As before, alternate between the pick and finger to keep the note short and choppy.

The final bars move down to the open position, descending down the E Blues scale (E, G, A, Bb, B, D).

Example 11a:

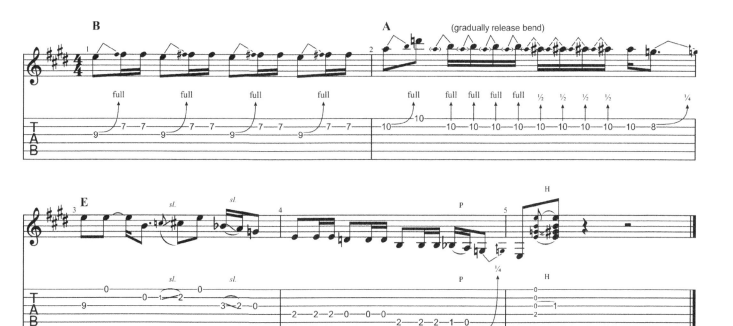

The second lick outlines an A chord with a classic country idea, similar to one covered in the Chet Atkins chapter. The 6ths played on the D and B strings imply an A, G, and D chord, and each is approached chromatically from a tone below.

As with the last example, alternate between the pick and the first finger to keep these notes as plucky as possible.

The final two bars demonstrate James' pedal steel influence; bending notes on the G while keeping double-stops on the A, and D string. The first double-stop implies a D, then a Bm, and ending on a classic voicing for A.

Example 11b:

The next lick continues with the chicken pickin' theme, this time descending down the B string while outlining an A major chord.

When learning licks like this, it's important to understand what note you're beginning on, and what note you're bending to. This makes the lick easier to understand conceptually. As an example, the first note is the 4th bending up to the 5th, the second is the 2nd bending up to the 3rd, then the root up to the 2nd. This is what gives licks like this context.

The ending of the lick outlines a D chord with some pedal steel bends using the D Major Pentatonic scale in the G shape.

Example 11c:

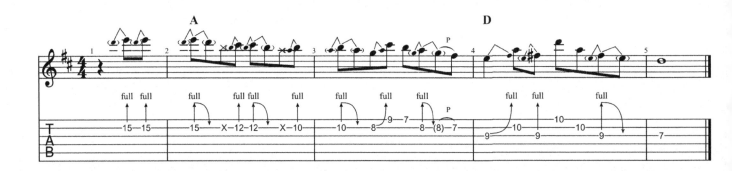

This lick shows how James might have played on a rock n' roll session, using his country pedal steel influences.

Bar one begins with notes from the E shape A Minor Pentatonic scale (A, C, D, E, G), then moves down to the G shape A Major Pentatonic scale (A, B, C#, E, F#) with a bend from the 2nd to the 3rd of the scale on the G string. The lick then moves back up to the E shape at the 5th fret.

The use of the same shape three frets apart, is a big part of many great country guitarists' vocabulary as lots of music can be found in each one.

Example 11d:

The final lick continues in the rock n' roll vein with a repeating two-bar idea on an E note played on the G and B strings. As with previous examples, careful use of staccato helps to bring these licks alive.

The second half of the bar uses notes of the A Minor Pentatonic, A Blues, and A Mixolydian scale, in fact, the same group of notes covered back in the Albert Lee chapter (A, B, C, C#, D, Eb, E, F#, G). That's a scale that contains nine notes, and it is easy to collapse into a chromatic mess if you're not careful. It's all about how you use these note, so pay attention to the details of the lick.

Example 11e:

Chapter Twelve: Jerry Donahue

Bending strings to imitate other instruments, such as the pedal steel, is nothing new in country guitar but there can be only one king of the string bend, and that'll probably always be Jerry Donahue.

Born in Manhattan in 1946, Jerry's family were big on the arts, and Jerry was encouraged to take guitar lessons (albeit classical) as a child. He would quickly be drawn to electric guitar, taking influence from Chet Atkins, Amos Garrett, and Duane Eddy.

Jerry moved to England early in his career and developed a reputation on the British folk-rock scene. During the late '60s and early '70s he would work with a few notable bands, including Fotheringay and Fairpoint Convention. Between 1969, and 1975, Jerry would appear on almost 25 records, as a player, singer, arranger, mixer, and more.

That's not to suggest that his career quietened down from then, in fact it went from strength to strength with a list of over 330 credits from the Beach Boys to the Proclaimers meaning that yes, he played on the Scottish anthem, I'm Gonna Be (500 Miles).

As a solo artist, Jerry has several albums to his name, and more with his country guitar trio supergroup, the Hellecasters (alongside Will Ray, and John Jorgenson), with 1994's Escape from Hollywood being a great place to start.

As a player, Jerry's style is dominated by his mind-numbing bending prowess, both behind the nut and fretted. He's a big user of multi-voice contrary and oblique motion, bending the strings in ways no one else has tried.

Gear-wise, Jerry has had numerous signature models over the years with Fender, Peavey, Fret King, and Vintage, although each guitar has been from the Telecaster family (aside from an old Fender Hellecaster Strat that is hard to come by), so a good Telecaster on the bridge pickup will get close to his tone.

The first lick here showcases some of Jerry's traditional country chicken pickin' ideas over a D chord

Where 'x' is used in the tab, just relax the fretting hand finger to dampen the string and create a clucky sound. It's not overly important which notes are muted, this is done freely while phrasing.

While bar one looks very much like the D Minor Pentatonic scale, the idea quickly shoots up the neck to the (G shape) D Major Pentatonic scale, then up to the E shape at the 10th fret for some double-stops and blues-rock phrasing.

Example 12a:

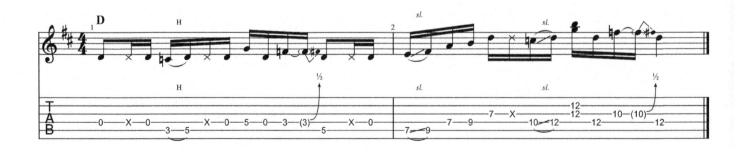

The second lick shows Jerry's wonderful hybrid pick-roll technique, and use of open strings to aid in position shifts.

Begin by picking the second fret with the pick, then pluck the A string with the second finger, then the D with the third finger. This basic forward roll over three strings is the base mechanic required to play the first bar, so take that technique and move it across the strings as required.

The second part of the lick requires you to move up the neck by plucking a note on the high E, pulling off to the open E string, then plucking a note on the B string before moving to the next position and ending on the 20th fret for a blues rock bend with an added open string.

Example 12b:

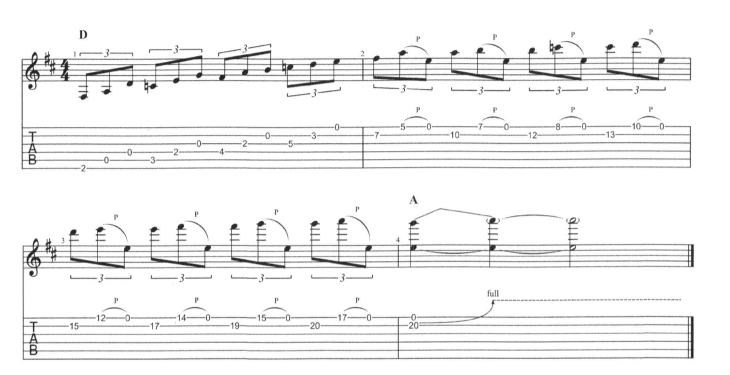

This next lick uses the same hybrid picked-roll technique and position shifts to outline an A chord in the open position. The real introduction is the use of behind the nut bends.

Behind-the-nut bends require a guitar with enough room behind the nut to push the strings down and raise their pitch. This works great on Telecasters, but is almost impossible on Les Pauls as the distance from the string to truss rod cover is so small.

At the end of the lick you need to play the open D and G strings, then bend both strings up a tone to create an A5 chord. This is extremely difficult (and taxing on the fingers), so it's a case of learning how much pressure to apply, and then doing that automatically.

Example 12c:

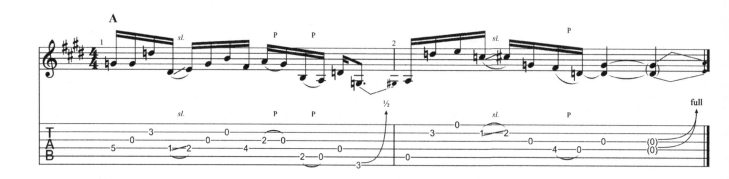

The next lick begins with traditional fretted bends with notes bent on the B string, and notes played against it on the E string. The first bar can be seen as the b7 to the root with the 3rd and 2nd on the high E string. The next bar can be seen as a C shape lick for a D chord.

The third bar becomes more challenging, pulling off to the open B string then bending the open string up tone with a behind-the-nut bend. This isn't too different from the previous bar but this time using behind-the-nut bends.

The final bar introduces a behind-the-nut bend featuring contrary motion. Contrary motion is where two voices go in different directions. The G string is pre-bent behind the nut, then gradually released, while the B string is bent up a tone behind the nut. Ideas like this are very hard to do well, but they're unlike anything you'll hear elsewhere.

Example 12d:

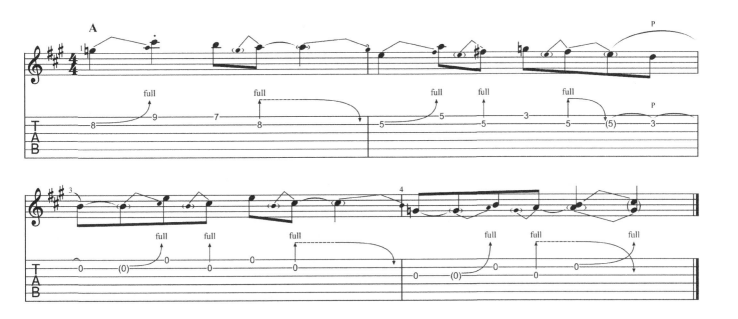

The final lick takes the previous idea to the extreme for what is probably the hardest lick in the entire book!

Beginning with a simple descending E Major scale using open strings (very much like one of the Chet Atkins licks), this lick really becomes difficult in the second bar as the open E string is played. You must hammer from F# to G# then bend this note up a semitone to A. It's important to bend this note upwards, towards the ceiling.

With those two notes ringing, pick the B note on the G string and bend it up a tone to C# by pulling the note down towards the floor. At this stage, all three notes should be ringing clearly.

With the first finger, catch the unbent B string in the same spot the G string is held. Now release the bends on the D and G strings, while pushing the B string up a semitone from D# to E. This is probably the hardest bending lick I've ever come across, so don't feel defeated and stick with it.

From here, play the 12th fret harmonics on the G, B, and E strings, and bend the G string harmonic up to G# with a behind the nut bend.

Example 12e:

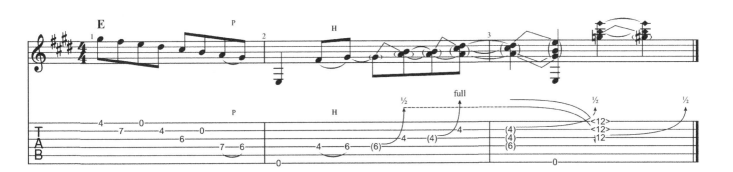

Chapter Thirteen: Jerry Reed

Born in Georgia in 1937, The Alabama Wildman, Jerry Reed Hubbard, would take the world by storm as a guitar player, composer, singer, and film star during his 50-year career. His influence is one of legend, and on a personal note, he is one of my all-time favourite guitarists.

After a rough start in life (spending almost 7 years in foster homes and orphanages), Jerry was reunited with his family in 1944. He would get a guitar around the age of 8, and quickly fall in love with the picking style of Merle Travis and banjo legend Earl Scruggs' claw hammer style.

Jerry showed promise as a player, singer, and composer, so much so that he was signed to a record label in 1954. This period in Jerry's career is an interesting one, as it's one he would completely disavow later in life. While he had hundreds of sessions and outings as a solo artist (check out Hully Gully Guitars), it wasn't until his 1967 RCA debut, The Unbelievable Guitar and Voice of Jerry Reed, that Jerry considered he'd officially launched.

This debut featured a wonderful display of guitar picking, singing, and writing. His style was so unique that when Elvis recorded Reed's Guitar Man, the only way to get it sounding the way it should was to fly Jerry in to play on it. The album also featured songs like If I Promise (which would be a hit for Tom Jones), and classics like Tupelo Mississippi Flash, U.S. Male, and instrumental tour de force, The Claw.

Jerry's style was dominated by his use of the thumb pick and complex multi-voice parts. He often refused to call himself a guitar player, instead opting for the title of 'guitar thinker' as he just thought the stuff up, recorded it (or even gave it to people like Chet to record), then never played it again.

Another important part of Jerry's sound was the use of nylon string guitars and the warmer sound they resulted in.

Jerry would go on to record nearly 50 albums before his death in 2008. Highlights include Me & Chet (with long-time collaborator and friend, Chet Atkins), Nashville Underground, and Alabama Wildman.

The first lick showcases Jerry's amazing double-stop style and chordal awareness.

When playing double-stops, it's important to not lose track of the underlying chord. It's not about just playing two random notes from the scale and hoping for the best.

Over the E chord the 5th and root are played with the 5th moving down a semitone to the b5 (11th fret B), then over to an A and C# on the G and B strings before sliding back into a G# and B (which sound like the underlying E chord).

The second part of the lick shifts down to the A shape, again using the b5 (Bb) to add some bluesy tensions to proceedings.

Example 13a:

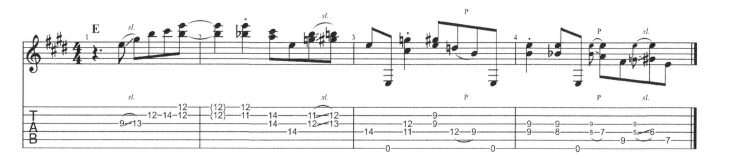

The next lick implies a G7 sound with a series of melodic double-stops and position shifts.

Beginning up at the C shape, the lick moves down the neck with some 6ths before resolving in the E shape.

Note-wise, there are some ear twisters, but they should all make sense. There's the Bb to B (b3 to 3) in bar one, and the C#/Db (b5) in bar two. Mixolydian with added b3 and b5 has been covered many times in the book so far.

Example 13b:

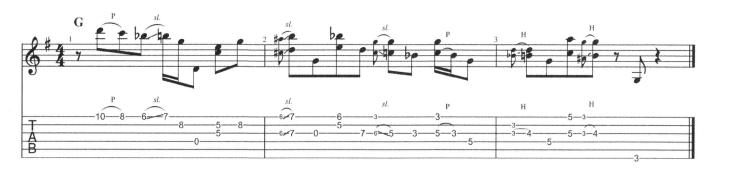

The next idea shows off Jerry's reverse roll technique, and how it's applied using open strings to create fast cascading ideas.

To play three-string descending patterns Jerry would use the third and second fingers and thumb, but don't be afraid to use the second and first fingers and thumb if it's easier. The pick directions show you where the thumb notes are played, the rest should easily fall into place.

Be careful with the position shift from the 7th fret area to the open position. Timing is everything, so don't rush!

Example 13c:

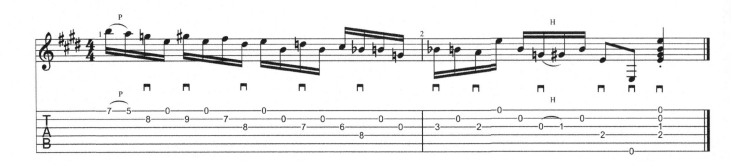

This next idea is a prime example of the 'guitar thinker' side of Jerry's playing. When listening to the audio, it just makes *sense* to the ear. Everything is pleasing and heads in a direction that sounds great.

When you look at the tab and try to play it though, problems quickly arise as it's much harder to play than hear!

Try learning the first two bars as a little lick for an E chord in the open position, then the lick in bar three, then bars four and five. Each function as their own individual ideas, and the descending nature of things ties them together nicely.

Example 13d:

The last idea looks at Jerry's jazzier influence. He really could play whatever he heard in his head!

Using the C Country scale over the Am and C, a phrase using notes from the Fdim7 arpeggio (F, Ab, B, D) is used over the E7 to imply an E7b9 sound. A great little arpeggio substitution.

The lick ends with notes of the A Blues scale to keep it cool.

Example 13e:

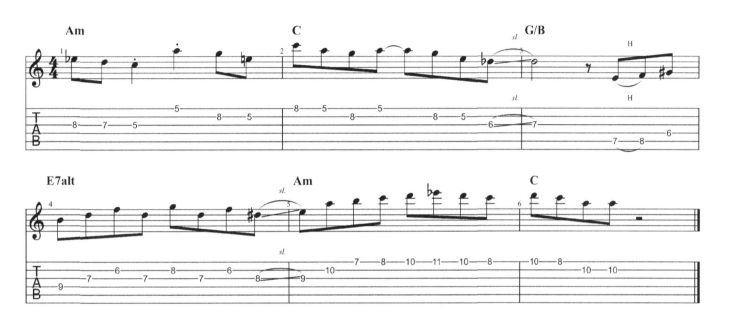

Chapter Fourteen: Jimmy Bryant

Born in Georgia in 1925, Jimmy Bryant took guitar playing to a whole new level in the '50s with his incredibly fast alternate picking and sweet twin-guitar harmonies.

Bryant began taking his guitar playing seriously in the mid-1940s, inspired by the gypsy jazz picking of Django Reinhardt. So much dedication to the style would inevitably add a heavy jazz influence to his note choice, and the aggressive picking of the genre translated well to electric guitar.

After moving to LA, Jimmy met pedal steel pioneer, Speedy West. The two would play together for many years, both as a featured duo and as part of the Capitol Records backing band. He's appeared as a guitar player, composer, arranger, bass player, vocalist, and even fiddle player over the years, but it was his solo guitar work that kept him on the map.

Jimmy's 1954 debut, Two Guitar Country Style, is a wonderful introduction to both Jimmy's exciting style and to the wonders of the pedal steel guitar, which features heavily on the album.

As mentioned, Jimmy appears on many albums and they're all worth a look. Speedy West's album Steel Guitar, Tennessee Ernie Ford's Sixteen Tons, and the duo album Country Cabin Jazz were all released in 1960!

Jimmy's sound was dominated by the Telecaster, an instrument that's more versatile than many think. Providing the harsh top-end twang when using the bridge pickup, switching to the neck gives a surprisingly warm, jazzy tone that Jimmy was no stranger to. Fender did release a Jimmy Bryant signature Telecaster (complete with leather scratch plate!), but these are pretty hard to come by. Featuring an ash body, nitro finish, and custom Nocaster style vintage pickups, this tone is something that can be achieved with any vintage-style Telecaster

The first lick takes influence from the blues with a jazzy motif that's adapted to fit the chords.

Over the G7 chord (E shape) the 3rd (B) is approached from below, but when the chord changes to C7, the chord is the A shape, and the top note is changed to the b7th (Bb) of the chord.

The second half of the lick repeats the G lick, but ends with a position shift up to the 8th fret, ending on the 3rd (B) of the underlying G chord.

The last two bars form a II-V in G, playing an A7 arpeggio with the added b9 (Bb) over the A, and a classic country jazz phrase over the D9.

Example 14a:

The next lick could be used in numerous settings, either static, or over chord changes. When looking at the actual arpeggios being played, the first four notes are a Bb triad (Bb, D, F), then an implied Bbdim7 (Bb, Db, E, G), followed by a Gm idea with chromaticism for the rest of the lick.

Licks like this are extremely hard to play at speed as there's lots of cross picking (the name given to lots of string crossing with single notes on each). As with any idea like this, the answer is good alternate picking, so keep that pick moving down and up!

Example 14b:

It would be impossible to talk about Jimmy without mentioning his incredible two-guitar arrangements.

For this lick, I've written a melody and then played the harmony immediately after so you can play both.

The idea fits loosely around a D chord, beginning on the root (in the A shape) with the 7th and 2nd around it, the second bar sees you move up to the E shape playing around the 3rd (F#).

The harmony isn't something theoretically solid, it simply sounds good, and remember; if something sounds good, it is good. As with the previous part, this part begins in the A shape, but plays the 3rd, the note a semitone below (this time a chromatic note) and the note a scale tone above (G). This then moves up to the E shape, taking a chord tone on the B string (the 5th), and playing a semitone below.

These kinds of harmonies (that don't adhere to a strict theoretical form) always sound more organic and musical to my ear.

Example 14c:

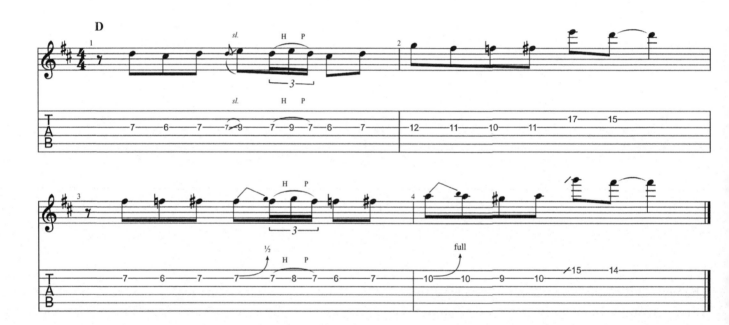

The next lick is a longer harmony idea that I'll present in two parts. Taking place over an Am – E7 chord change, the idea feels more in line with the gypsy approach to playing: connecting notes of the chord with scale tones, and using chromatic notes a semitone below chord tones for colour.

The real tricky part here is the speed at which Jimmy played ideas like this. Stick to strict alternate picking, and build up speed over time.

Example 14d:

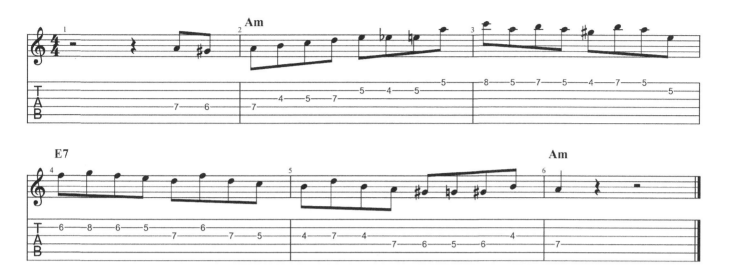

The harmony to this part just attempts to follow the contour of the lower part. So, while the lower harmony begins on the root (A), the harmony begins on the 3rd (C) as it's the next chord tone.

As with the previous idea, you'll note that any chord tone (A, C, E) can be approached by a note a semitone below.

The phrase over the E7 is particularly difficult to play at speed, but that's the nature of harmonising something that might have fit easily under the fingers in a lower inversion. The longer you spend with these types of harmony ideas, the faster your ear will tune in and hear the harmonies before you play them.

Example 14e:

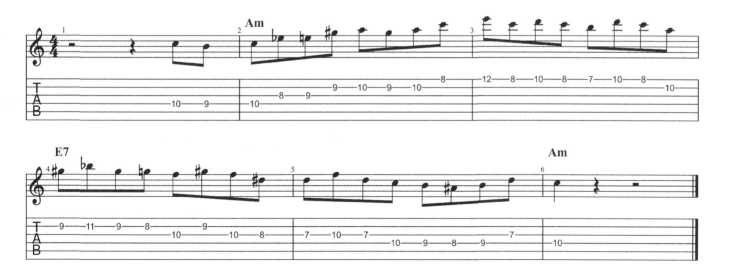

Chapter Fifteen: Johnny Hiland

Born in Maine in 1975, Johnny Hiland is one of the newer faces flying the high-tech country guitar flag.

Although his first widely available release didn't come out until 2004, Johnny began playing at an extremely young age, playing publicly in talent contests as young as five. He devoted a lot of time to music, being legally blind (suffering from nystagmus from birth) made it difficult to run around in parks with friends, but playing music was a great alternative.

In terms of sound and influence, Johnny grew up in a post Van Halen world, so a lot of the music he was captured by was actually classic rock, hair metal, and shred guitar players like Eddie Van Halen, and Joe Satriani. Growing up playing music with his family also meant that he was exposed to a lot of country music, too, and he's been very vocal about Jimmy Bryant, Albert Lee, Chet Atkins, and Danny Gatton.

This mix of influences sees Johnny slips between western swing, hot country, and high-tech rock from track to track (and sometimes on the same track). This means you need a good command of techniques associated with both country guitar (like alternate picking, hybrid picking, double-stops, and pedal steel bends), and also the shred style techniques (such as fast legato, and two-handed tapping). This makes Johnny's style one of the most technically demanding you'll ever learn.

Johnny moved to Nashville in 1996 to pursue a career in session guitar, quickly picking up a spot in the Don Kelley band. His manager eventually got Johnny a record deal on Steve Vai's Favoured Nations label... by playing his music into Steve's answerphone! His self-titled debut came in 2004, it features some incredible playing and is a must-own.

Guitar-wise, Johnny has worked with many companies, most notably Fender (being their first unsigned artist), PRS (his signature model was their first bolt on), and now Ernie Ball Music Man. He's a big fan of the Axis Sport model, but a good Telecaster is going to get you close to the sound on Johnny's first album. His old Fender was inspired by both Don Rich and Danny Gatton, and featured three Joe Barden pickups Fender had lying around for Gatton signature models.

This first lick mixes pedal steel bends, position shifts, and double-stops for a classic Albert Lee-esque hot country lick over E.

Beginning with a C shape bend, 2nd to 3rd on the B with the 5th on the high E (as played a few times in previous chapters), the lick moves down to the D shape in bar two with a first finger slide from E down to D.

The last few bars are in the open position and use notes of the E Mixolydian scale with added b3 and b5. The lick ends on an open A, as the progression changes to an A chord.

Example 15a:

The next lick showcases some of Johnny's western swing influences, characterised by lots of interesting notes. A theory book might tell you they're 'wrong', but in reality they sound great… so they are great!

Starting over an A7 chord in the A shape, there's a b3 (C) to 3 (C#) movement, before using a triplet to transition down into the C shape. The second bar features an A, G#, G, and F on the B string, that G# in particular (7th) clashes directly with the G in the A7 chord.

When the chord changes to D, the perspective changes to the D Major Pentatonic scale in the G shape (first half of bar three), sliding up to an ascending D7 arpeggio. The fourth bar uses notes of the D Mixolydian scale in the D shape, moving down to end on the 3rd of G (B).

Example 15b:

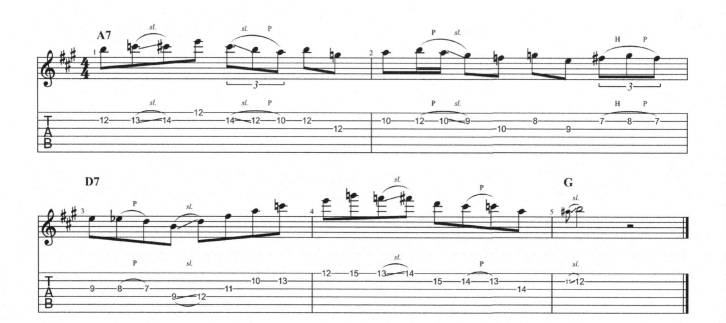

The next lick has a bit of Danny Gatton flavour to it, a common theme in Johnny's playing.

Beginning around an A shape the concept here is to play a melody around a repeating E, D#, E on the D string. That D# gives it a pedal steel, or even Jimmy Bryant sound. Remember that playing notes a semitone below a chord tone is always fair game in country music!

The second half of the lick features some higher notes that fit around the G shape. That position has been under-utilised thus far in this book, so pay attention because it's important to have as much vocabulary as you can in each part of the neck.

Example 15c:

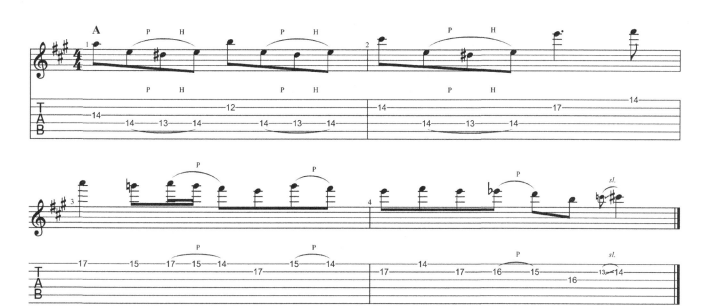

Here's a lick featuring some trickier pedal steel-type bends.

The first two bars look a lot more like a D chord, rather than the A chord being played, but this D/A is a common chord substitution. When thinking of it as D, it fits pretty neatly around the G shape D Major Pentatonic scale, though the pattern also fits well as the D shape A Minor Pentatonic.

The second part of the lick features triads (played as double-stops on the G, and B, followed by the D) moving down with bends added for colour on the G string. Very much like in the Brent Mason examples, you're playing an A major, G major, A major movement over the static A chord.

Example 15d:

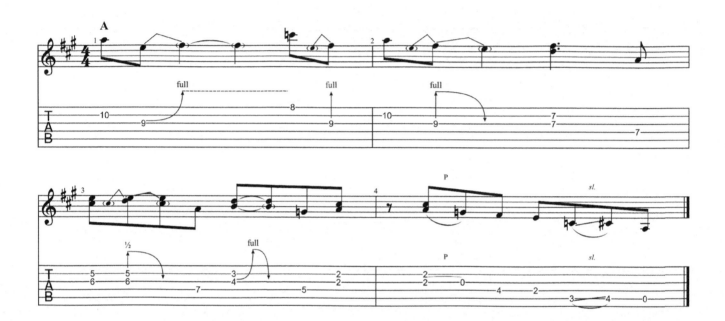

The final lick takes inspiration from rock players, but fits great in a country setting (and is not too dissimilar to licks that Keith Urban plays), conjuring up vibes of the Eagles.

Essentially it's just an A triad played around the E shape, and all about the E and A notes, with B, C#, and D used on top for colour.

Example 15e:

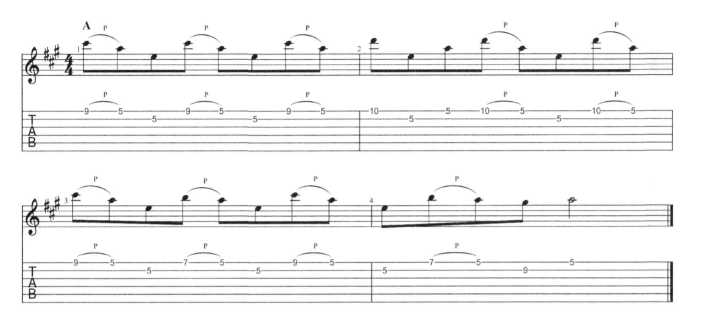

Chapter Sixteen: Keith Urban

Keith Urban is another player who shows that you don't need to be from the Southern States to be an icon of country music. Born in 1967, Urban is actually Australian, but that hasn't hurt his career; to date winning four Grammy awards and having twenty-two hit singles.

As far as iconic country guitar players go, Keith was a hard sell for this book, but it would be a shame to ignore one of the top faces of modern country music. There's definitely a country edge to his playing but he doesn't hide the fact that his heroes growing up were Mark Knopfler and Lindsey Buckingham.

As a composer and singer, Keith's early material made waves on the country scene, resulting a self-titled debut album with EMI in Australia in 1991. Understanding that the home of country music would never be in Australia, Keith relocated to Nashville in 1992 and forged a reputation as an up and coming singer and composer by writing several songs for other artists, and carrying out session guitar work around town.

Despite having a band (The Ranch) release an album in 1997, it was his 1999 solo album (also self-titled for added confusion!) that saw him really break out on the American market. This would lead to several more albums, each going platinum (some multiple times). 2004's Be Here, is a great starting place and mixes those country influences with pop.

As an instrumentalist, one really has to look no further than the Rollercoaster to hear that Keith is no slouch on the guitar, though that does take a backseat to his award-winning voice a lot of the time. Because of this, Keith's sound is more in the production than the gear, and he's seen playing everything from Telecasters to Les Pauls, SGs to Explorers. Having said that, I can't help but think of Keith holding a Strat.

The first lick here uses notes of the E Major Pentatonic scale (in the G shape), using classic double-stop vocabulary.

The second half of the lick is an idea Keith uses frequently, playing a melody on one string (the B), and keeping another string open (the high E). In this case, the melody is a descending E Major scale. Dig in on this one and don't be afraid to let the notes ring out.

Example 16a:

The second lick shows off more of Keith's pedal steel-type licks, beginning by sliding into the E shape, then shifting down for a great sounding bend on the G. Take the B note and bend it up to the C#, then play the D note on the high E string and let them ring into each other. This C# against a D causes a real clash to the ears which wouldn't work well with overdrive, but on a clean Strat, it's a winner.

Example 16b:

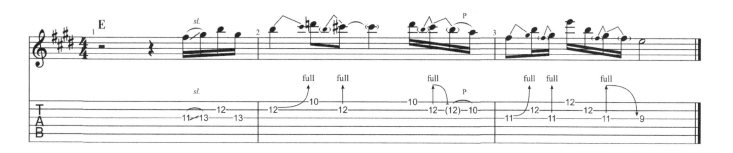

The next idea showcases some traditional country vocabulary outlining basic chord changes. Beginning in the E Major Pentatonic scale in the open position, when the chord changes to A, your perspective needs to change. This all makes sense as an 'A shape' A chord, with the b3 to 3 movement (C – C#) for that country edge.

The third bar outlines a B major and A major chord, beginning by outlining a B/D# triad in the G shape (D#, F#, B), then an A major idea in the E shape. The idea ends over the E chord with some simple great sounding bends, but when analysed you'll notice that the notes played/bent to are the B, E, and G# (notes of the E chord)

Example 16c:

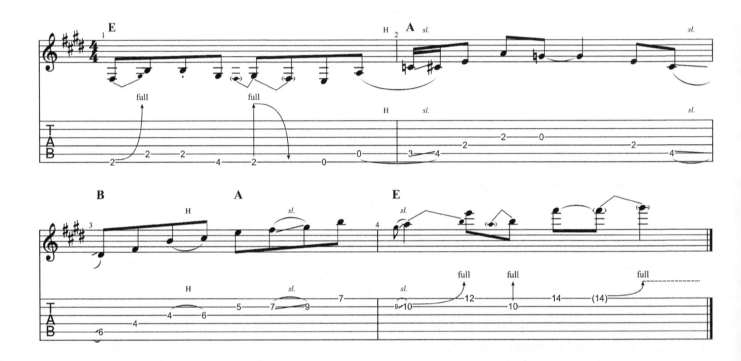

This lick is a flashier country idea covering different positions of an E major chord.

Beginning around a C shape E triad at the 4th fret, and using classic pedal steel-type bends on the B and E string, the lick shifts up to the G shape to help the melody continue up the neck.

While this has been written and recorded as 1/16th notes, ideas like this work just as well played at half the speed as 1/8th notes, so don't be overwhelmed.

Example 16d:

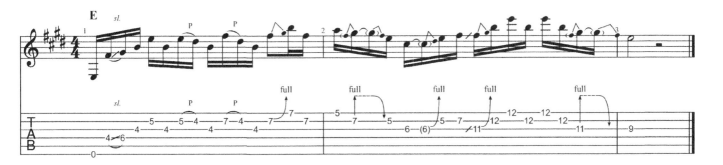

This final lick takes influence from some of Keith's rockier tracks, using fast pull-offs around an E major chord up at the 12th fret.

The notes come from the E Major scale and are played using a combination of picked notes and pull-offs.

In all honesty, if I were to record something like this in a session, I'd be inclined to put a capo on the 12th fret, to allow the use of pull-offs to 'open' notes. This sort of studio trick is a staple of an experienced session player like Keith.

Example 16e:

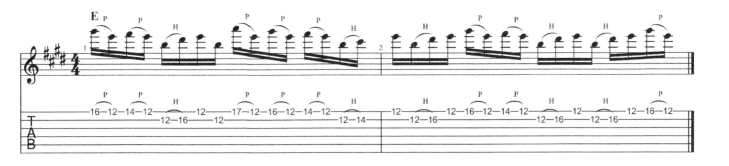

Chapter Seventeen: Redd Volkaert

Born in Vancouver in 1958, Redd Volkaert picked up the guitar around the age of 10 and kept with it after falling in love with Merle Haggard, Buck Owens, Led Zeppelin, Albert King, and Johnny Winter.

Redd moved to the US in the late '80s, making it to Nashville in November 1990. At 32, Redd certainly wasn't the youngest cat on the block, but he had enough experience trying to make it in new towns, and would soon land a spot in Don Kelley's band (a name you should be pretty familiar with now!).

In 1997 it became clear that the key to success wasn't just what you knew, but who you knew. Redd was recommended to Merle Haggard by five of his band members. This resulted in one of the biggest gigs in the genre, and a position he held for well over a decade.

Redd is probably the cult hero on this list, having kept a lot of his underground status for all these years by putting less effort into internet marketing, and more time into gigging, which he does regularly in his home of Austin, Texas.

He's released multiple albums since 1998, with every one being worth a listen. Start with his debut, Telewacker, and take it from there as you're bound to find some authentic and inspiring picking. 95% of his tone is the bridge pickup of a Telecaster going into a clean amp... you can't get much more country than that!

This first lick uses open strings allowing up to four notes to ring into one at any given time.

In the first bar, use the third finger to play the A note on the D string, pluck the B string with the middle finger, then fret the C# with the second finger and hammer-on to the D note with the fourth finger before plucking the open E with the middle finger again. The same idea is then repeated, but with a C instead of a C#, to create an A minor chord.

The final bar uses notes of the A Mixolydian scale with added b5 and open strings to create a cascading effect. As with the previous bars, allow notes to ring out for that country spice.

Example 17a:

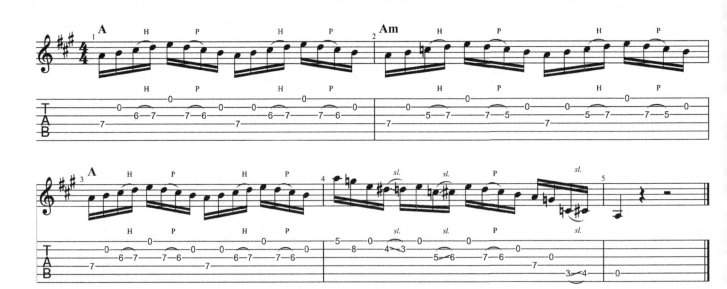

The next lick showcases how Redd might outline an E chord in the open position. As expected, you're using notes of the E Mixolydian scale with added b3, and b5, this combination of Mixolydian and approach notes is easy to solo with when you understand how the b3 and b5 are used.

Use the second and third fingers to hybrid pick the double-stops, alternating against the notes on the D string with the pick.

Example 17b:

This lick shows how Redd might apply double-stops and behind the nut bends to outline an A chord.

As with the previous lick, the second and third fingers are used to hybrid pick the double-stops, while the pick is used to play the notes on the D string.

As with the Jerry Donahue licks, the behind-the-nut bend should be executed with two fingers if possible. Pluck the open E, then the B and using the first and second fingers, press down on the string behind the nut to bend the open B up to a C#. This same idea is then repeated, but pre-bending the open G up to an A and releasing.

Example 17c:

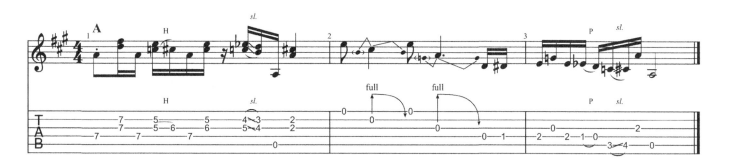

Here's a lick with some pedal steel-type bends on the G string. These are much harder to execute than the more common B string bends, but they have a distinct voice that cries guitar.

It's important to keep track of the CAGED positions you're using so these licks can be transposed. The first two beats fit around an A shape, bending the b7 to the root with the 3rd on the B. Beats 3 and 4 transition down to the E shape, before resolving to the G shape in the second bar. The lick then ends with a double-stop in the C shape.

Example 17d:

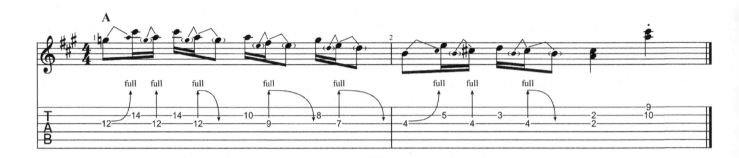

The final lick takes more of a western swing edge. Notice the use of both a G# (the 7th) and G (b7) in bar one which really twists the ear as you move from the A shape down to the C.

As the chord changes to D, 6ths are employed on the G and high E string, connected by chromatic passing notes on the G. Play the notes on the G string with the pick, and notes in the high E with the second finger of the picking hand.

The lick resolves to a G chord by playing the 3rd, and root of a G chord in the E shape.

Example 17e:

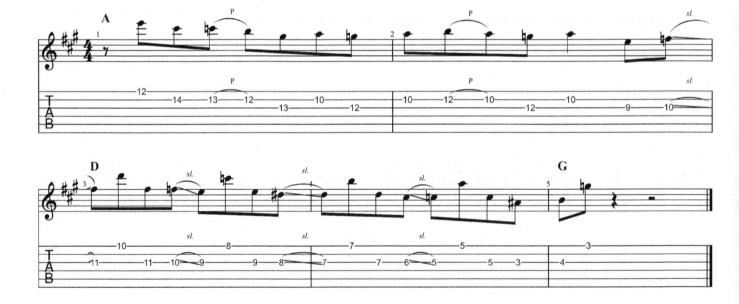

Chapter Eighteen: Roy Nichols

Born in Arizona in 1932, Roy Nichols is one of the true elder statesmen of country guitar, influencing millions along with Merle Haggard, who he played with for 22 years. He was instrumental in the spread of the Bakersfield sound, along with peers like Buck Owens and Don Rich.

Nichols began playing professionally around the age of 16, garnering quite the reputation on the scene for his fluid finger picking, and pedal steel influenced bends. A few recordings exist from this period, most notably his work with the Maddox Brothers & Rose, but from 1965 his main gig was alongside Merle Haggard. He was credited on over 40 releases, including publishing 19 of his own songs, and seeing Street Singer get recorded by Merle and be nominated for a Grammy.

Roy was never a band leader with his own albums, which is a great shame, but he does have some iconic solos with Merle where he was often allowed to cut loose and showcase his influential style.

Roy's style certainly isn't one that's going to give you technical challenges compared to the likes of Brent Mason, but it's one that came decades before the hot pickers of today began their careers. Because of this, Roy's melody-based style with great bends and interesting notes is an easy one to take influence from, but a hard one to master.

Each of these licks takes place over a G chord, and as such notes of the G Mixolydian scale (G, A, B, C, D, E, F) are added around a G Major Pentatonic framework (G, A, B, D, E), with added chromatic passing and approach notes.

The first note begins with a repeating ascending G Major Pentatonic scale idea around the E shape. This should be executed with alternate picking on 1/8th notes to allow the idea to be executed at faster speeds.

The second half of the lick remains in the E shape, using a Bb as an approach note to the B on the G string, then descending down a jazzy sounding pattern featuring both the b7 (F) and the 6th (E).

Example 18a:

Here's an idea that begins in a similar way, but takes it in another direction as the lick develops. This time playing the b5th (Db) and b3 (Bb) in bar 2 implies a blusier G Blues scale sound.

Bar three features a big part of Roy's approach to these jazzier notes, playing chromatic approach notes and sliding them up a semitone. In this instance, Db sliding up to a D (b5 to 5).

The final bar also features a chromatic approach note of F#, played between the F (b7) and G (root).

Example 18b:

The third lick begins with a similar melodic fragment, but an octave higher, in the A shape. This time adding the b9 (Ab) as a sliding approach note to the 9th (A).

The second bar features more slides into notes, first an F# (a non-scale tone) and then an E (a scale tone), it's the continuity of these slides on strong beats that helps tie the lick together.

The second part of the lick looks a lot more like the D Blues scale, but over G the Ab gives you the gritty b9 sound, one that indicates real confidence with jazz vocabulary.

Example 18c:

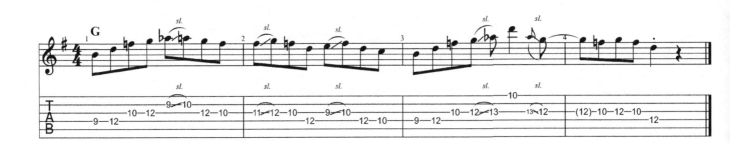

This next lick features more uses of the Bb (b3) and Ab (b9) in the first bar around the E shape, before moving between the 6th (E) and b6th (Eb) with sharp staccato notes to grab attention.

The next bar continues with melodic 1/8th notes around the G Major Pentatonic scale, along with the b3 to 3 movement covered numerous times before.

The final bar ascends up a G7 arpeggio and ends on the 6th (E). The aspect to focus on in a lick like this is the characteristic sound of the 6th (E), as found in the Major Pentatonic scale, and the darker sounding b7 (F) as found in the dominant 7 chord/Mixolydian scale.

Example 18d:

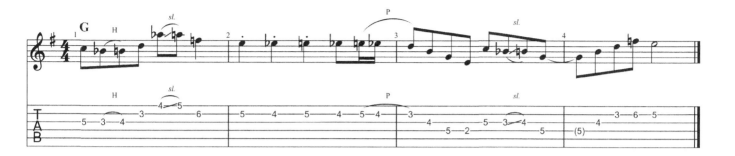

The final lick also takes place around the E shape, and uses the same outside notes found in the previous examples.

What sets this lick apart is the use of more syncopated rhythms in the second and third bars. In this particular setting I've outlined how Roy might have used the Blues scale to fit in around his rockier contemporaries, using 1/4 tone bends and gracenote hammer-ons.

Example 18e:

Chapter Nineteen: Steve Wariner

Born in Indiana, in 1954, Steve Wariner is one of just four players bestowed with the title of CGP (Certified Guitar Player), by the one and only Chet Atkins (The others being Jerry Reed, John Knowles, and Tommy Emmanuel). So, he's certainly not someone to underestimate!

As a youth, Steve took influence from George Jones, Chet Atkins, and later, Glen Campbell. After playing and touring professionally in many bands, he got his big break when Chet Atkins had him sign with RCA Records, in 1976.

Releasing his self-titled debut album in 1982, he began to find success with the release of the single, All Roads Lead to You, which reached the number 1 spot. There was an undeniable influence from Glen Campbell and the Nashville sound that Merle Haggard and Buck Owens had grown weary of all those years ago. While there's plenty of guitar playing, the songs are well produced and feature heavy string arrangements.

In 1991, Steve's tenth album, I Am Ready, would be his first to reach the gold certification of 500,000 sales. This album sounds a world apart from his debut, focusing more on the guitar and using crunchy rhythm parts (and no strings!).

From a guitar playing perspective, 1996's instrumental offering, No More Mr. Nice Guy is a great place to dig into Steve's playing. It showcases him to be a hot-picking machine, with a distinct voice on the instrument led by a largely Albert Lee-style 'Stratty' tone over the more traditional Telecaster vibes heard from his peers. Using the bridge and middle pick-up combined with enough compression and drive to add a little hair to the tone without losing that clean chime will get you close.

The first lick features faster 1/16th notes over an A chord, using notes of the A Mixolydian scale with the added b3 (C) as an approach to the 3rd. You may also notice the use of an Em7 arpeggio (E, G, B, D) in the final beat of the first bar, this use of arpeggio substitution shows a sophisticated, smooth jazz influence.

Position-wise, the idea fits around the E shape for the most part, with a brief visit to the D shape towards the end of the first bar, and then ending up around the C shape.

Example 19a:

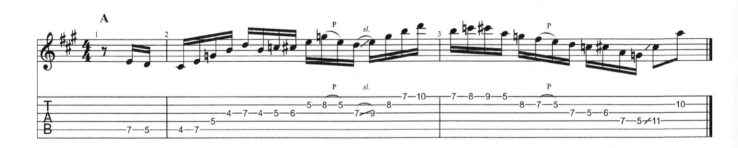

The second lick is played over a G chord, but looks very much like Em Minor Pentatonic in the E shape, this shares the notes of the G Major Pentatonic in the G shape.

As with the previous lick, this idea uses 1/16th notes to maintain a fast sound at a slower speed. Things really kick up a notch in the second bar, using pull-offs with 1/32nd notes to add some excitement.

Just as in previous examples, use the middle and ring fingers to pluck the double-stops, while using the pick to play the notes on the D string. This hybrid picking style is a standard technique among country players.

Example 19b:

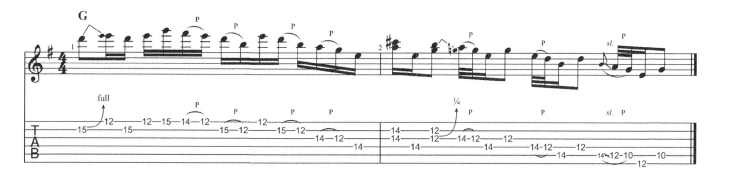

Here's another idea using the Major Pentatonic scale, but this time in E with the addition of the b3 (G).

The difference between this idea and the last is that this idea moves down the neck, one position at a time. It's a masterclass in position shifting, beginning in the G shape, moving down to the A in beat 3, and then the E shape (open position) towards the end of the second bar.

There's a definite Albert Lee sound to this one, especially with the tone, but as previously mentioned, Albert is a hard influence to avoid in this genre.

Example 19c:

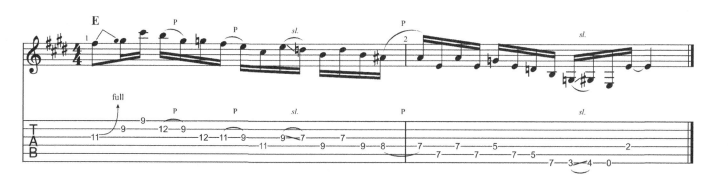

Example 19d fits around the G Major Pentatonic scale from the second lick, but this time adding the 4th (C) on the B string. As with many of Steve's licks, this idea is played at speed, so aim for consistent alternate picking, using down strokes on the 1st and 3rd 1/16th notes in groupings of four, and upstrokes on the 2nd and 4th.

The second half of the lick moves down the neck using repeating bends, bending from B to C# on the G string, then picking C# on the B string twice. This then moves down the G Major scale before resolving to a D chord using a pedal steel-type bend in the G shape.

Example 19d:

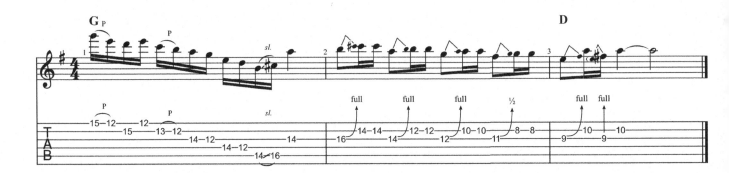

This final idea takes a simple Mixolydian idea and transposes it down through three different dominant 7 chords, first a C7, then a Bb7, then an A7. While many different approaches can be used to execute this, alternate picking will yield the most consistent results.

The final bar finishes the idea with a simple ending, very common to the country style.

Licks like this can be used over these exact chord changes, though they will also work as an outside approach on a static A7 chord.

Example 19e:

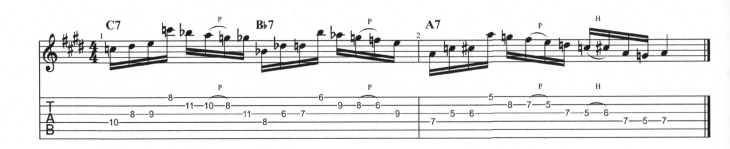

Chapter Twenty: Vince Gill

Born in Oklahoma in 1957, Vince Gill is the quintessential country guitar player and singer, having been awarded twenty (!) Grammy awards throughout his illustrious 40+ year career.

Vince grew up in a family passionate about music, learning to play guitar, bass, mandolin, dobro, and fiddle, all while showing promise as an aspiring singer and songwriter. He wouldn't debut professionally until he was 22, appearing on Pure Prairie League's 1979 album, Can't Hold Back.

In 1984, Vince released his debut album, Turn Me Loose, For RCA Records, but nothing charted higher than number 38. It was his third album, 1989's When I Call Your Name, which saw Vince achieve wider success, reaching the number 2 spot on the US Billboard Top Country Albums and eventually going twice platinum. The follow-up (Pocket Full of Gold) is a great place to start with Vince as it shows a man with full support of his label writing some excellent songs (like Liza Jane), and playing some head spinning guitar.

To date, Vince has almost 20 records to his name, including many fantastic solo albums and recordings with others like Olivia Newton-John and Nashville western swing outfit, The Time Jumpers. Their self-titled debut album is a great listen and features some great examples of Vince playing in a slightly jazzier setting.

Vince's style is a far-reaching one, being as comfortable in outlaw and Bakersfield country as he is in soul and western swing. He's most famous for his '53 Fender Telecaster, which he picked up for $450, and has been playing since 1980. One of his favourite tricks is to roll the tone off on the guitar enough to take the real high end off the sound without losing the clarity of the note, this helps dramatically when playing on the bridge pickup.

The first example showcases how Vince might move from the lower part of the neck to the higher when playing over an A chord.

Using a series of bends on the G with repeating notes on the B and shifting up from the open position to the G shape, the best way to keep track here is to focus on playing the E, G, A, and B notes on the B string, then keep the bend notes two frets higher.

The lick ends by slipping from the G shape down to the A with double-stops. As usual, these should be executed with the middle and ring fingers, while using the pick on the D string.

Example 20a:

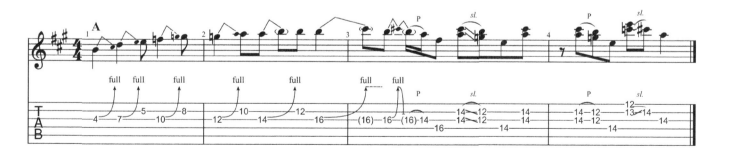

The second lick also outlines an A chord, using notes of the A Major Pentatonic scale and slick pedal steel-type bends. Vince is no stranger to good pedal steel players, playing with Paul Franklin.

Beginning with a 5th to 6th fret bend against the root in the G shape, bar two quickly moves down through the C shape, D shape, and ending in the E.

As with many of the licks in this book, the thing that sets these ideas apart from uninspired ideas you might have tried learning before, is the use of notes that aren't in the scale. In this case, the D#/Eb in bar four is just a little bit cooler than the D you might expect if you were only playing notes from the A Mixolydian scale.

Example 20b:

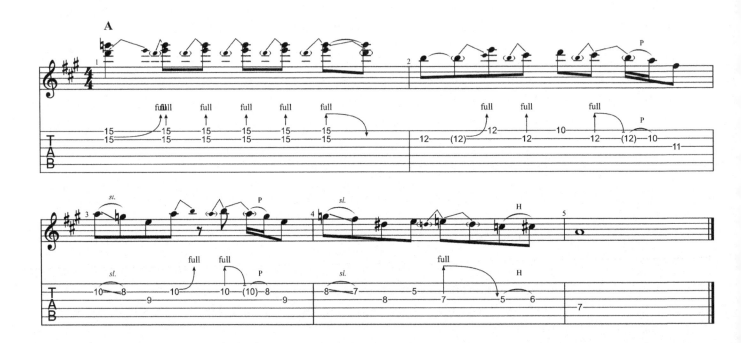

This next lick sits on an E chord and moves between three distinct positions.

Beginning around the E shape with some great little double-stops, the lick moves down to the G shape in the second bar. To execute this, go for the 10th fret with the second finger, allowing you to slide up and play the note on the G string with the first.

The second half of the lick plays a classic idea moving down the E Country scale, ending with a slide down to the A shape. It's important to play the pull-offs and slides in the right place to get the correct articulation.

Example 20c:

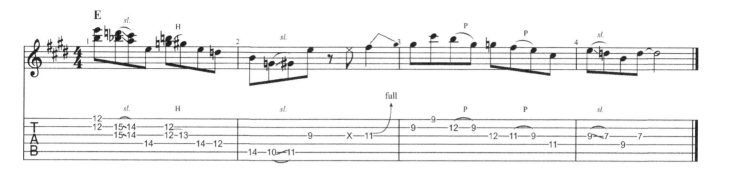

Another aspect of Vince's playing that's worth stealing is his use of pull-offs to open strings during position changes.

Taking place over a G chord, some basic chromaticism is used around the G Minor Pentatonic scale, before sliding up to the 7th fret, plucking the 5th fret G (with the second finger) and pulling off to the open G. This is then repeated, but two frets lower. This works well because while the fretted notes change, the open note stays the same and helps to keep it rooted in the key of G.

The lick ends by sliding up to the 3rd and root of G, this time in the C shape.

Example 20d:

The final lick takes this idea to the next level, moving down the neck from the G shape, to the D. The best way to look at this idea is to ask yourself how each note relates to G. First it's the 3rd and the root, then the 2nd and b7, then the root and 6th, then the b7 and 5th, then the 6th and 4th.

Ideas like this are great, but they're pretty key specific, doing the same thing in A is possible, but the open G string is now the darker sounding b7. Doing the same sort of thing in F# is virtually impossible, though, as the open G sounds awful, so open string ideas can be double edged swords.

The lick ends with a great little ascending idea based around the G Country scale in the C shape. To keep things interesting, I've played consecutive chromatic notes on the high E string.

Example 20e:

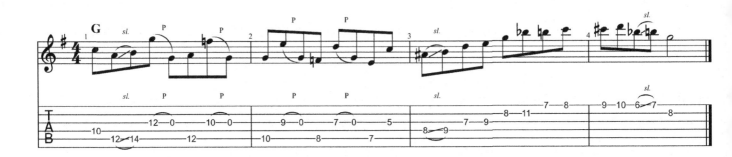

Chapter Twenty-One: Whit Smith

Originally hailing from Greenwich, Connecticut, Whit Smith gained a reputation as part of the western swing renaissance in 1998 when his band, The Hot Club of Cowtown, released their debut album, Swingin' Stampede.

Whit was raised by a musical family and by the time he was a teen he was out playing in rock bands inspired by his heroes, Eddie Van Halen, Jimmy Page, and Keith Richards. He took lessons with many people, the most notable being Chick Corea's one-time sideman, Bill Connors.

Eventually he would make the move to New York, and while working in a record shop he was exposed to the infectious sounds of western swing artists like Bob Wills and Milton Brown. This would lead him down a jazz path, and take the music of Django Reinhardt more seriously.

Around this period he would also meet Danny Gatton, who would help steer him in the direction of more country-flavoured jazz players. Richard Lieberson helped Whit screw down into his new passions, dissecting the music and understanding the evolution of players from 1927 to 1947.

The next step was relocating to Austin, Texas, in order to make a go at it with the Hot Club of Cowtown. It was a roaring success and to date the band have 13 albums available. Whit also has one solo album: a duo with Matt Munisteri and has also released excellent album with Bruce Forman and Rich O'Brien.

When it comes to Whit's sound, he tries to be as authentic as possible. While old swing players like Eldon Shamblin were happy to experiment with solid body electrics, Whit has a collection of pre-1930 Gibson L5s, and uses a 1946 L5 on the road. None of these originally came with pickups, but his '46 was fitted with one before he owned it. Someone even had it modified to include a cutaway!

Whereas a lot of the licks covered in this book take place over major chords, for the most part it's implied that they're dominant 7 chords. Whit's style is more rooted in jazz though, so when he sees a major chord, he's a lot more likely to treat it as major. So instead of C Mixolydian (C, D, E, F, G, A, Bb) Whit is more likely to play the C Major Pentatonic scale (C, D, E, G, A) or the C Major scale (C, D, E, F, G, A, B) That difference between B and Bb makes all the difference.

This first lick uses the C Major Pentatonic scale in the E shape, with the b3 (Eb) added as an approach note to the D in bar 2.

The lick is played in bars one and two, then repeated in bars three and four, this time with a slight variation in the ending.

Example 21a:

The next lick features some descending arpeggios played on two strings. Beats 1 and 2 contain an Em triad (E, G, B), this then moves down a semitone to Ebm (Eb, Gb, Bb) and then down another semitone to Dm (D, F, A). This approach of taking a musical idea and then moving it down chromatically is a great way to add some jazzy flavours to your playing.

The arpeggio idea then resolves to a C major in the C shape, then a C Major Pentatonic idea with added b3 (Eb) in the E shape.

Example 21b:

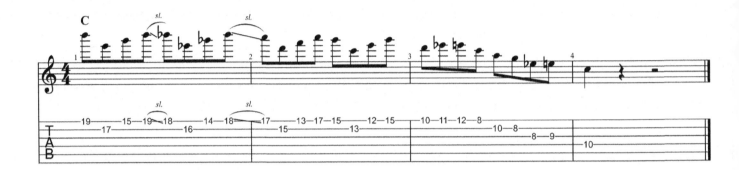

The third lick focuses on rhythm, playing strong staccato notes in the first bar, and simple rhythms with notes taken from a C major triad (C, E, G).

The final two bars feature basic triads, but with chromatic passing tones. The idea begins by playing a C major triad, that approaches the E from an Eb. Next a G major triad is played (G, B, D), but the E from the C chord, and the D in the G chord are connected with an Eb on the high E.

The idea then resolves to another C major triad, a perfect end to a swingin' lick!

Example 21c:

The penultimate lick features interesting notes around a C6 chord sound. So, beginning by hammering from the 5th (G) to the 6th (A) and back, the note then slides down a semitone to the #4 (F#).

This idea is then repeated, but on a lower string group. A chord tone is played (E) and then hammered to the next scale tone (F). Pull off and slide down to the note a semitone below the chord tone (Eb).

Bar three contains an F#m7b5 and Em7 arpeggios that resolve back to the root of C.

Example 21d:

The final lick implies lots of slightly different sounds over a C chord.

The first bar simply contains notes of the C Major Pentatonic scale. The second bar sharpens the 5th up to a G# , creating a C augmented triad sound. The next bar then takes that G# and move it up again to the 6th (A) creating a C6 sound. This gives you an inside sound in bar one, something a little spicy in bar two, then an inside sound in bar three, all tied together with a nice ascending chromatic melody.

The final bar reaches up for a Bb (the b7) and resolves to C via the b3 to 3 movement.

Example 21e:

Chapter Twenty-Two: Transposing Licks

Now that you've got a decent selection of licks under your fingers, it's time to start digging in to how you can use them. On the one hand, the worst part of learning licks is that you're learning the vocabulary of someone else, but on the other hand, it's important to have a sense of how the language works. The average lick book is great at teaching the first part, but often leaves you with nothing for the second part, so here's everything you need to know to make these licks work for you.

For the sake of authenticity, the one hundred licks are in the keys that the player recorded them in, but what we're going to do here is take six of those licks and transpose them (change their key) to work in the key of A.

This is an extremely useful skill, as from time to time you might hear a great lick in an uncommon key. You wouldn't want to be limited to using it only in Eb (for example), especially if you're recording a great track in A where you think it might work a treat.

As explained in the first chapter, every lick in this book has been described in relation to a CAGED chord shape. This should make it extremely easy to transpose any lick into a key that's useful to you.

As a first example, here's one of the Roy Nichols licks (Example 18a).

Example 22a:

This idea begins around the E shape barre chord at the 3rd fret, starting on the 3rd of the chord (B).

To transpose this idea it's as simple as seeing the same E shape barre chord, and 'moving' it to become an A chord. In this case at the 5th fret. From here you should be able to 'see' the lick around the chord form in the same way you learned it before. So, move up to the 3rd (C#) and play the same fingering as before.

The notes have changed, but the pattern/shape (or more importantly, the intervals) are exactly the same!

Example 22b:

Here's one of the Albert Lee licks (Example 2c) played in the original key of E.

Example 22c:

When learning the original lick, I can see that it's played in the G shape (I see the 9th fret D, G, and B strings played with the first finger), so moving this up to the key of A is as simple as moving that triad shape up to A, at the 14th fret.

From there, the other position shifts just fall into place as they're related to the shapes you're playing in, rather than the key the lick was learned in.

Example 22d:

This great little E Major Pentatonic lick is taken from the Steve Wariner chapter (Example 19c)

Example 22e:

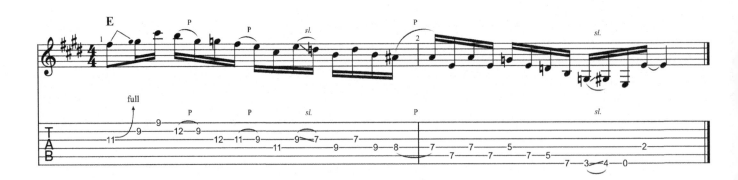

As with the previous lick, this too begins in the G shape. I track this by seeing the 12th fret of the high E played with the fourth finger, so moving this to the key of A means moving that finger up to the A at the 17th fret. This means the bend begins on the 16th fret, rather than the 11th.

In order to make this lick work in the key of A, I've made a small adjustment to the end as the original lick used an open E. Instead I played the A note on the D string.

Example 22f:

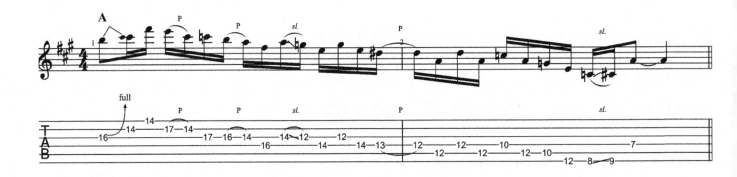

Here's one of the Danny Gatton licks (Example 7c), played over an E chord in the open position.

Example 22g:

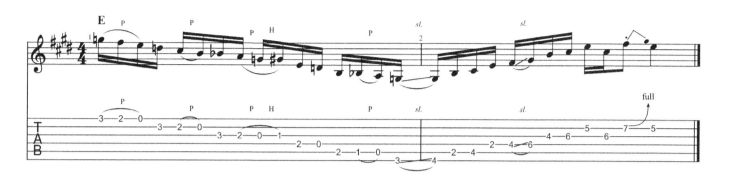

Even though this is in the open position, it's still based around a CAGED chord, an open E! So, moving the lick to the key of A means moving up to the 5th fret.

With the 5th fret low E as your root note; the first note is now the 8th fret high E (C).

You'll note I've adjusted the articulation ever so slightly; this makes the lick a little easier to play.

Example 22h:

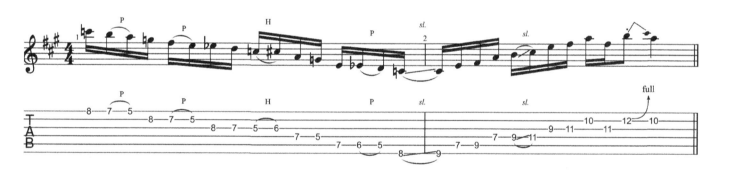

Here's one of the jazzier Brad Paisley phrases (Example 3d), originally in the key of G.

Example 22i:

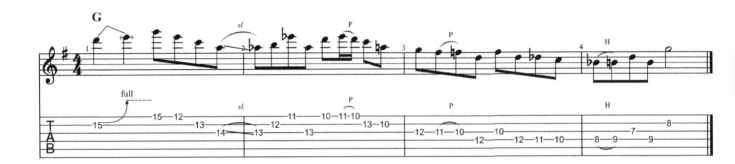

Hopefully by this stage the process is becoming automatic.

The next lick takes place over a G chord and is played in the G shape. This can be tracked by the little finger on the high E string.

Now move that up to an A (17th fret) and the lick has been transposed into the key of A. It really is as simple as that.

Example 22j:

The final example has been taken from the Jerry Donahue chapter (Example 12e), and features that mind-twisting bend in the key of E.

Example 22k:

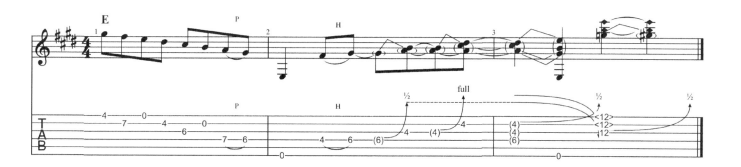

This lick presents some problems as the open string idea makes it much harder to just shift everything up to the key of A.

Instead, I tackle it in two sections, the later part is played in the A shape (which has the root at the 7th fret A, played with the fourth finger) so that part is moved up so that fourth finger is on an A, 12th fret A string.

For the open string lick, I've used the same approach, playing an open string A note, and descending down the scale as best I can, using open strings where possible.

You may also notice that the behind-the-nut bend is different too. This is because you're bending to notes in an open A chord, not an open E chord.

Example 22l:

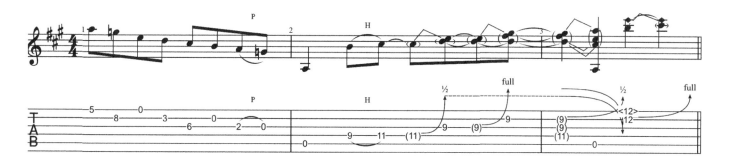

Now take a look back at some of the other licks in the book and try transposing them. The sky is the limit, the more you do, the easier it becomes.

Chapter Twenty-Three: Changing Context

Now that you've got a grip on putting the licks you've learned in different keys; the last skill is being able to adapt the quality of the licks so you can make them work in any key… and any context.

So, what exactly does this mean?

While a lot of country music takes place over major chords (like C major), that doesn't mean that you won't encounter other sounds. If you have a lick in C major, it makes sense that you're able to adapt it to work in C minor, or over a C7, or a Cmaj7, or anything else that might come up.

As an example, here's the start of a 12-bar blues, but played in a way a western swing player might approach it.

Example 23a:

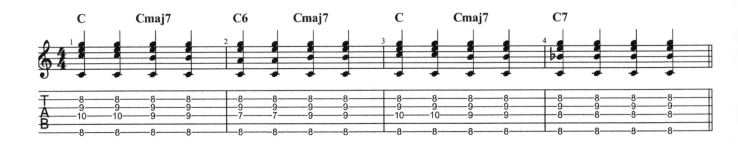

It's possible to look at this and say the first three bars are in the key of C, while the fourth bar is actually in the key of F (C7 being the V chord in the key of F), but I find this 'key centric' approach doesn't yield effective soloing results as playing a generic lick in the key of F over the C7 doesn't sound great.

To demonstrate that idea, here's Example 5d (a Don Rich lick) but transposed to the key of F. Technically it 'fits' but it just doesn't sound right. It sounds like an F tonality because it is. It doesn't work over C7.

Example 23b:

The more effective way to solo here is to have an understanding of what a C7 chord *is*, and how it differs from a C major, C6, or Cmaj7 chord. Then it becomes easy to make small adjustments to vocabulary you know to make it work where you need it.

When soloing over a C major chord, it's fair to assume that the C Major scale (C, D, E, F, G, A, B) will sound good over the top. When harmonising the scale, you create a Cmaj7 chord (C, E, G, B) so C Major is the perfect scale to fit over that a Cmaj7 chord too.

The problem with a maj7 chord is that it can sound a little bit jazzy, so often a C major chord is extended to a C6 (C, E, G, A) instead. That 6th has a sweet sound without being too jazzy.

For this reason, country players often favour playing the Major Pentatonic scale over major chords. C Major Pentatonic (C, D, E, G, A) contains the root, 2nd, 3rd, 5th, and 6th. It sounds a lot like a C6 chord as it contains that 6th and avoids the 7th. This has the added benefit of making any lick from this scale work over both Cmaj7 and C7 settings, as it doesn't contain the B or Bb contained in either of those chords.

As an example, here's a simple lick using the C Major Pentatonic scale.

Example 23c:

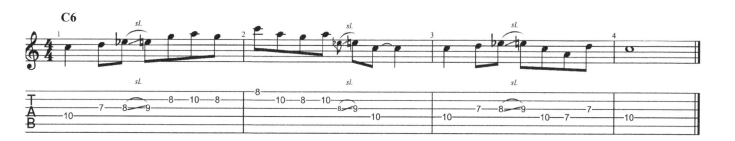

While that sounds great, it is possible to alter it slightly to fit better on a Cmaj7 chord. This example is the same as the previous idea, but you'll notice that the 7th (B) has been used in place of the 6th.

This note change doesn't happen every time, but when it does it creates some great melodic interest.

Example 23d:

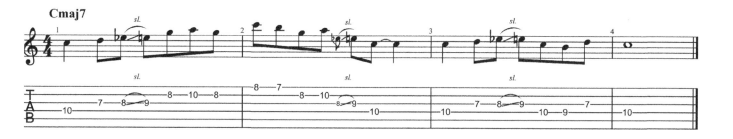

The same idea is now presented again, but instead of the 7th (B), the b7th is used (Bb). This has a much darker sound as it creates a C7 tonality.

Example 23e:

Here's a different lick based around the C Major Pentatonic scale. This would work on a C major, C6, Cmaj7, or C7, but it sounds most like a C6 chord.

Example 23f:

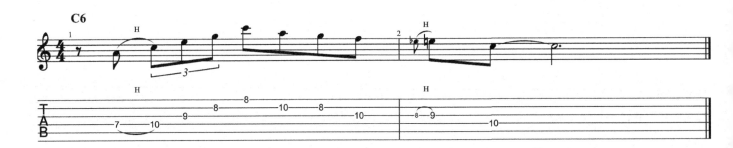

Now that same idea has been adapted to include the use of the B. Suddenly it won't work over a C7 as the B in the melody conflicts with the Bb in the chord. While it will still work over a C6, it definitely sits best over a Cmaj7.

Example 23g:

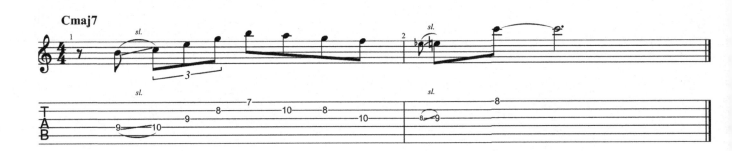

And now that idea has been adapted further to fit a C7. The Bb (b7) gives the lick some real character.

Example 23h:

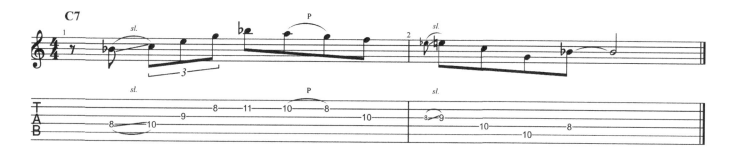

Finally, here's that basic idea developed to sequentially outline a C major, Cmaj7, C6, and C7, before resolving to an F7 (as it might appear in a blues).

Example 23i:

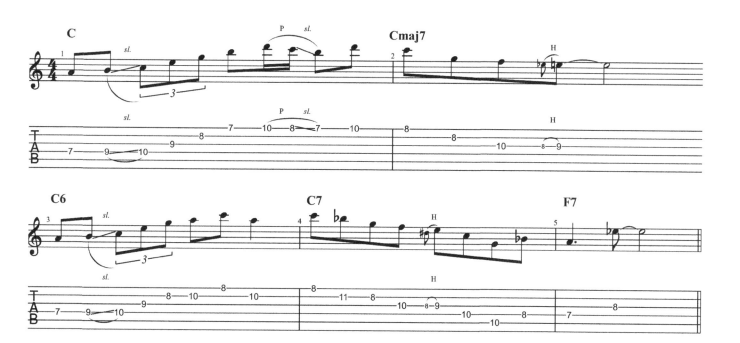

It's possible to apply the same logic to other chords.

If a C7 chord contains C, E, G, and Bb, and a Cm7 chord contains a C, Eb, G, and Bb, then taking C7 licks and flattening the 3rd should result in a lick that sounds great on a Cm7.

Here's a lick over a C7 chord in the C shape.

Example 23j:

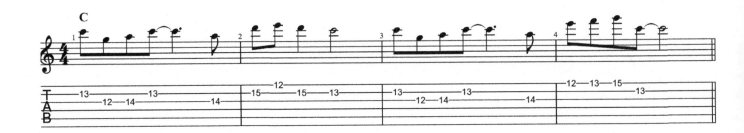

Next, the same basic idea is played, but adjusted to include Ebs instead of Es.

There's not just one way to do this, it's not maths. You may need to play around with ideas to make them work, but experimentation is what helps develop your ear.

Example 23k:

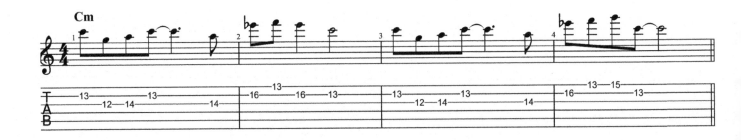

Using this method, the sky is the limit when learning any licks. If a lick works over C7, could you adapt it and make it a fit for a C6 chord?

This will also help with your ear training. When listening to a great player soloing, you'll be able to hear the difference between each of these subtle sounds as players are using them, and understand why a lick sounds the way it does.

Chapter Twenty-Four: Country Rock Solo

Now that you have some country licks under your belt, I've composed some solos using vocabulary taken exclusively from this book so you can see how it's possible to develop these licks into your own style.

This first example is a country rock-type track in A.

Before looking at the solo, here's the rhythm part transcribed fully so you can get to grips with the track. I cover this type of rhythm guitar playing in my book, Country Guitar for Beginners, but if you have some experience with the style, it should pose no real problems.

The main riff is played over A for the first four bars, then this idea is transposed up to D for two bars, and back to A for another two.

At this stage, you may think it feels like a blues, so to mix things up I've gone back to the D for two bars then up to an E chord. The space here allows you to play a few notes and stand out when soloing.

To finish, the chord switches back to an A chord for four bars. This basic form could then be repeated while people take turns to solo.

Example 24a:

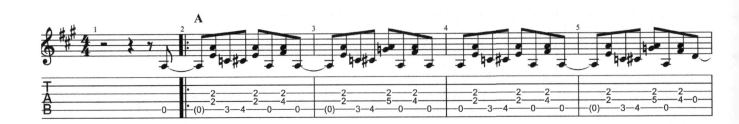

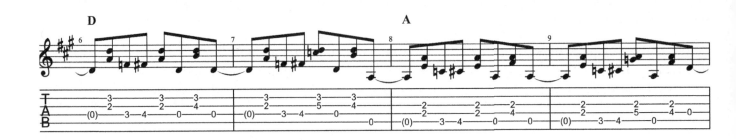

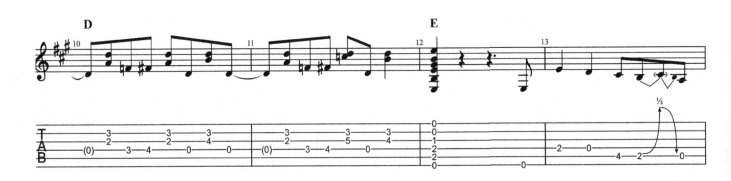

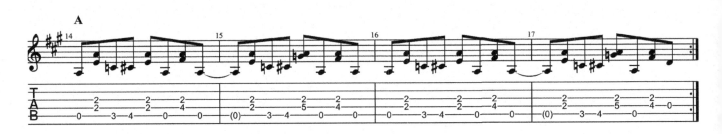

The solo begins with a Don Rich idea (Example 5d) that is transposed up a tone to work over the A chord.

Example 24b:

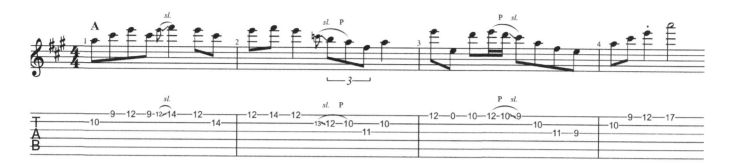

As the chord changes to D, I've used a Brent Mason lick (Example 4d) as it begins around the area that the last lick finished.

This is an important thing to consider when soloing as nothing sounds less natural than jumping around the neck playing ideas that don't flow into each other. When the chord changes back to A, I move to one of the Danny Gatton licks (Example 7d), again, transposed to fit the chord.

Example 24c:

At this point I've decided to up the excitement and develop the solo by picking an idea using 1/16th notes.

The first of these two ideas is another Danny Gatton lick (Example 7a), but transposed up to fit a D chord.

Example 24d:

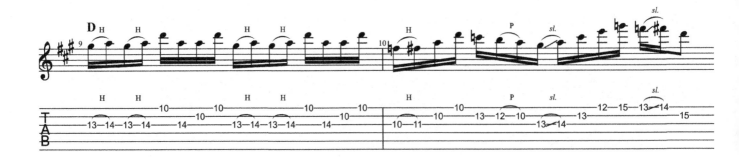

From here I wanted to keep the 1/16th note feel going, but the lick I wanted to play was an Albert Lee eight note idea (Example 2c) ending on the 7th fret E. Here I just doubled up the speed of the 1/8th notes. This kind of rhythmic variation is another way to develop a lick and put your own stamp on it.

Example 24e:

The final lick goes back to the 1/8th note feel, with a Johnny Hiland lick (Example 15a), but transposed up to fit in the key of A.

I've also added an ending to the phrase, another important aspect of using licks. Remember that they're not set in stone; they don't need to be played verbatim. You can play part of one lick, and then take it somewhere else.

Example 24f:

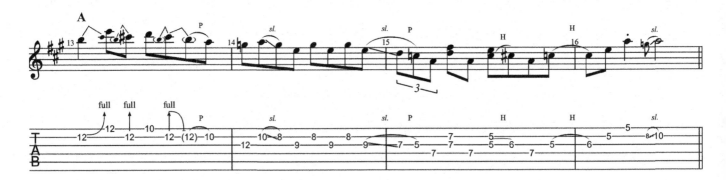

The backing track repeats this progression a few times so you can try this solo, but also experiment with some of the other ideas you've learned.

Chapter Twenty-Five: Country Boogie Solo

The final chapter in this book takes everything covered to the extreme, taking licks from the hundred, and applying them over an up-tempo country boogie.

The first step in developing licks and vocabulary for soloing over the track is to learn the chord progression. The basic idea is taken from Albert Lee's Fun Ranch Boogie, but I've adapted it to work in a 32-bar form.

Here's a basic rhythm guitar part to help you learn the chord progression. As with the previous chapter, this style of rhythm guitar is covered in more detail in my first book, Country Guitar for Beginners.

In order to learn this correctly, tackle it eight bars at a time.

Example 25a:

The first lick outlines an E and A chord. While none of the 100 licks are this specific, it's possible to easily adapt a lick to outline a chord.

To do this I took one of the Albert Lee licks (Example 2a) and moved just the third bar up a string set to fit an A chord.

Example 25b:

The next lick begins on an E major chord, and uses one of the Danny Gatton ideas (Example 7c) but played at an 1/8th note speed to fit the track.

After two bars the chords change to F# major and B major, so I've chosen to continue with the Danny idea, but adjusted it to fit the correct chords.

Example 25c:

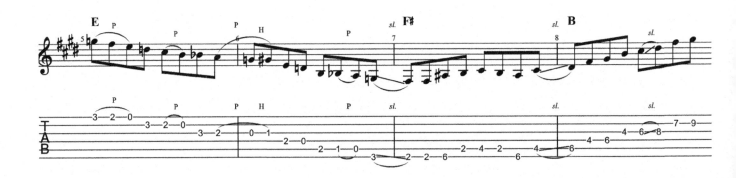

This next idea begins with some Albert Lee (Example 2b) before transitioning to Brent Mason for the third bar (Example 4b) and then Johnny Hiland (the third bar of Example 15a).

After a few years of playing country guitar, you'll soon find that fluidly combining and adapting ideas like this becomes quite simple.

Example 25d:

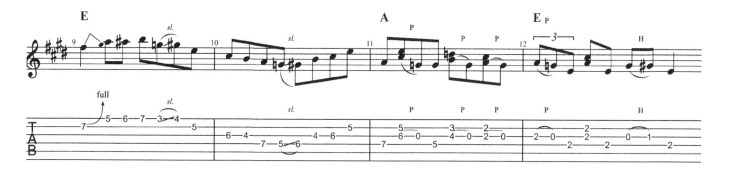

This lick ignores the B7 chord, using the bluesy colours to cover that sound. The lick is one of Redd Volkaert's ideas (Example 17b) but now played using 1/8th notes instead of the 1/16th note framework it was originally covered in.

Example 25e:

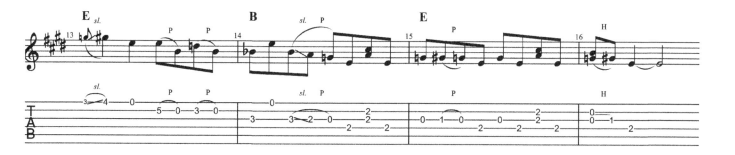

In the B section of the tune, I rely heavily on Brent Mason vocabulary (Examples 4a, and 4c). While I couldn't think of any examples of Brent playing over this particular set of chord changes, it's hard to not hear Hot Wired in the melody!

Example 25f:

To conclude the B section before returning to the first part, I've used a Hank Garland lick in bars one and two, (Example 10d) before adapting one of the Danny Gatton licks (the second half of Example 7a) to fit over F# major and B7.

Example 25g:

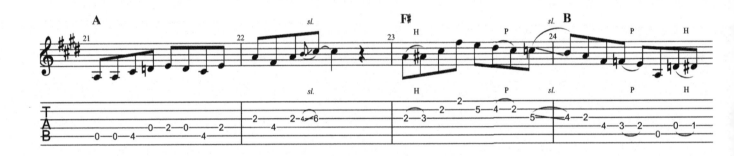

When returning to the first section, I've used the ending of a James Burton lick (Example 11a) to take you from the 2nd fret D down to the open E string.

Example 25h:

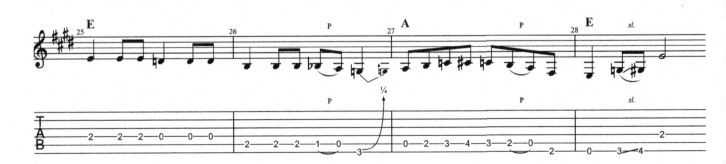

The final lick uses some more Hank Garland (Example 10e) but using notes of the E Mixolydian scale before ending on an adapted Brent Mason lick (Example 4d).

Example 25i:

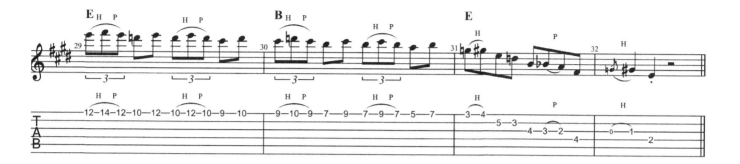

Once you have these licks down, use the backing track and play the solo in its entirety. It's not an easy one, but it shows you just how much mileage you can get out of knowing licks. It's entirely possible to turn licks into completely new ideas. We're all using a shared language here, so don't feel bad. As they say, good composers borrow… great composers steal!

Conclusion

Now you've got a big selection of licks in your arsenal, the most important thing is going out and using them in unique settings.

It's possible that you may not be able to imagine how this is done, or even if it's something that "real" country guitarists do. What I'd encourage you to do is listen to the greats like Albert Lee and Brent Mason and you'll soon start hearing similar ideas coming up again and again.

As musicians, our ears are our most valuable tools, so it's extremely important to listen to as much music as possible to help you internalize the vocabulary.

When you've started to hear these types of licks in real music, the next step is to begin transcribing things you hear that you enjoy. Transcribing can mean many things to many people, but in reality you don't need to be doing "proper" transcription (listening to music and writing it down), all you need to do is work out the bits you like! The most valuable tool I can recommend is the software called (fittingly) Transcribe!

Getting a copy of Transcribe means you're able to loop music, slow things down, retune them, EQ them, etc. Anything that allows you to listen more closely to licks you like and work them out on the guitar is a must have. This is honestly the quickest way to develop your ears. As a starting point, here are some album recommendations where you'll hear countless great licks that are all worth transcribing.

- Alan Jackson - The Greatest Hits Collection
- Albert Lee - Live at the Iridium
- Brad Paisley - Time Well Wasted
- Brent Mason - Hot Wired
- Buck Owens - The Very Best of Buck Owens - Vol. 1
- Buddy Emmons - Amazing Steel Guitar
- Chet Atkins - The Essential Chet Atkins
- Ernest Tubb - Texas Troubadour
- Hank Williams - The Best of Hank Williams
- The Hellecasters - The Return of The Hellecasters
- The Hot Club Of Cowtown - What Makes Bob Holler
- Jerry Reed - The Unbelievable Guitar and Voice Of Jerry Reed
- Keith Urban - Days Go By
- Maddie & Tae - Start Here
- Merle Haggard - The Very Best of Merle Haggard
- The Time Jumpers - The Time Jumpers

Good luck with your journey, I hope you've enjoyed these first steps, and I look forward to seeing you on the other side!

Levi Clay

Other Books from Fundamental Changes

*The Complete Guide to Playing Blues Guitar
Book One: Rhythm Guitar*

*The Complete Guide to Playing Blues Guitar
Book Two: Melodic Phrasing*

*The Complete Guide to Playing Blues Guitar
Book Three: Beyond Pentatonics*

*The Complete Guide to Playing Blues Guitar
Compilation*

*The CAGED System and 100 Licks for Blues
Guitar*

Minor ii V Mastery for Jazz Guitar

Jazz Blues Soloing for Guitar

Guitar Scales in Context

Guitar Chords in Context

The First 100 Chords for Guitar

Jazz Guitar Chord Mastery

Complete Technique for Modern Guitar

Funk Guitar Mastery

*The Complete Technique, Theory & Scales
Compilation for Guitar*

Sight Reading Mastery for Guitar

Rock Guitar Un-CAGED

*The Practical Guide to Modern Music Theory for
Guitarists*

Beginner's Guitar Lessons: The Essential Guide

Chord Tone Soloing for Jazz Guitar

Chord Tone Soloing for Bass Guitar

Voice Leading Jazz Guitar

Guitar Fretboard Fluency

The Circle of Fifths for Guitarists

First Chord Progressions for Guitar

The First 100 Jazz Chords for Guitar

100 Country Licks for Guitar

Pop & Rock Ukulele Strumming

Walking Bass for Jazz and Blues

Guitar Finger Gym

The Melodic Minor Cookbook

The Chicago Blues Guitar Method

Heavy Metal Rhythm Guitar

Heavy Metal Lead Guitar

Progressive Metal Guitar

Heavy Metal Guitar Bible

Exotic Pentatonic Soloing for Guitar

The Complete Jazz Guitar Soloing Compilation

The Jazz Guitar Chords Compilation

Fingerstyle Blues Guitar

The Complete DADGAD Guitar Method

Country Guitar for Beginners

Beginner Lead Guitar Method

The Country Fingerstyle Guitar Method

Beyond Rhythm Guitar

Rock Rhythm Guitar Playing

Fundamental Changes in Jazz Guitar

Neo-Classical Speed Strategies for Guitar

100 Classic Rock Licks for Guitar

The Beginner's Guitar Method Compilation

100 Classic Blues Licks for Guitar

The Country Guitar Method Compilation

Country Guitar Soloing Techniques

Made in the USA
Coppell, TX
21 July 2021